C-4759   CAREER EXAMINATION SERIES

This is your
PASSBOOK for...

Law Enforcement Aptitude Battery (LEAB)

Test Preparation Study Guide
Questions & Answers

COPYRIGHT NOTICE

This book is SOLELY intended for, is sold ONLY to, and its use is RESTRICTED to individual, bona fide applicants or candidates who qualify by virtue of having seriously filed applications for appropriate license, certificate, professional and/or promotional advancement, higher school matriculation, scholarship, or other legitimate requirements of education and/or governmental authorities.

This book is NOT intended for use, class instruction, tutoring, training, duplication, copying, reprinting, excerption, or adaptation, etc., by:

1) Other publishers
2) Proprietors and/or Instructors of "Coaching" and/or Preparatory Courses
3) Personnel and/or Training Divisions of commercial, industrial, and governmental organizations
4) Schools, colleges, or universities and/or their departments and staffs, including teachers and other personnel
5) Testing Agencies or Bureaus
6) Study groups which seek by the purchase of a single volume to copy and/or duplicate and/or adapt this material for use by the group as a whole without having purchased individual volumes for each of the members of the group
7) Et al.

Such persons would be in violation of appropriate Federal and State statutes.

PROVISION OF LICENSING AGREEMENTS – Recognized educational, commercial, industrial, and governmental institutions and organizations, and others legitimately engaged in educational pursuits, including training, testing, and measurement activities, may address request for a licensing agreement to the copyright owners, who will determine whether, and under what conditions, including fees and charges, the materials in this book may be used them. In other words, a licensing facility exists for the legitimate use of the material in this book on other than an individual basis. However, it is asseverated and affirmed here that the material in this book CANNOT be used without the receipt of the express permission of such a licensing agreement from the Publishers. Inquiries re licensing should be addressed to the company, attention rights and permissions department.

All rights reserved, including the right of reproduction in whole or in part, in any form or by any means, electronic or mechanical, including photocopying, recording, or by any information storage and retrieval system, without permission in writing from the Publisher.

Copyright © 2024 by
National Learning Corporation

212 Michael Drive, Syosset, NY 11791
(516) 921-8888 • www.passbooks.com
E-mail: info@passbooks.com

PASSBOOK® SERIES

THE *PASSBOOK® SERIES* has been created to prepare applicants and candidates for the ultimate academic battlefield – the examination room.

At some time in our lives, each and every one of us may be required to take an examination – for validation, matriculation, admission, qualification, registration, certification, or licensure.

Based on the assumption that every applicant or candidate has met the basic formal educational standards, has taken the required number of courses, and read the necessary texts, the *PASSBOOK® SERIES* furnishes the one special preparation which may assure passing with confidence, instead of failing with insecurity. Examination questions – together with answers – are furnished as the basic vehicle for study so that the mysteries of the examination and its compounding difficulties may be eliminated or diminished by a sure method.

This book is meant to help you pass your examination provided that you qualify and are serious in your objective.

The entire field is reviewed through the huge store of content information which is succinctly presented through a provocative and challenging approach – the question-and-answer method.

A climate of success is established by furnishing the correct answers at the end of each test.

You soon learn to recognize types of questions, forms of questions, and patterns of questioning. You may even begin to anticipate expected outcomes.

You perceive that many questions are repeated or adapted so that you can gain acute insights, which may enable you to score many sure points.

You learn how to confront new questions, or types of questions, and to attack them confidently and work out the correct answers.

You note objectives and emphases, and recognize pitfalls and dangers, so that you may make positive educational adjustments.

Moreover, you are kept fully informed in relation to new concepts, methods, practices, and directions in the field.

You discover that you are actually taking the examination all the time: you are preparing for the examination by "taking" an examination, not by reading extraneous and/or supererogatory textbooks.

In short, this PASSBOOK®, used directedly, should be an important factor in helping you to pass your test.

INTRODUCTION

This study guide has been designed to help you prepare for the Law Enforcement Aptitude Battery (LEAB). The LEAB consists of the following three test components: the Ability Test, the Work Styles Questionnaire, and the Life Experience Survey.

> The Ability Test is designed to test a series of abilities, such as Written Comprehension, Problem Sensitivity and Reasoning, determined to be important to the effective performance of entry-level law enforcement officers.

> The Work Styles Questionnaire is designed to assess certain motivational, value-related and attitudinal characteristics that are of potential relevance to successful performance of entry-level law enforcement officers.

> The Life Experience Survey consists of a series of multiple-choice questions related to candidates' past history and experience of potential relevance to successful performance of entry-level law enforcement officers.

TEST COMPONENT DESCRIPTIONS
SECTION 1: ABILITY TEST

The Ability Test is designed to test a series of abilities, such as Written Comprehension, Problem Sensitivity and Reasoning, determined to be important to the effective performance of entry-level law enforcement officers. The Ability Test contains 48 questions. Each question will be followed by four alternatives (A through D). For each question, candidates will be asked to identify the single best answer and record the response chosen (see examples below in the boxed area).

You should use approximately two hours of the total LEAB assessment time to complete the Ability Test. You should provide a response for every question. Questions that are left unanswered will be scored as incorrect. Therefore, even if you are not at all sure of the correct answer to a question, it is in your best interest to record a response rather than to leave the question blank.

The following examples are presented ONLY for illustrative purposes and do not actually appear on the Ability Test portion of the LEAB. These examples closely represent the kinds of questions that will be included on the Ability Test. Please note that the second example is preceded by a passage. Although there is only one question associated with the passage, during the Ability Test you may be presented with passages of information that apply to more than one question.

Example 1

1. As a law enforcement officer arrived at the scene of a disturbance in an abandoned warehouse, the officer noticed a van leaving the scene. Since the investigation revealed that the warehouse had been vandalized, the officer felt that the van leaving the scene should be included in the report. The most effective way for the officer to report this fact is to say:

   A. "As I arrived at the warehouse, I saw a van driving away from the scene."
   B. "A van which should not have been there, was at the warehouse."
   C. "The vandals escaped in a van."
   D. "I don't know if it's important but as I got there, I saw a vehicle leaving the scene."

Example 2

Use the information in the following passage to answer question 2.

Officer Thompson has noticed that in his patrol area, most of the assaults occur in the eastern and northern sections, while most automobile thefts occur in the southern and western sections and most traffic accidents occur in the western section.

The majority of automobile thefts take place between 3 a.m. and 7 a.m. Most of the traffic accidents occur either between 7 a.m. and 9 a.m. or between 5 p.m. and 8 p.m. Most of the assaults occur between 7 p.m. and 9 p.m. or between 11 p.m. and 4 a.m.

In addition, the traffic accidents almost always occur on Mondays and Fridays, the assaults take place on any day from Wednesday through Saturday, and automobile thefts typically take place on weekday mornings.

2. According to the preceding passage, Officer Thompson most likely would be able to reduce the number of assaults by patrolling the:

   A. eastern section between 5 a.m. and 1 p.m.
   B. eastern section between 11 a.m. and 5 p.m.
   C. western section between 10 p.m. and 6 a.m.
   D. northern section between 8 p.m. and 1 a.m.

WORK STYLES QUESTIONNAIRE

This component is an important part of the LEAB. In addition to the ability requirements placed upon law enforcement officers, successful performance requires certain motivational, value-related, and attitudinal characteristics. The Work Styles Questionnaire will be used to measure these important characteristics.

You should use a total of approximately 45 minutes of the total LEAB assessment time to complete the Work Styles Questionnaire and Life Experience Survey. No preparation is necessary (or expected) for this component of the LEAB. However, the Work Styles Questionnaire will be scored and your score will be combined with your scores on the Life Experience Survey and Ability Test to determine your continued eligibility in the selection process. Examples have been presented in the boxed area below so that you will know what to expect during the Work Styles Questionnaire.

The Work Styles Questionnaire contains a series of 103 short statements. You will read each statement (see examples below) and then decide the degree to which you agree or disagree with each statement as it applies to you by selecting a rating from 1 to 5 using the rating scale presented in the boxed area below.

In this questionnaire you will be instructed to:

- Rate yourself on a scale from 1 to 5 (see scale below) on a number of phrases or statements and record the rating you choose.

- Choose "Unsure" ONLY when you are truly not sure how to rate yourself.

- Work quickly through the questionnaire, provide honest responses and avoid spending too much time thinking about how to respond to any single statement.

- Respond to every statement, even if no single point on the rating scale describes you or the way you feel perfectly, since candidates who do not respond to all statements on the Work Styles Questionnaire may be disqualified from the selection process.

Strongly Disagree	Disagree	Unsure	Agree	Strongly Agree

The following examples are presented ONLY for illustrative purposes and do not actually appear on the Work Styles Questionnaire portion of the LEAB. These examples are closely representative of the kinds of statements that will be included on the Work Styles Questionnaire.

1. I set goals and strive to achieve them.
2. I prefer to work alone.
3. I take time to think about why people do things.
4. I find myself taking control in group situations.
5. I find that it is not necessary to have all of the facts before making a decision.
6. Insults don't bother me.

ABILITY AREAS

This section of the Guide is designed to familiarize you with the nature of the questions you will encounter on the Ability Test, and to provide you with some useful strategies for responding to these types of questions. This portion of the Guide is organized around the ability areas that will be tested. For each ability area, the following information is provided:

Definition.: In this section, the ability area is defined and you are provided with examples of how the ability applies to the job of an entry-level law enforcement officer.

A. ABILITY TEST-TAKING STRATEGIES

1. WRITTEN EXPRESSION

Definition: This ability involves using language in writing to communicate information or ideas to other people. These other people might include suspects, victims, witnesses, other law enforcement personnel, shop owners, or any individuals with whom the individual might come in contact. This ability includes vocabulary, knowledge of distinctions among words, and knowledge of grammar and the way words are ordered.

Examples of this ability include:

- documenting the details of an incident in a report
- composing a letter to a member of the community

Techniques: There are two types of Written Expression questions that you may encounter. The first type requires you to identify the most appropriate way to communicate a particular thought or idea to another individual. For these questions, it is important to ensure that the alternative chosen (a) accurately reflects the content of the original idea, and (b) expresses the original idea in the most clear and concise manner. Consider the example below.

Example 1:

As a law enforcement officer arrived at the scene of a disturbance in an abandoned warehouse, the officer noticed a van leaving the scene. Since the investigation revealed that the warehouse had been vandalized, the officer felt that the van leaving the scene should be included in the report. The most effective way for the officer to report this fact is to say:

A. "As I arrived at the warehouse, I saw a van driving away from the scene."
B. "A van which should not have been there, was at the warehouse."
C. "The vandals escaped in a van."
D. "I don't know if it's important but as I got there, I saw a vehicle leaving the scene."

Correct Response and Explanation:

A is the correct answer, because it correctly reflects the facts given in the question.

Answers B and C are incorrect, because they provide details which have not been established (the van should not have been there AND the vandals escaped in the van) in the question. The officer was only able to state that the vehicle was leaving the scene as the officer arrived.

Answer D is not the best answer because it leaves out the important fact that the vehicle was a van.

The second type of Written Expression question requires that you order your thoughts, or statements, in a logical sequence so that others will understand you. Such questions will start with a list of statements to be made by an individual. For example, the statements may represent sentences contained within a report describing the sequence of events that occurred at an incident. These statements will not be presented in the correct order. The response alternatives will present you with several possible ways to order the statements; however, only one correct possibility will be included among the alternatives provided.

LIFE EXPERIENCE SURVEY

The Life Experience Survey is designed to assess characteristics related to each candidate's past history and experience. In this survey you will be presented with 68 questions. These questions pertain to you and your personal experiences, and will cover many different topics. Each question will be followed by five response alternatives (A through E). For each question you will be asked to select which of the five response alternatives best describes your past experience and to record the response you choose (see the examples in the boxed area below).

You will be instructed to work at a steady pace through this survey, provide honest responses and avoid spending too much time thinking about how to respond to any single question. You will also be instructed to answer every question by selecting the response that best fits you and your personal experiences, even if no single response perfectly describes you or your personal experiences. You should respond to every question since candidates who do not respond to all questions on the Life Experience Survey may be disqualified from the selection process.

You should use a total of approximately 45 minutes of the total LEAB assessment time to complete the Life Experience Survey and Work Styles Questionnaire. Although no extended preparation is necessary (or expected) for this component of the LEAB, **we strongly recommend that you review your previous school and/or work related documents (e.g., school transcripts, resume, evaluations from previous supervisors and/or instructors) to ensure that you are able to answer the Life Experience Survey questions regarding your past experiences as accurately as possible.** The Life Experience Survey will be scored and your score will be combined with your scores on the Work Styles Questionnaire and Ability Test to determine your continued eligibility in the selection process.

Examples are presented below so that you will know what to expect during the administration of the Life Experience Survey. These examples are presented ONLY for illustrative purposes and do not actually appear on the survey but they closely represent the types of questions that you will see when you take this portion of the LEAB.

---

1. Your previous supervisor would describe you as someone who usually does:

    A. more than your fair share of the work that must be done.
    B. more work than most of your coworkers.
    C. about as much work as most of your coworkers.
    D. almost as much work as most of your coworkers.
    E. less work than most of your coworkers.

2. Within the past two years, how many times have you taken a day off because you did not feel like going to work?

    A. never.
    B. once.
    C. twice.
    D. three times.
    E. more than three times.

3. Since completing your high school education, how many days a month do you take part in some form of community-based activity (e.g., community service, athletics, clubs, drama, etc.) outside of work or school?

    A. 0.
    B. 1 - 2.
    C. 3 - 5.
    D. 6 - 8.
    E. 9 or more.

Example 2:

Officer Wilkins is preparing a report on a hit and run accident. The report will include the following sentences. (These sentences are NOT listed in the correct order.)

1. The Dodge struck the right rear fender of Mrs. Smith's Ford, and continued on its way.
2. Mrs. Smith stated that she was making a left turn from 40th St. onto Third Avenue.
3. As the car passed, Mrs. Smith noticed the rear license plate #412AEJ.
4. Mrs. Smith complained to police of back pains and was removed by ambulance to Bellevue Hospital.
5. A green Dodge traveling on Third Avenue went through the red light at 40th St. and Third Avenue.

The most logical order for the above sentences to appear in the report is:

A. 1, 3, 2, 5, 4.
B. 2, 5, 1, 3, 4.
C. 4, 5, 1, 2, 3.
D. 5, 3, 1, 2, 4.

When responding to this type of question, look at the content of each sentence separately and determine whether it can stand alone, or whether it must precede or follow another sentence. If it can't stand alone, look for the sentence that contains the information you need. However, don't forget to evaluate that sentence in the same way as the first. Ask the questions, what happened first and what happened next? Similarly, consider whether there are sentences that the sentence under consideration cannot precede or follow. This also will help to narrow down the choices.

While we suggest that you identify the pairs of sentences that must (or cannot) go together, we'd like to discourage you from attempting to determine the correct order of all of the sentences before checking the response alternatives provided. The reason for this is that there may be several logical ways in which to order the sentences. However, only one correct possibility will be included among the alternatives provided. Instead, we suggest that you work through each of the alternatives presented one-by-one, keeping in mind the sentences that must (or cannot) appear together. Alternatives that are not feasible should be eliminated until you find the one alternative that places the sentences in an appropriate order.

If you're not sure which sentence should be first, you may find it easier to note which sentence should be last. This will help you considerably in eliminating obviously wrong choices. If you don't know which sentence should be first nor last, then go by what you know for sure. In other words, even if you do not know the proper order of all of the sentences, nor which sentence should come first or last, you may know that one of the sentences should come after another. If so, you may be able to choose the correct answer by using just those two sentences to answer the question. **The key thing to remember is that you practically never need to know the correct order of all of the sentences to answer these types of questions.**

Correct Response and Explanation:

The correct answer is B. To identify the correct order, the sentences for the report need to be placed into the proper time sequence. Sentences 1, 2, 3 and 5 describe the events of the accident. The proper sequence for these four events is 2, 5, 1, 3. (Mrs. Smith is attempting a left turn, a Dodge ran the red light, struck her vehicle and continued on its way, and as it passed she noticed its license plate number.) Answer B is the only alternative with this sequence.

Sample Test Questions:

Sample Question 1:

1. A law enforcement officer is writing an outline for a presentation to a local citizen's group on the role of law enforcement in responding to domestic conflicts. During the presentation, the officer would like to explain that law enforcement officers are often contacted because a domestic conflict is disturbing neighbors. In addition, the officer will point out that many calls occur prior to a crime being committed. This is effective, because one of the objectives of law enforcement is to stop crime before it starts. The most effective way for the officer to sum up the role of law enforcement in responding to domestic conflicts during the presentation is to say:

    A. "Since frequently no crime has been committed, the role of law enforcement in domestic conflicts is fairly limited."
    B. "In responding to domestic conflicts, the officer's function is to restore order and prevent possible crimes from occurring."
    C. "The officer's main goal in responding to domestic conflicts is to protect the innocent."
    D. "Many people involved in domestic conflicts call the police in order to have an objective authority help settle disputes."

Sample Question 2:

2. Officer Turner is writing a report on a homicide investigation. The report will include the following five sentences. (These sentences are NOT listed in the correct order.)

    1. I noticed a display case for handguns was open, but there were no guns in it.

    2. We got a call reporting that the front door of a pawnshop was open, but the owner was not there.

    3. We interviewed tenants of the apartments in the upstairs sections of the same building.

    4. Upon arrival, we discovered the body of the shop owner, apparently dead from knife wounds to the chest.

    5. I called an ambulance to pick up the victim.

    The most logical order for the above sentences to appear in the report is:

    A. 2, 1, 4, 5, 3.
    B. 2, 4, 5, 1, 3.
    C. 2, 5, 1, 3, 4.
    D. 4, 5, 2, 3, 1.

2. WRITTEN COMPREHENSION

Definition: This is the ability to understand written language. This ability involves the understanding of individual words as well as patterns of words (sentences and phrases), so it is more than simply vocabulary. It is also the ability to read a sentence or series of sentences and understand the meaning. This involves receiving information, not giving it.

Examples of this ability include:

- reading narrative material, such as an arrest report
- following written instructions

Techniques: Items designed to test Written Comprehension will include a passage describing a police-related incident or set of operating procedures. These passages will be approximately one-half to a full page in length and will be followed by two or more test questions. These questions will test your understanding of the information presented in the passage.

For some candidates, these questions may prove to be difficult simply because of the initial amount of information you'll be given. Some of the techniques you can use on these questions have already been discussed as part of the general test-taking strategies.

A. One of the most useful techniques involves <u>reading the test questions and possible answers before reading the passage</u> to help you identify and focus on the information that is being sought. You may find that you locate the answer to one of the questions related to a passage before you even finish reading the passage. If so, answer the question right away. As you go from one sentence or paragraph to the next in the passage, you may have to glance back at the questions to remind yourself of the specific details for which you are searching.

B. Another extremely useful technique is to <u>identify key words</u> once you have read the questions related to a passage and know what to focus on. For example, if the questions related to the passage seek information about a particular person (e.g., Mr. Jones), then make note of Mr. Jones' name when you come to it in the passage, so that you don't waste time looking back through the passage later. Also, make the passage easier to understand by breaking sentences down into key phrases.

C. These tend to be time consuming questions which you may not have the opportunity to read more than once. A third technique is to <u>read for understanding the first time and avoid getting bogged down by individual words</u> that you do not understand. Sometimes you can tell the meaning of a word from the context within which it has been placed, or you may not need to understand the word at all to understand the passage. We caution you, however, do not try to read faster than you can read with comprehension.

D. Try to <u>form a picture in your mind as you read</u>. School books used to teach reading contain many pictures, since pictures aid in comprehension.

E. <u>Ask yourself questions as you read</u>. When you finish reading a paragraph or a long sentence, ask yourself what the passage or sentence was about. What was the point of the paragraph or sentence?

It's important to note that most of the suggested strategies for Written Comprehension questions are designed to help candidates understand the relatively lengthy passage of information which precede these questions. Thus, these strategies would be useful with any type of question that requires candidates to read and understand a large amount of information.

Sample Test Questions:

Use the information in the following passage to answer questions 3 and 4.

Two patrol vehicles were dispatched to a home on the evening of June 12, at 9:47 p.m. The owner of the home had reported a robbery which took place while he and his wife were out. The owner also stated that the suspects were still in the home when he and his wife arrived, but they fled the scene in a dark blue sedan.

Upon arrival at the home, Officers Baker and Reigner began to question Mr. Corneal. In the meantime, Officers Lucas and Gentry conducted a preliminary investigation of the home to determine the activities of the suspects. The questioning revealed that Mr. Corneal collected exotic guns and had accumulated an extensive collection. In addition, Mrs. Corneal had several sets of antique jewelry. When questioned as to who knew about the collections, Mr. Corneal stated that only friends of the family and members of the rifle club were aware of them. He was further questioned to determine whether any unusual events had occurred recently that might be related to this incident. Mr. Corneal stated that they had extensive remodeling done to the interior of the home during the past six weeks by several different companies. Officer Reigner asked if they had reason to suspect any of the workers. Mr. Corneal stated that several members of the crew had shown an interest in seeing and discussing his collection of guns, but that it would be very difficult to determine which individuals, if any, may have been involved. Officer Reigner requested the names of the companies and the services they performed.

After a few minutes, Officers Lucas and Gentry returned from their search of the home. They had determined that the suspects concentrated their efforts on the two collections, since the only other areas of the home that were disturbed were ones which typically contain money (e.g., dresser top, dresser drawers). They concluded that the suspects must have been aware of the collections before entering the home.

Sample Question 3:

3. According to the preceding passage, when the Corneals arrived home on the evening of June 12, they discovered that their home had been:

    A. ransacked, but nothing was stolen.
    B. entered, and the television, stereo, and computer were stolen.
    C. entered, and the suspects were still in the home.
    D. robbed, and five antique guns and several pieces of exotic jewelry were the items that were taken.

Sample Question 4:

4. According to the preceding passage, considering the robbery and subsequent investigation described above, the ONLY statement that accurately reflects the information gathered is:

    A. Officer Reigner requested the names of the companies and the services they performed.
    B. Mrs. Corneal seemed to be the one to answer all of the officers' questions.
    C. Officer Baker helped with the search of the home.
    D. The robbers fled the scene in a dark blue van.

3. PROBLEM SENSITIVITY

Definition: This is the ability to recognize or identify the existence of problems. It involves both the recognition of the problem as a whole and the elements of the problem. This ability does not include the ability to solve the problem, only the ability to identify or recognize the problem.

Examples of this ability include recognizing when:

- an explanation that someone provides is farfetched and probably not truthful
- to stop and question a group of individuals
- to call in information about roadway conditions
- to report a malfunction in the patrol car

Techniques: There are two types of Problem Sensitivity questions that you may encounter. The first type of Problem Sensitivity question will consist of stories or descriptions by victims and witnesses. For these questions, a problem exists when a victim or witness gives information that is different from information supplied by other victims or witnesses. Consider the example below.

Example 1:

Officer Dunn interviewed four witnesses to a stabbing that took place in a crowded bar and grill. Each of the witnesses saw the suspect as he was fleeing the bar. They described the suspect as follows:

Witness 1 - "He was a White male, about 25 to 30 years of age, with brown, shoulder-length hair. He was about 6'0" and weighed about 185 pounds. He wore black jeans and a brown leather jacket. He had a small scar on his forehead."

Witness 2 - "He was a male, White or Hispanic, late twenties, around 5'10", about 190 pounds, with long, brown hair. He was stocky and wore dark pants and a brownish jacket."

Witness 3 - "He was a light skinned male, possibly White or Hispanic, in his mid-twenties, about 6' weighing about 180 pounds. He had a tattoo of a panther on his right forearm. He had moderately long hair and wore a brown shirt and dark pants."

Witness 4 - "He was a White male, around 25 years old, about 5'11" and weighing about 185 pounds. His hair was brown and over his ears, fairly long. He wore darkish clothes, I'm not sure of the color of his jacket or pants."

Given the above information, Officer Dunn should recognize that there is a problem with the description given by witness:

A. 1.
B. 2.
C. 3.
D. 4.

Correct Response and Explanation:

C is the correct answer. There is agreement that the suspect was a White or Hispanic male in his mid-to-late twenties with long, brown hair who was approximately 6' tall and 185 pounds. In addition, his pants and jacket were dark in color. There were only two discrepancies across the descriptions. Witness 1 reported that the suspect had a small scar on his forehead. Witness 3 reported a tattoo of a panther on the suspect's right forearm. Of the two, it is much harder to explain how a tattoo of a panther could be overlooked by three of four witnesses AND how one witness could see it when the other three witnesses all stated that the suspect had a jacket on during the incident. Thus, C is the best answer.

The second type of Problem Sensitivity question will often begin with the presentation of rules, procedures or recommended practices followed by a description of an incident or situation in which these rules should be applied. Based on the applicable rules, you will be required to identify a problem (or the most serious of several problems) in the way the incident was handled. Because this type of Problem Sensitivity question typically involves the presentation of a large amount of initial information, many of the suggested strategies for Written Comprehension questions (e.g., identifying key information) will also assist you with these types of questions.

Example 2:

Use the information in the following passage to answer this question.

Police and Fire Departments have standard procedures for handling bomb threats that include the following:

1. Trained police personnel direct operations at the scene; fire personnel stand by and typically assist in rescue operations.
2. While radios may be left on at the scene of an unexploded device to receive instructions from the Communications Office, no radio transmissions are to be made from the scene, because radio signals can detonate an explosive device.
3. The decision to evacuate a building is to be made by the management of the building, unless an explosive device has been found; in such an instance, police personnel in charge of the scene make the evacuation decision.
4. No public statements are to be made to the media by police or fire personnel.
5. If one device detonates, there is always the possibility of a second or third device, so police and fire personnel should stay clear of the area until it has been determined (usually by Bomb Squad Personnel) to be safe.

According to the preceding passage, of the four actions described below, the potentially most serious error would occur if:

A. Immediately after a second bomb exploded in a bank, Firefighter Thomas entered the bank to conduct rescue operations.
B. While standing by at the scene of a bomb threat, Police Lieutenant Caffey provided information regarding the incident to a reporter.
C. While standing by at the scene of a bomb threat, Fire Lieutenant Griffin received instructions from the Communications Office via his radio.
D. After an unexploded device was discovered in an apartment building, Assistant Police Chief Johnson ordered the apartment building manager to evacuate the building.

Correct Response and Explanation:

A is the correct answer. Answers A and B represent the only mistakes. With respect to answer A, Firefighter Thomas should have waited to enter the bank until the Bomb Squad Personnel determined that it was safe (according to procedure 5). With respect to answer B, no police or fire personnel, should make a public statement to the media (according to procedure 4). Since the question asks for the "potentially most serious error," the best answer is A, since entering the bank without proper safety clearance is a direct risk to one's own life and to the life of anyone who follows.

C is incorrect, because it is acceptable to receive instructions via the radio as long as no transmissions are made (according to procedure 2).

D is incorrect, because the actions of Assistant Police Chief Johnson were appropriate (according to procedure 3).

Sample Test Questions:

Sample Question 5:

Use the information in the following passage to answer question 5.

Law enforcement officers should follow the guidelines presented below when dealing with individuals suspected of driving while under the influence of alcohol:

1. A separate citation shall be issued for any traffic offense that originally brought the driver to the attention of the officers (e.g., reckless operation of motor vehicle).

2. If the driver refuses to submit to a blood alcohol test or submits to such tests and scores above the limit, the arresting officer should order the driver to surrender his/her license and issue a citation for driving under the influence.

3. If the driver scores below the legal limit on the blood alcohol test, his/her license shall not be confiscated. The results of field tests (e.g., walking heel to toe on a straight line) have no influence on this guideline.

4. Even if the driver scores below the legal limit, the driver can still be charged with driving under the influence, if the officer can justify the charge through the use of field tests.

5. Consider the following situation:

Officer Kelley notices a car swerving in and out of its lane. Officer Kelley stops the car and asks the driver to submit to a test for driving under the influence of alcohol. The driver submits to the test and scores below the legal limit. However, based on the results of several field tests, Officer Kelley still charges the driver with driving under the influence. Officer Kelley then orders the driver to surrender his license.

According to the preceding passage, Officer Kelley's actions were:

A. appropriate, because they were consistent with the guidelines provided.
B. problematic, because the driver was forced to surrender his license.
C. problematic, because Officer Kelley did not have a witness to the field tests.
D. problematic, because Officer Kelley charged the driver with driving under the influence even though the driver passed the blood alcohol test.

Sample Question 6:

6. Officer Johnson interviewed four witnesses to a bank robbery. Each of the witnesses described the suspects as follows:

Witness 1 - "There were two of them. Both male, about 6'2" tall, with medium builds. One of them had dark hair and was wearing jeans, a leather jacket, and sunglasses. The other had short, blond hair and was wearing jeans and a red, light-weight jacket. Only the one with the sunglasses spoke, and he had a foreign accent."

Witness 2 - "Both of the men were about the same size. Maybe 6', about 180 pounds. One of them was wearing a leather jacket and the other one was wearing a light-weight, red jacket. I couldn't see their faces because one had on a ski mask and the other had on dark sunglasses. The one with the sunglasses had dark hair."

Witness 3 - "Both of the men were about 6'1" and 180 pounds. One had on a leather jacket, the other a red windbreaker. Both men were wearing jeans and tennis shoes. One had dark hair and sunglasses on. The other one was wearing some kind of stocking cap that was pulled down over his face."

Witness 4 - "Both men had on jeans, tennis shoes and jackets. One jacket was leather, the other bright red. One of the men had dark hair, and I could not see the other one's face because of a ski mask. They both looked a little over 6' tall. Only the one with the dark hair spoke."

Given the above information, Officer Johnson should recognize that there is a problem with the description provided by witness:

A. 1.
B. 2.
C. 3.
D. 4.

4. DEDUCTIVE REASONING

Definition: This is the ability to apply general rules or regulations to specific cases or to proceed from stated principles to logical conclusions.

Examples of this ability include:

- identifying a particular situation as a civil or criminal case
- distinguishing between burglary and trespass, or between assault and harassment
- determining whether a homeless person should be referred to a charitable organization or a public welfare agency
- determining which factors to take into account when drawing a weapon

Techniques: There are four types of Deductive Reasoning questions that you may encounter, questions based on verbal rules and procedures, questions based on quantitative rules, questions based on the assignment of a specific case to one of several given classifications, and law interpretation questions.

For Questions Based on Verbal or Quantitative Rules and Procedures: The first and second types of questions will start with the presentation of general verbal or quantitative rules and procedures and require candidates to apply the general rules to specific cases. The general quantitative rules and procedures will be presented in tabular fashion. Rules and procedures are intended to ensure that law enforcement officers make correct decisions in a wide variety of situations. There are four factors to attend to when answering questions about rules and procedures:

1. **PAY ATTENTION TO THE DEFINITE ORDER IN WHICH STEPS ARE TAKEN**: Many rules and procedures require law enforcement officers to go through a series of actions. There is often a correct order for these actions. Make sure the correct answer has that same sequence of steps.

2. **PAY ATTENTION TO WHEN A RULE OR PROCEDURE IS IN EFFECT**: Some rules apply only to certain types of situations or certain periods of time. Make sure the correct answer applies to the situation and time in question.

3. **PAY CLOSE ATTENTION TO EXCEPTIONS**: Pay particular attention to any exceptions given in the rule or procedure. Identify key words such as **except**, **unless**, **if**, and **only** that "harden" or "soften" statements.

4. **PAY ATTENTION TO COMPLETENESS**: If a procedure requires law enforcement officers to do several things, make certain the correct answer allows that all those things can be done. However, if the question is just focusing on a few things, or on a series of many, make sure the correct answer doesn't eliminate the possibility of the events taking place.

For Questions Based on the Assignment of a Specific Case to One of Several Given Classifications: The third type of question will start with the presentation of categories or classifications and require candidates to assign a specific case to one of the given categories or classifications. The following strategy may be helpful in responding to this type of Deductive Reasoning question.

1. Determine how the classifications or categories differ.

2. Review the particular incident presented in the question with regard to these differences.

3. Identify the classification or category that matches the particular incident with regard to these differences.

Example 1:

Use the information in the following passage to answer the next question.

Law enforcement officers categorize accidents into the four classes described below:

CLASS I - Any accident involving one vehicle but no injuries.

CLASS II - Any accident involving two vehicles but no injuries or one vehicle and at least one injury.

CLASS III - Any accident involving two or more vehicles and multiple injuries.

CLASS IV - Any accident involving a hazardous materials spill.

Consider the following situation:

A law enforcement officer was dispatched to the scene of an accident. When the officer arrived, the officer found a nine-year-old girl with a pair of roller blades lying on the road. Witnesses stated that a small blue car swerved to avoid hitting the girl, but the car's back bumper hit the girl as it passed. The driver did not stop to see if the girl was hurt. According to the preceding passage, the accident could be categorized most accurately as Class:

A. I.
B. II.
C. III.
D. IV.

Correct Response and Explanation:

B is the correct answer. The accident involved one vehicle and one injury.

A is incorrect because Class I involves one vehicle and no injuries, but the situation presented involved one injury.

C is incorrect because Class III involves two vehicles with multiple injuries, but the situation presented involved only one vehicle and one injury.

D is incorrect because Class IV involves a hazardous materials spill, but the situation presented did not involve a spill.

For Law Interpretation Questions: The fourth type of Deductive Reasoning question will provide you with a definition of a police-related term (usually a crime) and ask you to interpret the term with respect to a specific police-related situation. Like questions which list procedures (e.g., Information Ordering), these questions require great attention to detail. You must carefully analyze the definition of a crime.

Analyzing the Definition: The definition of a crime usually has several parts. Each part is referred to as an element. The elements are like the pieces of a puzzle; all the elements must be present to make up the crime. If any one of the elements is missing, that particular crime has not been committed.

There are usually several elements in a legal definition. The definition must be broken down into these separate elements. Once the elements of the definition are separated, identify key words and take note of words that "harden" or "soften" statements in the definition. Then, check to see if the elements apply to the situation. The elements must be compared to the situation on an item-by-item basis. Specifically, watch out for the words **AND** and **OR**.

AND means that one element must be present in addition to another for the crime to be present.

OR means there is a choice of elements; only one of the choices must be present for the crime to be committed.

For example, consider the definition of **DISORDERLY CONDUCT:** When, with intent to cause public inconvenience, annoyance or alarm or recklessly creating a risk thereof, a person engages in fighting or in violent, tumultuous or threatening behavior.

The slash marks below indicate how you can separate the definition to make it easier to understand:

DISORDERLY CONDUCT: When, / with intent to cause public inconvenience, annoyance or alarm / or recklessly creating a risk thereof, / a person engages in fighting / or in violent, tumultuous or threatening behavior.

For the crime of **DISORDERLY CONDUCT**:

Is it necessary to intend public inconvenience, annoyance or alarm? No. The definition says "intent to cause... **OR** recklessly create a risk thereof..."

Is it necessary to be fighting? No. The definition says "engages in fighting **OR** in violent, tumultuous **OR** threatening behavior."

Practice using this strategy with the example below:

Example 2:

Criminal Mischief - the crime of criminal mischief is committed when:

1. A person intentionally damages property belonging to another and the amount of the damage is 250 dollars or more; or
2. A person intentionally damages property, in any amount, by means of explosives.

According to the definition given, the following is the best example of criminal mischief:

A. Frank is playing baseball with his friends when he hits a ball that breaks the 2,000 dollar window of Ford Motors.
B. Tony is chopping down a tree in his backyard. The tree falls the wrong way and hits the neighbor's house, causing 3,500 dollars worth of damage.
C. Harold gets mad after an argument with his wife and throws his 600 dollar T.V. through the 200 dollar picture window of his house.
D. Lloyd decides to get even with a neighbor and throws an M-80 firecracker onto his neighbor's porch on Halloween night. The only damage is to his neighbor's milk box, about 15 dollars.

Correct Response and Explanation:

D is the correct answer. Intentional damage using explosives fits part 2 of the Criminal Mischief definition.

A and B are incorrect because there was no intent in either case to damage property (the window or the house, respectively).

C is incorrect because, although there was intent, no explosives were used **AND** the damage to property <u>belonging to another</u> was not equal to or greater than 250 dollars, because Harold damaged his own property.

Sample Test Questions:

Sample Question 7:

Use the information in the following table to answer question 7.

Law enforcement officers are required to call for backup when responding to certain offenses. Examples of offenses requiring backup are listed below, along with the number of backup officers needed:

OFFENSES	NUMBER OF BACKUP OFFICERS
Speeding violations of more than 30 mph over the posted speed limit.	1
Robbery whereby the police are notified within 30 minutes after the incident.	1
Fatal traffic accident where two or less people are killed.	2
Any situation involving hostages.	3
Any situation where three or more people are killed.	3
Any situation where there are two or more armed suspects.	3

7. According to the preceding table, Officer Latimer should call for backup in the following situation:

   A. A manager of a store reported a robbery that occurred more than 30 minutes ago after untying himself from a chair.
   B. A motorist traveled 35 mph in a 65 mph zone because of poor road conditions.
   C. A suspect armed with an automatic rifle has been holding employees and customers of a liquor store hostage for 40 minutes.
   D. Two people suffered broken bones in a traffic accident.

Sample Question 8:

Use the information in the following passage to answer question 8.

The following dress code guidelines apply to law enforcement officers.

1. The Antron Jacket will be worn for outside duty during the months of November through February and whenever the temperature is below 55 degrees.
2. The Eisenhower Jacket shall be worn for outside duty during the months of March, April, May, September, and October, only if the temperature is below 65 degrees. Officers at the rank of Captain or above may wear the Double Breasted Blouse instead of the Eisenhower Jacket.
3. A navy blue, long sleeve uniform shirt shall be the standard shirt to be worn with all jackets. All individuals at the rank of Captain or above will substitute a white shirt.
4. The short sleeve shirt may be worn whenever the temperature is above 70 degrees during the months of May through September.
5. Officers assigned to indoor duty may also substitute the short sleeve shirt for the long sleeve shirt.
6. Regulation trousers shall be worn. The black trouser braid or stripe shall be worn by individuals at the rank of Lieutenant and above.

TYPICAL RANKS (from highest rank to lowest rank):	1. Chief of Police	4. Lieutenant
	2. Deputy Chief	5. Sergeant
	3. Captain	6. Patrol Officer

8. Consider the following situation:

The temperature for the day is expected to stay right around 60 degrees. The date is September 15. According to the preceding passage, if Captain Cross was assigned to outside duty she should wear:

A. an Eisenhower Jacket, a white, long sleeve shirt and regulation trousers with a black stripe.
B. a Double Breasted Blouse, a navy blue, long sleeve shirt and regulation trousers.
C. an Antron Jacket, a white, long sleeve shirt and regulation trousers with a black braid.
D. a Double Breasted Blouse, a white, short sleeve shirt and regulation trousers with a black braid.

5. INDUCTIVE REASONING

Definition: This is the ability to find a rule or concept that fits the situation. This would include coming up with a logical explanation for a series of events that seem to be unrelated. In addition, this ability involves understanding how a string of objects or events might be connected.

Examples of this ability include:

- coming upon an accident scene and correctly guessing what must have happened from the position of the cars, the skid marks, and the road conditions
- recognizing that the same pattern applies to a series of burglaries or purse snatchings
- examining a log book for previous days in order to see if there is some pattern that can be found for a series of events

Techniques: Inductive Reasoning questions require that you notice something common among a series of events or objects. In order to do this, you have to be able to identify the details that are important to answering a question. The majority of questions for Inductive Reasoning will start with a passage which provides you with all the information you will need to answer the question. Scan the passage to get an idea of what it's about and then read the questions. The questions may ask you to identify which parts of the passage are similar or different. For example there may be a description of four different incidents of rape and you may be asked which ones might have been committed by the same suspect. This will require you to compare the four descriptions, point-by-point and to note differences that would rule out the same suspect. For example, if a heavy, White male, committed one rape and a thin, Black male committed another rape, they could not have been committed by the same suspect. You might find it useful to compare objects or suspects by asking, 'Are they the same or different?" The table below shows how you might compare four rape suspects to answer this question.

	Suspect Description				
	Height	Weight	Race	Age	Scars
Rape 1	5'10"	170	W	30	No
Rape 2	5'3"	120	W	16	Face
Rape 3	5'8"	155	B	26	No
Rape 4	5'9"	165	W	35	No

From looking at this table, you can be fairly sure that the suspect in Rape 3 was not involved in rapes 1, 2, or 4 since he was described as Black and the other suspects are White. Also, the suspect in Rape 2 was probably not involved in 1 or 4, because he is too short (5'3") and the other two suspects are described as average in height. On the other hand, the same suspect could have committed Rape 1 and Rape 4, since there are only slight differences in estimated height, weight and age.

Remember, when you are reading the question, identify the pieces of important information. This might include color of clothing or the physical characteristics of a suspect. When considering the example on the next page, compare the suspects in a similar way and ask if they are the same or different.

Example 1:

Officer Crawford received a series of reports from victims who were mugged in the early evening as they were exiting from the Spruce Street subway station. The description of each suspect is as follows:

Report 1 (November 16) - male, White, early 30s, around 5'10", about 180 pounds, dark hair, mustache, one gold earring, blue jeans, black jacket, running shoes.

Report 2 (November 20) - male, White, 25-30, about 5'6", around 120 pounds, dark hair, dark glasses, one gold earring, blue jeans, green sweatshirt, running shoes.

Report 3 (November 21) - male, White, 40-45, almost 5'10", about 130-140 pounds, dark hair, mustache, one gold earring, blue jeans, black jacket, running shoes.

On November 23rd, a male who was loitering near the subway station mugged another person. However, a witness saw the mugging, called 911, and the male was apprehended two blocks away. The description of the suspect is as follows:

Report 4 (November 23) - male, White, 25-30, 5'10", 175 pounds, dark hair, mustache, blue jeans, black jacket, green ski cap, boots.

Based on the description given above of the suspects in the first three reports, the suspect in report 4 should also be considered a suspect in report(s):

A. 1 only.
B. 1 and 2 only.
C. 2 and 3 only.
D. 1, 2, and 3.

Correct Response and Explanation:

The important differences among the suspects in the four reports center around three characteristics -- age, height and weight. Report 4 does not match Report 2, because the suspects differ substantially with respect to height and weight. Report 4 does not match Report 3, because the suspects differ substantially with respect to age and weight. Report 4 does closely match Report 1. Comparing the suspects in the reports allow us to determine the correct answer, A.

Sample Test Questions:

Sample Question 9:

Use the information in the following passage to answer question 9.

Officer Thompson has noticed that in his patrol area, most of the assaults occur in the eastern and northern sections, while most automobile thefts occur in the southern and western sections and most traffic accidents occur in the western section.

The majority of automobile thefts take place between 3 a.m. and 7 a.m. Most of the traffic accidents occur either between 7 a.m. and 9 a.m. or between 5 p.m. and 8 p.m. Most of the assaults occur between 7 p.m. and 9 p.m. or between 11 p.m. and 4 a.m.

In addition, the traffic accidents almost always occur on Mondays and Fridays, the assaults take place on any day from Wednesday through Saturday, and automobile thefts typically take place on weekday mornings.

9. According to the preceding passage, Officer Thompson most likely would be able to reduce the number of assaults by patrolling the:

   A. eastern section between 5 a.m. and 1 p.m.
   B. eastern section between 11 a.m. and 5 p.m.
   C. western section between 10 p.m. and 6 a.m.
   D. northern section between 8 p.m. and 1 a.m.

Sample Question 10:

10. Officer Riggins received a series of reports from victims who were mugged outside the South Side Shopping Plaza. The description of each suspect is as follows:

Incident 1: (May 7) - male, Black, early 20s, almost 5'9", about 170 pounds, black hair, tattoo on his upper arm, blue jeans and t-shirt.

Incident 2: (May 13) - male, Black, 20-26, about 5'10", around 175 pounds, black hair, tattoo on left hand, tank top, jeans and sneakers.

Incident 3: (May 15) - male, Black, late teens, about 5'11", around 190 pounds, brown hair, snake tattoos on both forearms and red tank top.

Incident 4: (May 20) - male, Black, 17-21, 6'1"-6'2", about 210 pounds, brown hair, brown pants, a three-quarter length sleeve shirt, and no jewelry.

Incident 5: (May 21) - male, Black, 16-20, about 6'7", around 230 pounds, black hair, an earring in the left ear, blue jeans and a tank top.

On June 3rd, a suspect was apprehended after mugging a person outside the South Side Shopping Plaza. The description of the suspect is as follows:

Incident 6: (June 3) – male, Black, 23, 5'10", 180 pounds, black hair, a tattoo of a cobra on his bicep, cut-off blue jeans and a muscle shirt.

Based on the descriptions given above of the suspects in the first five incidents, the suspect in incident 6 should also be considered a suspect in incident:

   A. 1.
   B. 2.
   C. 3.
   D. 5.

6. INFORMATION ORDERING

Definition: This is the ability to apply rules to a situation for the purpose of putting the information in the best or most appropriate sequence. In order to use this ability, rules or instructions must exist for the person to know what the correct order of information is. This ability also involves the application of specified sequences or procedures to a given situation. This ability would come into play particularly when deciding which set of procedures to follow first, which to follow next, and so on.

Examples of this ability include:

- determining what should be done first, second, and so on in a first aid situation
- arranging the importance of certain activities in a traffic accident or domestic dispute
- determining whether traffic control or first aid procedures take priority and should be implemented first at a traffic accident on a busy street when a serious injury is involved

Techniques: These questions usually start with the relevant rules, procedures, or other items of information. In some instances, procedures are presented in the order in which they must be performed. Candidates are then given a specific set of events and asked to identify the next step which must be followed (based on the sequence of procedures specified in the initial passage). Such questions require you to closely follow the sequence of procedures presented in the initial passage. Consider the example below.

Example 1:

Use the information in the following passage to answer the next question.

When responding to an incident involving a person needing medical assistance, law enforcement officers should follow these steps in the order given:

1. Render reasonable aid to the sick or injured person.
2. Request an ambulance or doctor, if necessary.
3. Notify the Radio Dispatcher if the person is wearing a Medic-Alert emblem, indicating that the person suffers from diabetes, heart disease, or other serious medical problems.
4. Wait to direct the ambulance to the scene, or instruct someone else at the scene to do so.
5. Make a second call in 20 minutes if the ambulance does not arrive.
6. Make an Activity Log entry, including the name of the person notified regarding the Medic-Alert emblem.

While on foot patrol, Officer Grayson is approached by a woman who informs the officer that an elderly man has just collapsed on the sidewalk around the corner. Officer Grayson, while offering aid to the man, notices that the man is wearing a Medic-Alert emblem indicating heart disease. Officer Grayson, requests an ambulance to respond. According to the preceding passage, the next step the officer should take is to:

A. wait for the ambulance to arrive.
B. have another person direct the ambulance to the scene.
C. place a second call for the ambulance after 20 minutes.
D. inform the Radio Dispatcher of the Medic-Alert emblem.

Correct Response and Explanation:

The correct answer is D. There are two key points to this question. First, the last step completed by Officer Grayson was to request an ambulance (step 2). Second, the next step is a conditional one. The radio dispatcher is only notified if "the person is wearing a Medic-Alert emblem." According to the description of the incident, prior to calling for the ambulance, Grayson "notices that the man is wearing a Medic-Alert emblem." Thus, the next step would be number 3 (as indicated by answer D). Answers A, B and C are incorrect, because they correspond to steps 4, 4 and 5, respectively.

In other Information Ordering questions, the initial items of information may be presented out of order and you may be asked to arrange the information in the most logical order.

Example 2:

Law enforcement officers may discover firearms at crime scenes. The following steps should be used when discovering a firearm at a crime scene. (These steps are NOT listed in the correct order.)

1. Note the position of the hammer, and whether the safety latch is on or off.
2. Unload the firearm, if possible, to ensure safe transportation.
3. Place each recovered spent cartridge separately in an envelope or box.
4. Carefully transport the firearm, cartridges, and cartridge casings to the lab for analysis.
5. Photograph the firearm close up and sketch each cartridge case position.
6. Wrap recovered cartridges in tissue paper.

The most logical order for the above steps is:

A. 1, 5, 2, 6, 3, 4.
B. 2, 6, 3, 5, 1, 4.
C. 5, 1, 3, 6, 2, 4.
D. 5, 4, 1, 6, 3, 2.

The approach recommended for these types of questions is similar to the approach recommended for the second type of Written Expression question. That is, put in order only as much information as you need to answer the question. Don't try to put all of the steps in correct order. You could be wasting valuable time doing this, because you usually do not need to put all of the steps in order to identify the correct answer. Consider only the order shown in each of the response alternatives. Go through the alternatives one-by-one. Examine each alternative only as far as the point where you find it to be wrong. Then proceed to the next response alternative.

If you're not sure which step should be first on the list, you may find it easier to note which step should be last. This will help you considerably in eliminating obviously wrong choices. If you don't know which step should be first nor last, then go by what you know for sure. In other words, even if you do not know the proper order of all of the steps, nor which step should come first or last, you may know that one of the steps should come after another. If so, you may be able to choose the correct answer by using just those two steps to answer the question. **The key thing to remember is that you practically never need to know the correct order of all of the steps to answer these types of questions.**

Correct Response and Explanation:

The correct answer is A. To determine the correct answer, the steps must be listed in the correct time sequence. Steps 2, 3, 5 and 6 deal with handling the cartridges (or cartridge casings) which are either in the firearm or ejected to the ground. In terms of these four steps, 5 must occur before 2, 2 before 6 and 6 before 3. In other words, you must sketch the cartridge positions before unloading cartridges from the firearm. The firearm must be unloaded before the cartridges can be wrapped. Once the cartridges are wrapped, then the recovered cartridges are placed in a separate envelope or box. The only answer with the 5, 2, 6, 3 sequence is answer A.

Sample Test Questions:

Sample Question 11:

Use the information in the following passage to answer question 11.

When dusting objects at a crime scene for fingerprints, law enforcement officers should follow these steps in the order given:

1. Choose a powder color in contrast with the surface to be dusted.
2. Dip a brush into the powder and work the powder into the fibers of the brush.
3. Lift the brush out of the powder, checking to make sure there is not too much powder on the brush.
4. Holding the brush lightly, shake a light dusting of powder onto the suspected area.
5. If a light pattern shows up, brush more powder into the pattern lightly with the flow of the ridges.
6. Lightly clean up the pattern by brushing excess powder out of the voids between the ridges to define the print.
7. Photograph the impression and proceed to lift the impression with transparent tape.

11. An officer is dusting the top of a dresser for fingerprints and notices a pattern emerging. According to the preceding passage, the officer's next step should be to:

    A. follow along the pattern with additional powder on the brush.
    B. shake a light dusting of powder over the entire area.
    C. shake the brush lightly to make sure there is no excess powder on it.
    D. photograph the impression and lift the impression with transparent tape.

Sample Question 12:

12. Law enforcement officers are required to search all individuals that have been taken into custody prior to placing individuals in a station holding cell. The following steps should be used when searching a prisoner. (These steps are NOT listed in the correct order.)

    1. Lower both of your hands to the base of the prisoner's neck and proceed with the search by covering the chest, stomach, and back.
    2. Have the prisoner empty all pockets in pants, shirt, coat and jacket.
    3. Be sure no other prisoners are in the room when the search takes place.
    4. From the waistline, proceed down the legs, using both hands on one leg and then the other.
    5. Have the prisoner stand facing a wall, back to you, legs spread and arms extended straight out.
    6. From behind, using both hands, start at the forehead and run your fingers or a comb through the prisoner's hair.

The most logical order for the above steps is:

A. 2, 1, 4, 3, 5, 6.
B. 3, 2, 5, 6, 1, 4.
C. 3, 5, 2, 6, 4, 1.
D. 3, 5, 4, 2, 6, 1.

B. SAMPLE TEST QUESTIONS: ANSWERS AND EXPLANATIONS

The answers to the sample test questions for the six ability areas are listed below. Explanations of the answers follow this list.

1. B	5. B	9. D
2. B	6. A	10. A
3. C	7. C	11. A
4. A	8. A	12. B

Written Expression questions - 1 and 2.

1. B is the correct answer. It correctly reflects the role of law enforcement in responding to domestic conflicts -- 1) handling a conflict that disturbs the neighbors AND 2) stopping crime before it starts.

    Although alternatives A, C and D do relate (in varying degrees) to other aspects of law enforcement involvement in domestic conflicts, none of these aspects are directly mentioned as information in the question.

2. The correct answer is B. To identify the correct order, the sentences to be included in the report need to be ordered into the proper time sequence. The clearest clues involve sentences 4 and 2.

    Sentence 4 begins "Upon arrival..." Therefore, sentence 4 must separate the actions that occurred prior to arriving at the scene from those events occurring after arriving at the scene. Sentence 2 is the only statement regarding actions prior to arriving (i.e., getting the call). Thus, sentence 2 must occur first and be followed by sentence 4. Only answer B begins with the sequence 2, 4. In addition, the rest of the sequence (5, 1, 3) is also appropriate.

Written Comprehension questions - 3 and 4.

3. C is the correct answer. As stated in the passage, "The owner of the home had reported a robbery...**AND**... the suspects were in the home when he and his wife arrived home."

    Although the information in the passage does not indicate the exact number and type of items taken from the Corneal home, Officers Lucas and Gentry did determine that the suspects concentrated their efforts on the exotic gun collection, the antique jewelry collection and the areas of the house that typically contain money.

    A- is incorrect, because it states that nothing was stolen;

    B- is incorrect, because the wrong items are listed;

    D- is incorrect, because it states specific numbers of items stolen which were not stated in the passage.

4. A is the correct answer. Officer Reigner was the officer who "requested the names of the companies and the services they performed."

    B- is incorrect, Mr. Corneal seemed to answer all of the officers' questions.

    C- is incorrect, because Officers Lucas and Gentry searched the home. Officer Baker assisted with questioning Mr. Corneal.

    D- is also incorrect, the suspects fled the scene in a dark blue sedan, not a dark blue van.

Problem Sensitivity questions - 5 and 6.

5. B is the correct answer. The driver submitted to the blood alcohol test and scored below the legal limit. According to guideline 3, "the driver's license SHALL NOT be confiscated." Officer Kelley did take the license and that was problematic.

   A- is incorrect, given the fact there was a problem with the license (response B).

   C- is incorrect, because the original guidelines did not mention that it was necessary to have someone witness the field tests.

   D- is incorrect, because (according to guideline 4) even if a driver passes the blood alcohol test, "the driver can still be charged with driving under the influence, if the officer can justify the charge through the use of field tests." Officer Kelley did base the charge on the results of the field tests.

6. A is the correct answer, because the only inconsistency between the various descriptions was provided by witness 1. Specifically, witnesses 2, 3 and 4 stated that the second robber's face was hidden by a ski mask/stocking cap. Witness 1 not only failed to mention the mask, but also was the only witness who claimed that this suspect had blonde hair. All other details were confirmed by at least two of the four witnesses.

Deductive Reasoning questions - 7 and 8.

7. C is the correct answer. According to the fourth example listed under offenses, any situation involving hostages would require backup.

   A- does not require backup because the crime was not reported within 30 minutes as indicated by the second example listed under offenses.

   B- does not require backup because the motorist traveled 30 mph under the speed limit. Backup would be required if the motorist traveled 30 mph over the speed limit as indicated by the first example listed under offenses.

   D- does not require backup because the accident was not fatal as indicated by the third example listed under offenses.

8. A is the correct answer. Based on the six guidelines, the Captain's work assignment, the date and temperature, Captain Cross may wear either the Eisenhower Jacket or the Double Breasted Blouse, a white, long sleeve shirt, and regulation trousers with either the black trouser braid or stripe.

   B- is incorrect, because according to guideline 3, a Captain "will substitute a white shirt" for the navy blue, long sleeve shirt.

   C- is incorrect, because according to guideline 1, it is too early in the year (September) and too warm (60 degrees) to wear the Antron Jacket.

   D- is incorrect, because according to guidelines 4 and 5, the Captain cannot wear the short sleeve shirt because the temperature is too cold (60 degrees) and the Captain is serving outside duty.

Inductive Reasoning questions - 9 and 10.

9. When examining the alternatives, they include the section of the city and time of day. There is no indication of the day of the week. Thus, the information provided in paragraph 3 is irrelevant in responding to this question. According to the first two paragraphs, assaults occur "in the eastern and northern sections" and "between 7 p.m. and 9 p.m. OR between 11 p.m. and 4 a.m."

    D is the correct answer. It includes both an appropriate section of the city and time of day.

    C- is incorrect, because it includes the wrong section of the city for assaults.

    A and B- are incorrect, because they do not include any hours of the day when assaults typically occur.

10. A is the correct answer. To answer this question it is helpful to compare the physical characteristics of the suspects in incidents 1, 2, 3 and 5 (4 is not one of the alternatives provided) and for the suspect in incident 6. Using this method, the other three answers can be eliminated.

    B- is incorrect, because the suspect's only tattoo is on the left hand, not on the bicep. Since this suspect was wearing a tank top, a cobra tattoo on the arm would be hard to miss.

    C- is incorrect, because the suspect's tattoos are on the forearms, not on the bicep.

    D- is incorrect, because the suspect is too tall and heavy (6'7" and 230 pounds).

Information Ordering questions - 11 and 12.

11. The correct answer is A. The key phrase in this question is "notices a pattern emerging." Step 5 reads "If a light pattern shows up,... the next step is to...brush more powder into the pattern lightly with the flow of the ridges."

    B, C and D- are incorrect because they correspond to procedures 4, 3 and 7, respectively.

12. The correct answer is B. To determine the correct answer, the steps must be listed in the correct time sequence. Steps 2, 3 and 5 deal with the preparation for the search and steps 1, 4 and 6 deal with conducting the search. In terms of the last three steps, 6 must be first, because it instructs the officer to "start at the forehead." Step 1 must be next because it states "Lower both of your hands to the base of the prisoner's neck and proceed..." Step 4 is a continuation of step 1, since you finish 1 at the mid-section and begin 4 at the waistline. Answer B is the only one ending with the sequence 6, 1, 4 AND the order for the initial three steps (3, 2, 5) is appropriate.

HOW TO TAKE A TEST

I. YOU MUST PASS AN EXAMINATION

A. *WHAT EVERY CANDIDATE SHOULD KNOW*

Examination applicants often ask us for help in preparing for the written test. What can I study in advance? What kinds of questions will be asked? How will the test be given? How will the papers be graded?

As an applicant for a civil service examination, you may be wondering about some of these things. Our purpose here is to suggest effective methods of advance study and to describe civil service examinations.

Your chances for success on this examination can be increased if you know how to prepare. Those "pre-examination jitters" can be reduced if you know what to expect. You can even experience an adventure in good citizenship if you know why civil service exams are given.

B. *WHY ARE CIVIL SERVICE EXAMINATIONS GIVEN?*

Civil service examinations are important to you in two ways. As a citizen, you want public jobs filled by employees who know how to do their work. As a job seeker, you want a fair chance to compete for that job on an equal footing with other candidates. The best-known means of accomplishing this two-fold goal is the competitive examination.

Exams are widely publicized throughout the nation. They may be administered for jobs in federal, state, city, municipal, town or village governments or agencies.

Any citizen may apply, with some limitations, such as the age or residence of applicants. Your experience and education may be reviewed to see whether you meet the requirements for the particular examination. When these requirements exist, they are reasonable and applied consistently to all applicants. Thus, a competitive examination may cause you some uneasiness now, but it is your privilege and safeguard.

C. *HOW ARE CIVIL SERVICE EXAMS DEVELOPED?*

Examinations are carefully written by trained technicians who are specialists in the field known as "psychological measurement," in consultation with recognized authorities in the field of work that the test will cover. These experts recommend the subject matter areas or skills to be tested; only those knowledges or skills important to your success on the job are included. The most reliable books and source materials available are used as references. Together, the experts and technicians judge the difficulty level of the questions.

Test technicians know how to phrase questions so that the problem is clearly stated. Their ethics do not permit "trick" or "catch" questions. Questions may have been tried out on sample groups, or subjected to statistical analysis, to determine their usefulness.

Written tests are often used in combination with performance tests, ratings of training and experience, and oral interviews. All of these measures combine to form the best-known means of finding the right person for the right job.

II. HOW TO PASS THE WRITTEN TEST

A. NATURE OF THE EXAMINATION

To prepare intelligently for civil service examinations, you should know how they differ from school examinations you have taken. In school you were assigned certain definite pages to read or subjects to cover. The examination questions were quite detailed and usually emphasized memory. Civil service exams, on the other hand, try to discover your present ability to perform the duties of a position, plus your potentiality to learn these duties. In other words, a civil service exam attempts to predict how successful you will be. Questions cover such a broad area that they cannot be as minute and detailed as school exam questions.

In the public service similar kinds of work, or positions, are grouped together in one "class." This process is known as *position-classification*. All the positions in a class are paid according to the salary range for that class. One class title covers all of these positions, and they are all tested by the same examination.

B. FOUR BASIC STEPS

1) Study the announcement

How, then, can you know what subjects to study? Our best answer is: "Learn as much as possible about the class of positions for which you've applied." The exam will test the knowledge, skills and abilities needed to do the work.

Your most valuable source of information about the position you want is the official exam announcement. This announcement lists the training and experience qualifications. Check these standards and apply only if you come reasonably close to meeting them.

The brief description of the position in the examination announcement offers some clues to the subjects which will be tested. Think about the job itself. Review the duties in your mind. Can you perform them, or are there some in which you are rusty? Fill in the blank spots in your preparation.

Many jurisdictions preview the written test in the exam announcement by including a section called "Knowledge and Abilities Required," "Scope of the Examination," or some similar heading. Here you will find out specifically what fields will be tested.

2) Review your own background

Once you learn in general what the position is all about, and what you need to know to do the work, ask yourself which subjects you already know fairly well and which need improvement. You may wonder whether to concentrate on improving your strong areas or on building some background in your fields of weakness. When the announcement has specified "some knowledge" or "considerable knowledge," or has used adjectives like "beginning principles of…" or "advanced … methods," you can get a clue as to the number and difficulty of questions to be asked in any given field. More questions, and hence broader coverage, would be included for those subjects which are more important in the work. Now weigh your strengths and weaknesses against the job requirements and prepare accordingly.

3) Determine the level of the position

Another way to tell how intensively you should prepare is to understand the level of the job for which you are applying. Is it the entering level? In other words, is this the position in which beginners in a field of work are hired? Or is it an intermediate or advanced level? Sometimes this is indicated by such words as "Junior" or "Senior" in the class title. Other jurisdictions use Roman numerals to designate the level – Clerk I, Clerk II, for example. The word "Supervisor" sometimes appears in the title. If the level is not indicated by the title, check the description of duties. Will you be working under very close supervision, or will you have responsibility for independent decisions in this work?

4) Choose appropriate study materials

Now that you know the subjects to be examined and the relative amount of each subject to be covered, you can choose suitable study materials. For beginning level jobs, or even advanced ones, if you have a pronounced weakness in some aspect of your training, read a modern, standard textbook in that field. Be sure it is up to date and has general coverage. Such books are normally available at your library, and the librarian will be glad to help you locate one. For entry-level positions, questions of appropriate difficulty are chosen – neither highly advanced questions, nor those too simple. Such questions require careful thought but not advanced training.

If the position for which you are applying is technical or advanced, you will read more advanced, specialized material. If you are already familiar with the basic principles of your field, elementary textbooks would waste your time. Concentrate on advanced textbooks and technical periodicals. Think through the concepts and review difficult problems in your field.

These are all general sources. You can get more ideas on your own initiative, following these leads. For example, training manuals and publications of the government agency which employs workers in your field can be useful, particularly for technical and professional positions. A letter or visit to the government department involved may result in more specific study suggestions, and certainly will provide you with a more definite idea of the exact nature of the position you are seeking.

III. KINDS OF TESTS

Tests are used for purposes other than measuring knowledge and ability to perform specified duties. For some positions, it is equally important to test ability to make adjustments to new situations or to profit from training. In others, basic mental abilities not dependent on information are essential. Questions which test these things may not appear as pertinent to the duties of the position as those which test for knowledge and information. Yet they are often highly important parts of a fair examination. For very general questions, it is almost impossible to help you direct your study efforts. What we can do is to point out some of the more common of these general abilities needed in public service positions and describe some typical questions.

1) General information

Broad, general information has been found useful for predicting job success in some kinds of work. This is tested in a variety of ways, from vocabulary lists to questions about current events. Basic background in some field of work, such as sociology or economics, may be sampled in a group of questions. Often these are principles which have become familiar to most persons through exposure rather than through formal training. It is difficult to advise you how to study for these questions; being alert to the world around you is our best suggestion.

2) Verbal ability

An example of an ability needed in many positions is verbal or language ability. Verbal ability is, in brief, the ability to use and understand words. Vocabulary and grammar tests are typical measures of this ability. Reading comprehension or paragraph interpretation questions are common in many kinds of civil service tests. You are given a paragraph of written material and asked to find its central meaning.

3) Numerical ability

Number skills can be tested by the familiar arithmetic problem, by checking paired lists of numbers to see which are alike and which are different, or by interpreting charts and graphs. In the latter test, a graph may be printed in the test booklet which you are asked to use as the basis for answering questions.

4) Observation

A popular test for law-enforcement positions is the observation test. A picture is shown to you for several minutes, then taken away. Questions about the picture test your ability to observe both details and larger elements.

5) Following directions

In many positions in the public service, the employee must be able to carry out written instructions dependably and accurately. You may be given a chart with several columns, each column listing a variety of information. The questions require you to carry out directions involving the information given in the chart.

6) Skills and aptitudes

Performance tests effectively measure some manual skills and aptitudes. When the skill is one in which you are trained, such as typing or shorthand, you can practice. These tests are often very much like those given in business school or high school courses. For many of the other skills and aptitudes, however, no short-time preparation can be made. Skills and abilities natural to you or that you have developed throughout your lifetime are being tested.

Many of the general questions just described provide all the data needed to answer the questions and ask you to use your reasoning ability to find the answers. Your best preparation for these tests, as well as for tests of facts and ideas, is to be at your physical and mental best. You, no doubt, have your own methods of getting into an exam-taking mood and keeping "in shape." The next section lists some ideas on this subject.

IV. KINDS OF QUESTIONS

Only rarely is the "essay" question, which you answer in narrative form, used in civil service tests. Civil service tests are usually of the short-answer type. Full instructions for answering these questions will be given to you at the examination. But in case this is your first experience with short-answer questions and separate answer sheets, here is what you need to know:

1) Multiple-choice Questions

Most popular of the short-answer questions is the "multiple choice" or "best answer" question. It can be used, for example, to test for factual knowledge, ability to solve problems or judgment in meeting situations found at work.

A multiple-choice question is normally one of three types—
- It can begin with an incomplete statement followed by several possible endings. You are to find the one ending which *best* completes the statement, although some of the others may not be entirely wrong.
- It can also be a complete statement in the form of a question which is answered by choosing one of the statements listed.

- It can be in the form of a problem – again you select the best answer.

Here is an example of a multiple-choice question with a discussion which should give you some clues as to the method for choosing the right answer:

When an employee has a complaint about his assignment, the action which will *best* help him overcome his difficulty is to
- A. discuss his difficulty with his coworkers
- B. take the problem to the head of the organization
- C. take the problem to the person who gave him the assignment
- D. say nothing to anyone about his complaint

In answering this question, you should study each of the choices to find which is best. Consider choice "A" – Certainly an employee may discuss his complaint with fellow employees, but no change or improvement can result, and the complaint remains unresolved. Choice "B" is a poor choice since the head of the organization probably does not know what assignment you have been given, and taking your problem to him is known as "going over the head" of the supervisor. The supervisor, or person who made the assignment, is the person who can clarify it or correct any injustice. Choice "C" is, therefore, correct. To say nothing, as in choice "D," is unwise. Supervisors have and interest in knowing the problems employees are facing, and the employee is seeking a solution to his problem.

2) True/False Questions

The "true/false" or "right/wrong" form of question is sometimes used. Here a complete statement is given. Your job is to decide whether the statement is right or wrong.

SAMPLE: A roaming cell-phone call to a nearby city costs less than a non-roaming call to a distant city.

This statement is wrong, or false, since roaming calls are more expensive.

This is not a complete list of all possible question forms, although most of the others are variations of these common types. You will always get complete directions for answering questions. Be sure you understand *how* to mark your answers – ask questions until you do.

V. RECORDING YOUR ANSWERS

Computer terminals are used more and more today for many different kinds of exams.

For an examination with very few applicants, you may be told to record your answers in the test booklet itself. Separate answer sheets are much more common. If this separate answer sheet is to be scored by machine – and this is often the case – it is highly important that you mark your answers correctly in order to get credit.

An electronic scoring machine is often used in civil service offices because of the speed with which papers can be scored. Machine-scored answer sheets must be marked with a pencil, which will be given to you. This pencil has a high graphite content which responds to the electronic scoring machine. As a matter of fact, stray dots may register as answers, so do not let your pencil rest on the answer sheet while you are pondering the correct answer. Also, if your pencil lead breaks or is otherwise defective, ask for another.

Since the answer sheet will be dropped in a slot in the scoring machine, be careful not to bend the corners or get the paper crumpled.

The answer sheet normally has five vertical columns of numbers, with 30 numbers to a column. These numbers correspond to the question numbers in your test booklet. After each number, going across the page are four or five pairs of dotted lines. These short dotted lines have small letters or numbers above them. The first two pairs may also have a "T" or "F" above the letters. This indicates that the first two pairs only are to be used if the questions are of the true-false type. If the questions are multiple choice, disregard the "T" and "F" and pay attention only to the small letters or numbers.

Answer your questions in the manner of the sample that follows:

32. The largest city in the United States is
    A. Washington, D.C.
    B. New York City
    C. Chicago
    D. Detroit
    E. San Francisco

1) Choose the answer you think is best. (New York City is the largest, so "B" is correct.)
2) Find the row of dotted lines numbered the same as the question you are answering. (Find row number 32)
3) Find the pair of dotted lines corresponding to the answer. (Find the pair of lines under the mark "B.")
4) Make a solid black mark between the dotted lines.

VI. BEFORE THE TEST

Common sense will help you find procedures to follow to get ready for an examination. Too many of us, however, overlook these sensible measures. Indeed, nervousness and fatigue have been found to be the most serious reasons why applicants fail to do their best on civil service tests. Here is a list of reminders:

- Begin your preparation early – Don't wait until the last minute to go scurrying around for books and materials or to find out what the position is all about.
- Prepare continuously – An hour a night for a week is better than an all-night cram session. This has been definitely established. What is more, a night a week for a month will return better dividends than crowding your study into a shorter period of time.
- Locate the place of the exam – You have been sent a notice telling you when and where to report for the examination. If the location is in a different town or otherwise unfamiliar to you, it would be well to inquire the best route and learn something about the building.
- Relax the night before the test – Allow your mind to rest. Do not study at all that night. Plan some mild recreation or diversion; then go to bed early and get a good night's sleep.
- Get up early enough to make a leisurely trip to the place for the test – This way unforeseen events, traffic snarls, unfamiliar buildings, etc. will not upset you.
- Dress comfortably – A written test is not a fashion show. You will be known by number and not by name, so wear something comfortable.

- Leave excess paraphernalia at home – Shopping bags and odd bundles will get in your way. You need bring only the items mentioned in the official notice you received; usually everything you need is provided. Do not bring reference books to the exam. They will only confuse those last minutes and be taken away from you when in the test room.
- Arrive somewhat ahead of time – If because of transportation schedules you must get there very early, bring a newspaper or magazine to take your mind off yourself while waiting.
- Locate the examination room – When you have found the proper room, you will be directed to the seat or part of the room where you will sit. Sometimes you are given a sheet of instructions to read while you are waiting. Do not fill out any forms until you are told to do so; just read them and be prepared.
- Relax and prepare to listen to the instructions
- If you have any physical problem that may keep you from doing your best, be sure to tell the test administrator. If you are sick or in poor health, you really cannot do your best on the exam. You can come back and take the test some other time.

VII. AT THE TEST

The day of the test is here and you have the test booklet in your hand. The temptation to get going is very strong. Caution! There is more to success than knowing the right answers. You must know how to identify your papers and understand variations in the type of short-answer question used in this particular examination. Follow these suggestions for maximum results from your efforts:

1) Cooperate with the monitor
The test administrator has a duty to create a situation in which you can be as much at ease as possible. He will give instructions, tell you when to begin, check to see that you are marking your answer sheet correctly, and so on. He is not there to guard you, although he will see that your competitors do not take unfair advantage. He wants to help you do your best.

2) Listen to all instructions
Don't jump the gun! Wait until you understand all directions. In most civil service tests you get more time than you need to answer the questions. So don't be in a hurry. Read each word of instructions until you clearly understand the meaning. Study the examples, listen to all announcements and follow directions. Ask questions if you do not understand what to do.

3) Identify your papers
Civil service exams are usually identified by number only. You will be assigned a number; you must not put your name on your test papers. Be sure to copy your number correctly. Since more than one exam may be given, copy your exact examination title.

4) Plan your time
Unless you are told that a test is a "speed" or "rate of work" test, speed itself is usually not important. Time enough to answer all the questions will be provided, but this does not mean that you have all day. An overall time limit has been set. Divide the total time (in minutes) by the number of questions to determine the approximate time you have for each question.

5) Do not linger over difficult questions

If you come across a difficult question, mark it with a paper clip (useful to have along) and come back to it when you have been through the booklet. One caution if you do this – be sure to skip a number on your answer sheet as well. Check often to be sure that you have not lost your place and that you are marking in the row numbered the same as the question you are answering.

6) Read the questions

Be sure you know what the question asks! Many capable people are unsuccessful because they failed to *read* the questions correctly.

7) Answer all questions

Unless you have been instructed that a penalty will be deducted for incorrect answers, it is better to guess than to omit a question.

8) Speed tests

It is often better NOT to guess on speed tests. It has been found that on timed tests people are tempted to spend the last few seconds before time is called in marking answers at random – without even reading them – in the hope of picking up a few extra points. To discourage this practice, the instructions may warn you that your score will be "corrected" for guessing. That is, a penalty will be applied. The incorrect answers will be deducted from the correct ones, or some other penalty formula will be used.

9) Review your answers

If you finish before time is called, go back to the questions you guessed or omitted to give them further thought. Review other answers if you have time.

10) Return your test materials

If you are ready to leave before others have finished or time is called, take ALL your materials to the monitor and leave quietly. Never take any test material with you. The monitor can discover whose papers are not complete, and taking a test booklet may be grounds for disqualification.

VIII. EXAMINATION TECHNIQUES

1) Read the general instructions carefully. These are usually printed on the first page of the exam booklet. As a rule, these instructions refer to the timing of the examination; the fact that you should not start work until the signal and must stop work at a signal, etc. If there are any *special* instructions, such as a choice of questions to be answered, make sure that you note this instruction carefully.

2) When you are ready to start work on the examination, that is as soon as the signal has been given, read the instructions to each question booklet, underline any key words or phrases, such as *least, best, outline, describe* and the like. In this way you will tend to answer as requested rather than discover on reviewing your paper that you *listed without describing*, that you selected the *worst* choice rather than the *best* choice, etc.

3) If the examination is of the objective or multiple-choice type – that is, each question will also give a series of possible answers: A, B, C or D, and you are called upon to select the best answer and write the letter next to that answer on your answer paper – it is advisable to start answering each question in turn. There may be anywhere from 50 to 100 such questions in the three or four hours allotted and you can see how much time would be taken if you read through all the questions before beginning to answer any. Furthermore, if you come across a question or group of questions which you know would be difficult to answer, it would undoubtedly affect your handling of all the other questions.

4) If the examination is of the essay type and contains but a few questions, it is a moot point as to whether you should read all the questions before starting to answer any one. Of course, if you are given a choice – say five out of seven and the like – then it is essential to read all the questions so you can eliminate the two that are most difficult. If, however, you are asked to answer all the questions, there may be danger in trying to answer the easiest one first because you may find that you will spend too much time on it. The best technique is to answer the first question, then proceed to the second, etc.

5) Time your answers. Before the exam begins, write down the time it started, then add the time allowed for the examination and write down the time it must be completed, then divide the time available somewhat as follows:
   - If 3-1/2 hours are allowed, that would be 210 minutes. If you have 80 objective-type questions, that would be an average of 2-1/2 minutes per question. Allow yourself no more than 2 minutes per question, or a total of 160 minutes, which will permit about 50 minutes to review.
   - If for the time allotment of 210 minutes there are 7 essay questions to answer, that would average about 30 minutes a question. Give yourself only 25 minutes per question so that you have about 35 minutes to review.

6) The most important instruction is to *read each question* and make sure you know what is wanted. The second most important instruction is to *time yourself properly* so that you answer every question. The third most important instruction is to *answer every question*. Guess if you have to but include something for each question. Remember that you will receive no credit for a blank and will probably receive some credit if you write something in answer to an essay question. If you guess a letter – say "B" for a multiple-choice question – you may have guessed right. If you leave a blank as an answer to a multiple-choice question, the examiners may respect your feelings but it will not add a point to your score. Some exams may penalize you for wrong answers, so in such cases *only*, you may not want to guess unless you have some basis for your answer.

7) Suggestions
   a. Objective-type questions
      1. Examine the question booklet for proper sequence of pages and questions
      2. Read all instructions carefully
      3. Skip any question which seems too difficult; return to it after all other questions have been answered
      4. Apportion your time properly; do not spend too much time on any single question or group of questions

5. Note and underline key words – *all, most, fewest, least, best, worst, same, opposite*, etc.
6. Pay particular attention to negatives
7. Note unusual option, e.g., unduly long, short, complex, different or similar in content to the body of the question
8. Observe the use of "hedging" words – *probably, may, most likely*, etc.
9. Make sure that your answer is put next to the same number as the question
10. Do not second-guess unless you have good reason to believe the second answer is definitely more correct
11. Cross out original answer if you decide another answer is more accurate; do not erase until you are ready to hand your paper in
12. Answer all questions; guess unless instructed otherwise
13. Leave time for review

   b. Essay questions
1. Read each question carefully
2. Determine exactly what is wanted. Underline key words or phrases.
3. Decide on outline or paragraph answer
4. Include many different points and elements unless asked to develop any one or two points or elements
5. Show impartiality by giving pros and cons unless directed to select one side only
6. Make and write down any assumptions you find necessary to answer the questions
7. Watch your English, grammar, punctuation and choice of words
8. Time your answers; don't crowd material

8) Answering the essay question

Most essay questions can be answered by framing the specific response around several key words or ideas. Here are a few such key words or ideas:

M's: manpower, materials, methods, money, management
P's: purpose, program, policy, plan, procedure, practice, problems, pitfalls, personnel, public relations

   a. Six basic steps in handling problems:
1. Preliminary plan and background development
2. Collect information, data and facts
3. Analyze and interpret information, data and facts
4. Analyze and develop solutions as well as make recommendations
5. Prepare report and sell recommendations
6. Install recommendations and follow up effectiveness

   b. Pitfalls to avoid
1. *Taking things for granted* – A statement of the situation does not necessarily imply that each of the elements is necessarily true; for example, a complaint may be invalid and biased so that all that can be taken for granted is that a complaint has been registered

2. *Considering only one side of a situation* – Wherever possible, indicate several alternatives and then point out the reasons you selected the best one
3. *Failing to indicate follow up* – Whenever your answer indicates action on your part, make certain that you will take proper follow-up action to see how successful your recommendations, procedures or actions turn out to be
4. *Taking too long in answering any single question* – Remember to time your answers properly

IX. AFTER THE TEST

Scoring procedures differ in detail among civil service jurisdictions although the general principles are the same. Whether the papers are hand-scored or graded by machine we have described, they are nearly always graded by number. That is, the person who marks the paper knows only the number – never the name – of the applicant. Not until all the papers have been graded will they be matched with names. If other tests, such as training and experience or oral interview ratings have been given, scores will be combined. Different parts of the examination usually have different weights. For example, the written test might count 60 percent of the final grade, and a rating of training and experience 40 percent. In many jurisdictions, veterans will have a certain number of points added to their grades.

After the final grade has been determined, the names are placed in grade order and an eligible list is established. There are various methods for resolving ties between those who get the same final grade – probably the most common is to place first the name of the person whose application was received first. Job offers are made from the eligible list in the order the names appear on it. You will be notified of your grade and your rank as soon as all these computations have been made. This will be done as rapidly as possible.

People who are found to meet the requirements in the announcement are called "eligibles." Their names are put on a list of eligible candidates. An eligible's chances of getting a job depend on how high he stands on this list and how fast agencies are filling jobs from the list.

When a job is to be filled from a list of eligibles, the agency asks for the names of people on the list of eligibles for that job. When the civil service commission receives this request, it sends to the agency the names of the three people highest on this list. Or, if the job to be filled has specialized requirements, the office sends the agency the names of the top three persons who meet these requirements from the general list.

The appointing officer makes a choice from among the three people whose names were sent to him. If the selected person accepts the appointment, the names of the others are put back on the list to be considered for future openings.

That is the rule in hiring from all kinds of eligible lists, whether they are for typist, carpenter, chemist, or something else. For every vacancy, the appointing officer has his choice of any one of the top three eligibles on the list. This explains why the person whose name is on top of the list sometimes does not get an appointment when some of the persons lower on the list do. If the appointing officer chooses the second or third eligible, the No. 1 eligible does not get a job at once, but stays on the list until he is appointed or the list is terminated.

X. HOW TO PASS THE INTERVIEW TEST

The examination for which you applied requires an oral interview test. You have already taken the written test and you are now being called for the interview test – the final part of the formal examination.

You may think that it is not possible to prepare for an interview test and that there are no procedures to follow during an interview. Our purpose is to point out some things you can do in advance that will help you and some good rules to follow and pitfalls to avoid while you are being interviewed.

What is an interview supposed to test?

The written examination is designed to test the technical knowledge and competence of the candidate; the oral is designed to evaluate intangible qualities, not readily measured otherwise, and to establish a list showing the relative fitness of each candidate – as measured against his competitors – for the position sought. Scoring is not on the basis of "right" and "wrong," but on a sliding scale of values ranging from "not passable" to "outstanding." As a matter of fact, it is possible to achieve a relatively low score without a single "incorrect" answer because of evident weakness in the qualities being measured.

Occasionally, an examination may consist entirely of an oral test – either an individual or a group oral. In such cases, information is sought concerning the technical knowledges and abilities of the candidate, since there has been no written examination for this purpose. More commonly, however, an oral test is used to supplement a written examination.

Who conducts interviews?

The composition of oral boards varies among different jurisdictions. In nearly all, a representative of the personnel department serves as chairman. One of the members of the board may be a representative of the department in which the candidate would work. In some cases, "outside experts" are used, and, frequently, a businessman or some other representative of the general public is asked to serve. Labor and management or other special groups may be represented. The aim is to secure the services of experts in the appropriate field.

However the board is composed, it is a good idea (and not at all improper or unethical) to ascertain in advance of the interview who the members are and what groups they represent. When you are introduced to them, you will have some idea of their backgrounds and interests, and at least you will not stutter and stammer over their names.

What should be done before the interview?

While knowledge about the board members is useful and takes some of the surprise element out of the interview, there is other preparation which is more substantive. It *is* possible to prepare for an oral interview – in several ways:

1) Keep a copy of your application and review it carefully before the interview

This may be the only document before the oral board, and the starting point of the interview. Know what education and experience you have listed there, and the sequence and dates of all of it. Sometimes the board will ask you to review the highlights of your experience for them; you should not have to hem and haw doing it.

2) Study the class specification and the examination announcement

Usually, the oral board has one or both of these to guide them. The qualities, characteristics or knowledges required by the position sought are stated in these documents. They offer valuable clues as to the nature of the oral interview. For example, if the job involves supervisory responsibilities, the announcement will usually indicate that knowledge of modern supervisory methods and the qualifications of the candidate as a supervisor will be tested. If so, you can expect such questions, frequently in the form of a hypothetical situation which you are expected to solve. NEVER go into an oral without knowledge of the duties and responsibilities of the job you seek.

3) Think through each qualification required

Try to visualize the kind of questions you would ask if you were a board member. How well could you answer them? Try especially to appraise your own knowledge and background in each area, *measured against the job sought*, and identify any areas in which you are weak. Be critical and realistic – do not flatter yourself.

4) Do some general reading in areas in which you feel you may be weak

For example, if the job involves supervision and your past experience has NOT, some general reading in supervisory methods and practices, particularly in the field of human relations, might be useful. Do NOT study agency procedures or detailed manuals. The oral board will be testing your understanding and capacity, not your memory.

5) Get a good night's sleep and watch your general health and mental attitude

You will want a clear head at the interview. Take care of a cold or any other minor ailment, and of course, no hangovers.

What should be done on the day of the interview?

Now comes the day of the interview itself. Give yourself plenty of time to get there. Plan to arrive somewhat ahead of the scheduled time, particularly if your appointment is in the fore part of the day. If a previous candidate fails to appear, the board might be ready for you a bit early. By early afternoon an oral board is almost invariably behind schedule if there are many candidates, and you may have to wait. Take along a book or magazine to read, or your application to review, but leave any extraneous material in the waiting room when you go in for your interview. In any event, relax and compose yourself.

The matter of dress is important. The board is forming impressions about you – from your experience, your manners, your attitude, and your appearance. Give your personal appearance careful attention. Dress your best, but not your flashiest. Choose conservative, appropriate clothing, and be sure it is immaculate. This is a business interview, and your appearance should indicate that you regard it as such. Besides, being well groomed and properly dressed will help boost your confidence.

Sooner or later, someone will call your name and escort you into the interview room. *This is it.* From here on you are on your own. It is too late for any more preparation. But remember, you asked for this opportunity to prove your fitness, and you are here because your request was granted.

What happens when you go in?

The usual sequence of events will be as follows: The clerk (who is often the board stenographer) will introduce you to the chairman of the oral board, who will introduce you to the other members of the board. Acknowledge the introductions before you sit down. Do not be surprised if you find a microphone facing you or a stenotypist sitting by. Oral interviews are usually recorded in the event of an appeal or other review.

Usually the chairman of the board will open the interview by reviewing the highlights of your education and work experience from your application – primarily for the benefit of the other members of the board, as well as to get the material into the record. Do not interrupt or comment unless there is an error or significant misinterpretation; if that is the case, do not hesitate. But do not quibble about insignificant matters. Also, he will usually ask you some question about your education, experience or your present job – partly to get you to start talking and to establish the interviewing "rapport." He may start the actual questioning, or turn it over to one of the other members. Frequently, each member undertakes the questioning on a particular area, one in which he is perhaps most competent, so you can expect each member to participate in the examination. Because time is limited, you may also expect some rather abrupt switches in the direction the questioning takes, so do not be upset by it. Normally, a board member will not pursue a single line of questioning unless he discovers a particular strength or weakness.

After each member has participated, the chairman will usually ask whether any member has any further questions, then will ask you if you have anything you wish to add. Unless you are expecting this question, it may floor you. Worse, it may start you off on an extended, extemporaneous speech. The board is not usually seeking more information. The question is principally to offer you a last opportunity to present further qualifications or to indicate that you have nothing to add. So, if you feel that a significant qualification or characteristic has been overlooked, it is proper to point it out in a sentence or so. Do not compliment the board on the thoroughness of their examination – they have been sketchy, and you know it. If you wish, merely say, "No thank you, I have nothing further to add." This is a point where you can "talk yourself out" of a good impression or fail to present an important bit of information. Remember, *you close the interview yourself.*

The chairman will then say, "That is all, Mr. _____, thank you." Do not be startled; the interview is over, and quicker than you think. Thank him, gather your belongings and take your leave. Save your sigh of relief for the other side of the door.

How to put your best foot forward

Throughout this entire process, you may feel that the board individually and collectively is trying to pierce your defenses, seek out your hidden weaknesses and embarrass and confuse you. Actually, this is not true. They are obliged to make an appraisal of your qualifications for the job you are seeking, and they want to see you in your best light. Remember, they must interview all candidates and a non-cooperative candidate may become a failure in spite of their best efforts to bring out his qualifications. Here are 15 suggestions that will help you:

1) Be natural – Keep your attitude confident, not cocky

If you are not confident that you can do the job, do not expect the board to be. Do not apologize for your weaknesses, try to bring out your strong points. The board is interested in a positive, not negative, presentation. Cockiness will antagonize any board member and make him wonder if you are covering up a weakness by a false show of strength.

2) Get comfortable, but don't lounge or sprawl

Sit erectly but not stiffly. A careless posture may lead the board to conclude that you are careless in other things, or at least that you are not impressed by the importance of the occasion. Either conclusion is natural, even if incorrect. Do not fuss with your clothing, a pencil or an ashtray. Your hands may occasionally be useful to emphasize a point; do not let them become a point of distraction.

3) Do not wisecrack or make small talk

This is a serious situation, and your attitude should show that you consider it as such. Further, the time of the board is limited – they do not want to waste it, and neither should you.

4) Do not exaggerate your experience or abilities
In the first place, from information in the application or other interviews and sources, the board may know more about you than you think. Secondly, you probably will not get away with it. An experienced board is rather adept at spotting such a situation, so do not take the chance.

5) If you know a board member, do not make a point of it, yet do not hide it
Certainly you are not fooling him, and probably not the other members of the board. Do not try to take advantage of your acquaintanceship – it will probably do you little good.

6) Do not dominate the interview
Let the board do that. They will give you the clues – do not assume that you have to do all the talking. Realize that the board has a number of questions to ask you, and do not try to take up all the interview time by showing off your extensive knowledge of the answer to the first one.

7) Be attentive
You only have 20 minutes or so, and you should keep your attention at its sharpest throughout. When a member is addressing a problem or question to you, give him your undivided attention. Address your reply principally to him, but do not exclude the other board members.

8) Do not interrupt
A board member may be stating a problem for you to analyze. He will ask you a question when the time comes. Let him state the problem, and wait for the question.

9) Make sure you understand the question
Do not try to answer until you are sure what the question is. If it is not clear, restate it in your own words or ask the board member to clarify it for you. However, do not haggle about minor elements.

10) Reply promptly but not hastily
A common entry on oral board rating sheets is "candidate responded readily," or "candidate hesitated in replies." Respond as promptly and quickly as you can, but do not jump to a hasty, ill-considered answer.

11) Do not be peremptory in your answers
A brief answer is proper – but do not fire your answer back. That is a losing game from your point of view. The board member can probably ask questions much faster than you can answer them.

12) Do not try to create the answer you think the board member wants
He is interested in what kind of mind you have and how it works – not in playing games. Furthermore, he can usually spot this practice and will actually grade you down on it.

13) Do not switch sides in your reply merely to agree with a board member
Frequently, a member will take a contrary position merely to draw you out and to see if you are willing and able to defend your point of view. Do not start a debate, yet do not surrender a good position. If a position is worth taking, it is worth defending.

14) Do not be afraid to admit an error in judgment if you are shown to be wrong

The board knows that you are forced to reply without any opportunity for careful consideration. Your answer may be demonstrably wrong. If so, admit it and get on with the interview.

15) Do not dwell at length on your present job

The opening question may relate to your present assignment. Answer the question but do not go into an extended discussion. You are being examined for a *new* job, not your present one. As a matter of fact, try to phrase ALL your answers in terms of the job for which you are being examined.

Basis of Rating

Probably you will forget most of these "do's" and "don'ts" when you walk into the oral interview room. Even remembering them all will not ensure you a passing grade. Perhaps you did not have the qualifications in the first place. But remembering them will help you to put your best foot forward, without treading on the toes of the board members.

Rumor and popular opinion to the contrary notwithstanding, an oral board wants you to make the best appearance possible. They know you are under pressure – but they also want to see how you respond to it as a guide to what your reaction would be under the pressures of the job you seek. They will be influenced by the degree of poise you display, the personal traits you show and the manner in which you respond.

ABOUT THIS BOOK

This book contains tests divided into Examination Sections. Go through each test, answering every question in the margin. We have also attached a sample answer sheet at the back of the book that can be removed and used. At the end of each test look at the answer key and check your answers. On the ones you got wrong, look at the right answer choice and learn. Do not fill in the answers first. Do not memorize the questions and answers, but understand the answer and principles involved. On your test, the questions will likely be different from the samples. Questions are changed and new ones added. If you understand these past questions you should have success with any changes that arise. Tests may consist of several types of questions. We have additional books on each subject should more study be advisable or necessary for you. Finally, the more you study, the better prepared you will be. This book is intended to be the last thing you study before you walk into the examination room. Prior study of relevant texts is also recommended. NLC publishes some of these in our Fundamental Series. Knowledge and good sense are important factors in passing your exam. Good luck also helps. So now study this Passbook, absorb the material contained within and take that knowledge into the examination. Then do your best to pass that exam.

EXAMINATION SECTION

SAMPLE QUESTIONS
BIOGRAPHICAL INVENTORY

The questions included in the Biographical Inventory ask for information about you and your background. These kinds of questions are often asked during an oral interview. For years, employers have been using interviews to relate personal history, preferences, and attitudes to job success. This Biographical Inventory attempts to do the same and includes questions which have been shown to be related to job success. It has been found that successful employees tend to select some answers more often than other answers, while less successful employees tend to select different answers. The questions in the Biographical Inventory do not have a single correct answer. Every choice is given some credit. More credit is given for answers selected more often by successful employees.

These Biographical Inventory questions are presented for illustrative purposes only. The answers have not been linked to the answers of successful employees; therefore, we cannot designate any "correct" answer(s).

DIRECTIONS: You may only mark ONE response to each question. It is possible that none of the answers applies well to you. However, one of the answers will surely be true (or less inaccurate) for you than others. In such a case, mark that answer. <u>Answer each question honestly.</u> The credit that is assigned to each response on the actual test is based upon how successful employees described themselves when honestly responding to the questions. *PRINT THE LETTER OF THE CORRECT ANSWER IN THE SPACE AT THE RIGHT.*

1. Generally, in your work assignments, would you prefer 1.____
   A. to work on one thing at a time
   B. to work on a couple of things at a time
   C. to work on many things at the same time

2. In the course of a week, which of the following gives you the GREATEST satisfaction? 2.____
   A. Being told you have done a good job.
   B. Helping other people to solve their problems.
   C. Coming up with a new or unique way to handle a situation.
   D. Having free time to devote to personal interests.

PERSONALITY/AUTOBIOGRAPHICAL INVENTORY
EXAMINATION SECTION
TEST 1

DIRECTIONS: Each question or incomplete statement is followed by several suggested answers or completions. Select the one that BEST answers the question or completes the statement. *PRINT THE LETTER OF THE CORRECT ANSWER IN THE SPACE AT THE RIGHT.*

1. While a senior in high school, I was absent 1.____
   A. never
   B. seldom
   C. frequently
   D. more than 10 days
   E. only when I felt bored

2. While in high school, I failed classes 2.____
   A. never
   B. once
   C. twice
   D. more than twice
   E. at least four times

3. During class discussions in my high school classes, I usually 3.____
   A. listened without participating
   B. participated as much as possible
   C. listened until I had something to add to the discussion
   D. disagreed with others simply for the sake of argument
   E. laughed at stupid ideas

4. My high school grade point average (on a 4.0 scale) was 4.____
   A. 2.0 or lower
   B. 2.1 to 2.5
   C. 2.6 to 3.0
   D. 3.1 to 3.5
   E. 3.6 to 4.0

5. As a high school student, I completed my assignments 5.____
   A. as close to the due date as I could manage
   B. whenever the teacher gave me an extension
   C. frequently
   D. on time
   E. when they were interesting

6. While in high school, I participated in 6.____
   A. athletic and nonathletic extracurricular activities
   B. athletic extracurricular activities
   C. nonathletic extracurricular activities
   D. no extracurricular activities
   E. mandatory after-school programs

7. In high school, I made the honor roll
   A. several times
   B. once
   C. more than once
   D. twice
   E. I can't remember if I made the honor role

8. Upon graduation from high school, I received
   A. academic and nonacademic honors
   B. academic honors
   C. nonacademic honors
   D. no honors
   E. I can't remember if I received honors

9. While attending high school, I worked at a paid job or as a volunteer
   A. never
   B. every so often
   C. 5 to 10 hours a month
   D. more than 10 hours a month
   E. more than 15 hours a month

10. During my senior year of high school, I skipped school
    A. whenever I could
    B. once a week
    C. several times a week
    D. not at all
    E. when I got bored

11. I was suspended from high school
    A. not at all
    B. once or twice
    C. once or twice, for fighting
    D. several times
    E. more times than I can remember

12. During high school, my fellow students and teachers considered me
    A. above average
    B. below average
    C. average
    D. underachieving
    E. underachieving and prone to fighting

13. The ability to _____ is most important to a Police Officer
    A. draw his/her gun quickly
    B. see over great distances and difficult terrain
    C. verbally and physically intimidate criminals
    D. communicate effectively in circumstances which can be dangerous
    E. hear over great distances

14. I began planning for college 14.____
    A. when my parents told me to
    B. when I entered high school
    C. during my junior year
    D. during my senior hear
    E. when I signed up for my SAT (or other standardized exam)

15. An effective leader is someone who 15.____
    A. inspires confidence in his/her followers
    B. inspires fear in his/her followers
    C. tells subordinates exactly what they should do
    D. creates an environment in which subordinates feel insecure about their job security and performance
    E. makes as few decisions as possible

16. I prepared myself for college by 16.____
    A. learning how to get extensions on major assignments
    B. working as many hours as possible at my after-school job
    C. spending as much time with my friends as possible
    D. getting good grades and participating in extracurricular activities
    E. watching television shows about college kids

17. I paid for college by 17.____
    A. supplementing my parents contributions with my own earnings
    B. relying on scholarships, loans, and my own earnings
    C. relying on my parents and student loans
    D. relying on my parents to pay my tuition, room and board
    E. relying on sources not listed here

18. While a college student, I spent my summers and holiday breaks 18.____
    A. in summer or remedial classes   B. traveling
    C. working   D. relaxing
    E. spending time with my friends

19. My final college grade point average (on a 4.0 scale) was 19.____
    A. 3.8 to 4.0   B. 3.5 to 3.8   C. 3.0 to 3.5
    D. 2.5 to 3.0   E. 2.0 to 2.5

20. As a college student, I cut classes 20.____
    A. frequently   B. when I didn't like them
    C. sometimes   D. rarely
    E. when I needed the sleep

21. In college, I received academic honors 21.____
    A. not at all
    B. once
    C. twice
    D. several times
    E. I can't remember if I received academic honors

22. While in college, I declared a major
    A. during my first year
    B. during my sophomore year
    C. during my junior year
    D. during my senior year
    E. several times

23. While on patrol as a Police Officer, you spot someone attempting to flee the scene of a crime. Your first reaction is to
    A. draw your weapon
    B. observe the person until he or she completes the fleeing
    C. identify yourself as a Police Officer
    D. fire your weapon over the person's head in order to scare him or her
    E. call immediately for backup

24. As a college student, I failed _____ classes.
    A. no
    B. two
    C. three
    D. four
    E. more than four

25. Friends describe me as
    A. introverted
    B. hot-tempered
    C. unpredictable
    D. quiet
    E. easygoing

KEY (CORRECT ANSWERS)

PLEASE NOTE: The answers listed are the best answers. However, you are to answer the exam honestly. Your personal answer may differ from the *best* answers.

1. A
2. A
3. C
4. E
5. D
6. A
7. A
8. A
9. E
10. D
11. A
12. A
13. D
14. B
15. A
16. D
17. B
18. C
19. A
20. D
21. D
22. A
23. C
24. A
25. E

TEST 2

DIRECTIONS: Each question or incomplete statement is followed by several suggested answers or completions. Select the one that BEST answers the question or completes the statement. *PRINT THE LETTER OF THE CORRECT ANSWER IN THE SPACE AT THE RIGHT.*

1. As a Police Officer, you apprehend three men whom you believe are in the country illegally. However, none of the men speaks English, and you don't speak their language.
   Your reaction should be to
   A. draw your weapon so that they understand the seriousness of the situation
   B. take them into custody, where they will have access to a translator
   C. attempt to communicate through hand gestures and shouting
   D. call for a translator to come and meet you at your location
   E. pretend you understand their language and apprehend them

   1.____

2. During my college classes, I preferred to
   A. remain silent during class discussions
   B. do other homework during class discussions
   C. participate frequently in class discussions
   D. argue with others as much as possible
   E. laugh at the stupid opinions of others

   2.____

3. As a Police Officer, you are chasing a small group of people who are running away from the scene of a crime. During your pursuit, one member of the group is left behind. You see that she is injured and in need of medical attention.
   Your reaction is to
   A. fire your weapon at the group members to get them to stop
   B. cease pursuit of the group members and take the woman into custody
   C. continue pursuit of the group members, leaving the woman behind since acting ill is a common trick
   D. radio for backup to stay with the woman while medical help arrives while you continue pursuit of the group members
   E. radio for backup to continue pursuit of the group members while you stay with the woman and wait for medical help to arrive

   3.____

4. As a college student, I was placed on academic probation
   A. not at all   B. once
   C. twice   D. three times
   E. more than three times

   4.____

5. At work, being a team player means to
   A. compromise your ideals and beliefs
   B. compensate for the incompetence of others
   C. count on others to compensate for my inexperience
   D. cooperate with others to get a project finished
   E. rely on others to get the job done

   5.____

6. As a Police Officer, you confront someone you believe has just committed a crime. After identifying yourself, you notice the suspect holding something that looks like a knife.
   Your FIRST reaction should be to
   A. draw your weapon and fire
   B. call immediately for backup
   C. keep your weapon drawn until you get the suspect into a position that is controllable
   D. ask the suspect if he is armed
   E. talk to the suspect without drawing your weapon

7. My friends from college remember me primarily as a(n)
   A. person who loved to party
   B. ambitious student
   C. athlete
   D. joker
   E. fighter

8. My college experience is memorable primarily because of
   A. the friends I made
   B. the sorority/fraternity I was able to join
   C. the social activities I participated in
   D. my academic achievements
   E. the money I spent

9. A friend who is applying for a job asks you to help him pass the mandatory drug test by substituting a sample of your urine for his.
   You should
   A. help him by supplying the sample
   B. help him by supplying the sample and insisting he seek drug counseling
   C. supply the sample, but tell him that this is the only time you'll help in this way
   D. call the police
   E. refuse

10. As a college student, I handed in my assignments
    A. when they were due
    B. whenever I could get an extension
    C. when they were interesting
    D. when my friends reminded me to
    E. when I was able

11. At work you are accused of a minor infraction which you didn't commit.
    Your FIRST reaction is to
    A. call a lawyer
    B. speak to your supervisor about the mistake
    C. call the police
    D. yell at the person who did commit the infraction
    E. accept the consequences regardless of your guilt or innocence

12. While on patrol, you are surprised by a large group of disorderly teenage gang members. You are greatly outnumbered.
    As a Police Officer, your FIRST reaction is to
    A. draw your weapon and identify yourself
    B. get back into your vehicle and wait for help to arrive
    C. call for backup
    D. pretend you are part of a large group of police in the area
    E. identify yourself and get the group members into a controllable position

13. As a college student, I began to prepare for final exams
    A. the night before taking them
    B. when the professor handed out the review sheets
    C. several weeks before taking them
    D. when my friends began to prepare for their exams
    E. the morning of the exam

14. As a Police Officer in the field, you confront a small group of people you believe to be wanted criminals.
    Your MOST important consideration during this exchange should be
    A. apprehension of criminals
    B. safety of county citizens in nearby towns
    C. safety of the criminals
    D. number of criminals you must apprehend in order to receive a commendation'
    E. the amount of respect the criminals show to you and your position

15. At work, I am known as
    A. popular   B. quiet   C. intense
    D. easygoing   E. dedicated

16. The MOST important quality in a coworker is
    A. friendliness   B. cleanliness
    C. a good sense of humor   D. dependability
    E. good listening skills

17. In the past year, I have stayed home from work
    A. frequently   B. only when I felt depressed
    C. rarely   D. only when I felt overwhelmed
    E. only to run important errands

18. As a Police Officer, the BEST way to collect information from a suspect during an interview is to
    A. physically intimidate the suspect
    B. verbally intimidate the suspect
    C. threaten the suspect's family and/or friend with criminal prosecution
    D. encourage a conversation with the suspect
    E. sit in silence until the suspect begins speaking

19. For me, the BEST thing about college was the
    A. chance to strengthen my friendships and develop new ones
    B. chance to test my abilities and develop new ones
    C. number of extracurricular activities and clubs
    D. chance to socialize
    E. chance to try several different majors

20. As an employee, my WEAKEST skill is
    A. controlling my temper
    B. my organizational ability
    C. my ability to effectively understand directions
    D. my ability to effectively manage others
    E. my ability to communicate my thoughts in writing

21. As a Police Officer, my GREATEST strength would be
    A. my sense of loyalty
    B. my organizational ability
    C. punctuality
    D. dedication
    E. my ability to intimidate others

22. As a Police Officer, you find a group of suspicious youths gathered around a truck which is on fire.
    Your FIRST reaction is to
    A. call the fire department
    B. arrest them all for destruction of property
    C. draw your weapon and begin questioning them
    D. return to your vehicle and wait for the fire department
    E. instruct the group to remain while you return to your vehicle and request backup

23. If asked by my company to learn a new job-related skill, my reaction would be to
    A. ask for a raise
    B. ask for overtime pay
    C. question the necessity of the skill
    D. cooperate with some reluctance
    E. cooperate with enthusiasm

24. When I disagree with others, I tend to
    A. listen quietly despite my disagreement
    B. laugh openly at the person I disagree with
    C. ask the person to explain their views before I respond
    D. leave the conversation before my anger gets the best of me
    E. point out exactly why the person is wrong

25. When I find myself in a situation which is confusing or unclear, my reaction is to
    A. pretend I am not confused
    B. remain calm and, if necessary, ask someone else for clarification
    C. grow frustrated and angry
    D. walk away from the situation
    E. immediately insist that someone explain things to me

25.____

KEY (CORRECT ANSWERS)

PLEASE NOTE: The answers listed are the best answers. However, you are to answer the exam honestly. Your personal answer may differ from the *best* answers.

1.	B		11.	B
2.	C		12.	E
3.	E		13.	C
4.	A		14.	A
5.	D		15.	E
6.	C		16.	D
7.	B		17.	C
8.	D		18.	D
9.	E		19.	B
10.	A		20.	E

21. D
22. A
23. E
24. C
25. B

TEST 3

DIRECTIONS: Each question or incomplete statement is followed by several suggested answers or completions. Select the one that BEST answers the question or completes the statement. *PRINT THE LETTER OF THE CORRECT ANSWER IN THE SPACE AT THE RIGHT.*

1. While on patrol as a Police Officer, you find a dead body lying in the open. Hiding a few feet away, behind some rocks, you find a suspicious person who is holding items which seem to have been taken from the dead body, including a pair of shoes and some jewelry.
   You should
   A. apprehend the suspect and bring him to the station for further questioning
   B. arrest the suspect for murder and robbery
   C. arrest the suspect for murder
   D. subdue the suspect with force and check the area for his accomplices
   E. subdue the suspect with force and call for backup to check the area for his accomplices

   1.____

2. If you were placed in a supervisory position, which of the following abilities would you consider to be MOST important to your job performance?
   A. Stubborness
   B. The ability to hear all sides of a story before making a decision
   C. Kindness
   D. The ability to make and stick to a decision
   E. Patience

   2.____

3. What is your HIGHEST level of education?
   A. Less than a high school diploma
   B. A high school diploma or equivalency
   C. A graduate of community college
   D. A graduate of a four-year accredited college
   E. A degree from graduate school

   3.____

4. When asked to supervise other workers, your approach should be to
   A. ask for management wages since you're doing management work
   B. give the workers direction and supervise every aspect of the process
   C. give the workers direction and then allow them to do the job
   D. and the workers their job specifications
   E. do the work yourself, since you're uncomfortable supervising others

   4.____

5. Which of the following BEST describes you?
   A. Need little or no supervision
   B. Resent too much supervision
   C. Require as much supervision as my peers
   D. Require slightly more supervision than my peers
   E. Require close supervision

   5.____

6. You accept a job which requires an ability to perform several tasks at once. What is the BEST way to handle such a position?
   A. With strong organizational skills and a close attention to detail
   B. By delegating the work to someone with strong organizational skills
   C. Staying focused on one task at a time, no matter what happens
   D. Working on one task at a time until each task is successfully completed
   E. Asking my supervisor to help me

7. As a Police Officer, you take a suspected perpetrator into custody. After returning to the field, you notice that your gun is missing.
   You should
   A. retrace your steps to see if you dropped it somewhere
   B. report the loss immediately
   C. ask your partner to borrow his or her gun
   D. pretend that nothing's happened
   E. rely on your hands for defense and protection

8. Which of the following BEST describes your behavior when you disagree with someone?
   You
   A. state your own point of view as quickly and loudly as you can
   B. listen quietly and keep your opinions to yourself
   C. listen to the other person's perspective and then carefully point out all the flaws in their logic
   D. list all of the ignorant people who agree with the opposing point of view
   E. listen to the other person's perspective and then explain your own perspective

9. As a new Police Officer, you make several mistakes during your first week of work.
   You react by
   A. learning from your mistakes and moving on
   B. resigning
   C. blaming it on your supervisor
   D. refusing to talk about it
   E. blaming yourself

10. My ability to communicate effectively with others is _____ average.
    A. below   B. about   C. above
    D. far above   E. far below

11. In which of the following areas are you MOST highly skilled?
    A. Written communication
    B. Oral communication
    C. Ability to think quickly in difficult situations
    D. Ability to work with a broad diversity of people and personalities
    E. Organizational skills

12. As a Police Officer, you are assigned to work with a partner whom you dislike. You should
    A. immediately report the problem to your supervisor
    B. ask your partner not to speak to you during working hours
    C. tell your colleagues about your differences
    D. tell your partner why you dislike him/her
    E. work with your partner regardless of your personal feelings

13. During high school, what was your MOST common after-school activity?
    A. Remaining after school to participate in various clubs and organizations (such as band, sports, etc.)
    B. Remaining after school to make up for missed classes
    C. Remaining after school as punishment (detention, etc.)
    D. Going straight to an after-school job
    E. Spending the afternoon at home or with friends

14. During high school, in which of the following subjects did you receive the HIGHEST grades?
    A. English, History, Social Studies
    B. Math, Science
    C. Vocational classes
    D. My grades were consistent in all subjects
    E. Classes I liked

15. When faced with an overwhelming number of duties at work, your reaction is to
    A. do all of the work yourself, no matter what the cost
    B. delegate some responsibilities to capable colleagues
    C. immediately ask your supervisor for help
    D. put off as much work as possible until you can get to it
    E. take some time off to relax and clear your mind

16. As a Police Officer, your supervisor informs you that a prisoner whom you arrested has accused you of beating him. You know you are innocent. You react by
    A. quitting your job
    B. hiring a lawyer
    C. challenging your supervisor to prove the charges against you
    D. calmly tell your supervisor what really happened and presenting evidence to support your position
    E. insisting that you be allowed to speak alone to the prisoner

17. Which of the following BEST describes your desk at your current or most recent job?
    A. Messy and disorganized   B. Neat and organized
    C. Messy but organized   D. Neat but disorganized
    E. Messy

18. The _____ BEST describes your reasons for wanting to become a Police Officer.
    A. ability to carry and use a weapon
    B. excitement and challenges of the career
    C. excellent salary and benefits package
    D. chance to tell other people what to do
    E. chance to help people find a better life

19. As a Police Officer in the field, you are approached by a man who is frantic but unable to speak English. After several minutes of trying to communicate, you realize that the man is asking you to come with him in order to help someone who has been hurt.
    You should
    A. ignore him, since it might be a trap
    B. call for backup
    C. immediately offer to help the man
    D. return to your vehicle and wait for the man to leave
    E. radio your position and situation to another officer, then go with the man to offer help

20. When asked to take on extra responsibility at work, in order to help out a coworker who is overwhelmed, your response is to
    A. ask for overtime pay
    B. complain to your supervisor that you are being taken advantage of
    C. help the coworker to the best of your ability
    D. ask the coworker to come back some other time
    E. give the coworker some advice on how to get his/her job done

21. At my last job, I was promoted
    A. not at all   B. once
    C. twice   D. three times
    E. more than three times

22. As a Police Officer, you discover the body of a person whom you suspect to be a gang member. You also suspect that there are several other gang members hiding in the nearby vicinity.
    Your FIRST reaction should be to
    A. begin a search of the nearby area for the other gang members
    B. return to your vehicle and call for backup
    C. return to your vehicle with the body of the person you found
    D. check whether the person you found is dead or alive
    E. draw your weapon and identify yourself

23. You are faced with an overwhelming deadline at work.   23.____
Your reaction is to
    A. procrastinate until the last minute
    B. procrastinate until someone notices you need some help
    C. notify your supervisor that you can't complete the work on your own
    D. work in silence without asking any questions
    E. arrange your schedule so that you can get the work done before the deadline

24. When you feel yourself under deadline pressures at work, your response   24.____
is to
    A. make sure you keep to a schedule which allows you to complete the work on time
    B. wait until just before the deadline to complete the work
    C. ask someone else to do the work
    D. grow so obsessive about the work that your coworkers feel compelled to help you
    E. ask your supervisor immediately for help

25. Which of the following BEST describes your appearance at your current or   25.____
most recent position?
    A. Well-groomed, neat, and clean
    B. Unkempt, but dressed neatly
    C. Messy and dirty clothing
    D. Unshaven and untidy
    E. Clean-shaven, but sloppily dressed

KEY (CORRECT ANSWERS)

PLEASE NOTE: The answers listed are our preferred answers. However, you are to answer the exam honestly. Your personal answer may differ from our answers.

1.	A		11.	C
2.	D		12.	E
3.	E		13.	A
4.	C		14.	D
5.	A		15.	B
6.	A		16.	D
7.	B		17.	B
8.	E		18.	B
9.	A		19.	E
10.	C		20.	C

21.	C
22.	D
23.	E
24.	A
25.	A

TEST 4

DIRECTIONS: Each question or incomplete statement is followed by several suggested answers or completions. Select the one that BEST answers the question or completes the statement. *PRINT THE LETTER OF THE CORRECT ANSWER IN THE SPACE AT THE RIGHT.*

1. Which of the following BEST describes the way you react to making a difficult decision?   1.____
   A. Consult with the people you're closest to before making the decision
   B. Make the decision entirely on your own
   C. Consult only with those people whom your decision will affect
   D. Consult with everyone you known, in an effort to make a decision that will please everyone
   E. Forget about the decision until you have to make it

2. If placed in a supervisory role, which of the following characteristics would you rely on most heavily when dealing with the employees you supervise?   2.____
   A. Kindness   B. Cheeriness   C. Honesty
   D. Hostility   E. Aloofness

3. As a Police Officer, you are pursuing a suspect when he turns and pulls something out of his pocket that looks like a gun.
   You should   3.____
   A. run away and call for backup
   B. assure the man that you mean him no harm
   C. draw your gun and order the man to stop and drop his weapon
   D. draw your gun and fire a warning shot
   E. draw your gun and fire immediately

4. In addition to English, in which of the following languages are you also fluent?   4.____
   A. Spanish   B. French   C. Italian
   D. German   E. Other

5. When confronted with gossip at work, your typical reaction is to   5.____
   A. participate
   B. listen without participating
   C. notify your supervisor
   D. excuse yourself from the discussion
   E. confront your coworkers about their problem

6. In the past two years, how many jobs have you held?   6.____
   A. None   B. One   C. Two
   D. Three   E. More than three

7. In your current or most recent job, you favorite part of the job is the part which involves
   A. telling other people what they're doing wrong
   B. supervising others
   C. working without supervision to finish a project
   D. written communication
   E. oral communication

   7.____

8. Your supervisor asks you about a colleague who is applying for a position which you also want.
   You react by
   A. commenting honestly on the person's work performance
   B. enhancing the person's negative traits
   C. informing your supervisor about your colleague's personal problems
   D. telling your supervisor that would be better in the position
   E. refusing to comment

   8.____

9. As a Police Officer, you confiscate some contraband which was being imported by an illegal alien who is now in your custody. Your partner asks you not to turn the contraband in to your supervisor.
   Your response is to
   A. inform your supervisor of your partner's request immediately
   B. tell your partner you feel uncomfortable with his request
   C. pretend you didn't hear you partner's request
   D. tell your supervisor and all your colleagues about your partner's request
   E. give the contraband to your partner and let him handle it

   9.____

10. Which of the following BEST describes your responsibilities in your last job?
    A. Entirely supervisory
    B. Much supervisory responsibility
    C. Equal amounts of supervisory and nonsupervisory responsibility
    D. Some supervisory responsibilities
    E. No supervisory responsibilities

    10.____

11. How much written communication did your previous or most recent job require of you?
    A. A great deal of written communication
    B. Some written communication
    C. I don't remember
    D. A small amount of written communication
    E. No written communication

    11.____

12. In the past two years, how many times have you been fired from a job?
    A. None   B. Once
    C. Twice   D. Three times
    E. More than three times

    12.____

13. How much time have you spent working for volunteer organizations in the past year? 13._____
    A. 10 to 20 hours per week
    B. 5 to 10 hours per week
    C. 3 to 5 hours per week
    D. 1 to 3 hours per week
    E. I have spent no time volunteering in the past year

14. Your efforts at volunteer work usually revolve around which of the following types of organizations? 14._____
    A. Religious
    B. Community-based organizations working to improve the community
    C. Charity organizations working on behalf of the poor
    D. Charity organizations working on behalf of the infirm or handicapped
    E. Other

15. Which of the following BEST describes your professional history? 15._____
    Promoted at _____ coworkers
    A. a much faster rate than
    B. a slightly faster rate than
    C. the same rate as
    D. a slightly slower rate than
    E. a much slower rate than

16. Which of the following qualities do you MOST appreciate in a coworker? 16._____
    A. Friendliness   B. Dependability   C. Good looks
    D. Silence   E. Forgiveness

17. When you disagree with a supervisor's instructions or opinion about how to complete a project, your reaction is to 17._____
    A. inform your supervisor that you refuse to complete the project according to his or her instructions
    B. inform your colleague of you supervisor's incompetence
    C. accept your supervisor's instructions in silence
    D. voice your concerns and then complete the project according to your own instincts
    E. voice your concerns and then complete the project according to your supervisor's instructions

18. Which of the following BEST describes your reaction to close supervision and specific direction from your supervisor? 18._____
    You
    A. listen carefully to the directions, and then figure out a way to do the job more effectively
    B. complete the job according to the given specifications
    C. show some initiative by doing the job your way
    D. ask someone else to do the job for you
    E. listen carefully to the directions, and then figure out a better way to do the job which will save more money

19. How should a Police Officer handle a situation in which he or she is offered a bribe not to issue a traffic ticket?
    A. Pretend the bribe was never offered
    B. Accept the money as evidence and release the person
    C. Draw your weapon and call for backup
    D. Refuse the bribe and then arrest the person
    E. Accept the bribe and then arrest the person

19.____

20. At work you are faced with a difficult decision.
    You react by
    A. seeking advice from your colleagues
    B. following your own path regardless of the consequences
    C. asking your supervisor what you should do
    D. keeping the difficulties to yourself
    E. working for a solution which will please everyone

20.____

21. If asked to work with a person whom you dislike, your response would be
    A. to ask your supervisor to allow you to work with someone else
    B. to ask your coworker to transfer to another department or project
    C. talk to your coworker about the proper way to behave at work
    D. pretend the coworker is your best friend for the sake of your job
    E. to set aside your personal differences in order to complete the job

21.____

22. As a supervisory, which of the following incentives would you use to motivate your employees?
    A. Fear of losing their jobs
    B. Fear of their supervisors
    C. Allowing employees to provide their input on a number of policies
    D. Encouraging employees to file secret reports regarding colleagues' transgressions
    E. All of the above

22.____

23. A fellow Police Officer, with whom you enjoy a close friendship, has a substance-abuse problem which has gone undetected. You suspect the problem may be affecting his job.
    You would
    A. ask the Police Officer if the problem is affecting his job performance
    B. warn the Police Officer that he must seek counseling or you will report him
    C. wait a few weeks to see whether the officer's problem really is affecting his job
    D. discuss it with your supervisor
    E. wait for the supervisor to discover the problem

23.____

24. In the past two months, you have missed work
    A. zero times   B. once
    C. twice   D. three times
    E. more than three times

24.____

25. As a Police Officer, you are pursuing a group of robbers when you discover two small children who have been abandoned near a railroad crossing.
You should
   A. tell the children to stay put while you continue your pursuit
   B. lock the children in your vehicle and continue your pursuit
   C. stay with the children and radio for help in the pursuit of the robbers
   D. use the children to set a trap for the robbers
   E. ignore the children and continue your pursuit

KEY (CORRECT ANSWERS)

PLEASE NOTE: The answers listed are our preferred answers. However, you are to answer the exam honestly. Your personal answer may differ from our answers.

1. A
2. C
3. C
4. A
5. D

6. B
7. C
8. A
9. A
10. D

11. B
12. A
13. C
14. B
15. A

16. B
17. E
18. B
19. D
20. A

21. E
22. C
23. D
24. A
25. C

EXAMINATION SECTION
TEST 1

DIRECTIONS: This inventory contains 50 questions about yourself. You are to read each question and select the answer that best describes you from the choices provided. *PRINT THE LETTER OF YOUR ANSWER IN THE SPACE AT THE RIGHT.*

1. What has given you the most difficulty in any job that you have had? 1.____

    A. A supervisor who watched over my work too closely
    B. A supervisor who gave inconsistent direction
    C. Disagreements or gossip among co-workers
    D. Having to deal with too many insignificant details

2. I _____ put off doing a chore that I could have taken care of right away. 2.____

    A. often B. sometimes C. seldom D. never

3. During high school, the number of clubs or organizations I belonged/ belong to is: 3.____

    A. 0 B. 1 or 2 C. 2 to 3 D. more than 3

4. In the past, when I have given a speech or presentation, I was likely to have prepared ahead of time: 4.____

    A. much less than others did
    B. less than others
    C. more than others
    D. about the same as others

5. When working as a member of a team, I prefer to: 5.____

    A. take on challenging tasks but not take the lead
    B. do less complex tasks
    C. take the lead
    D. keep a low profile

6. Generally, in my work assignments, I would prefer to work: 6.____

    A. on one thing at a time.
    B. on a couple of things at a time.
    C. on many things at the same time.
    D. on something I have never done before.

7. In the course of a week, the thing that gives me the greatest satisfaction is 7.____

    A. coming up with a new or unique way to handle a situation.
    B. helping other people to solve problems.
    C. having free time to devote to personal interests.
    D. being told I have done a good job.

8. My health or fitness has _____ limited my ability to perform certain tasks.

   A. often   B. sometimes   C. seldom   D. never

9. In the past, when faced with an ethical dilemma, my first step has usually been to

   A. identify the issues that are in conflict
   B. reflect on the punishment or rewards likely to result from either course of action
   C. try to find someone else who is more appropriate for making such a decision
   D. identify the people and organizations likely to be affected by the decision

10. My leadership style could be best described as

    A. autocratic
    B. democratic/participative
    C. permissive/laissez faire
    D. motivational

11. In the past, when I have been part of a team, I most often felt

    A. as if I were a cut above, and ready to lead
    B. a sense of equality and belonging
    C. uncertain about the next step
    D. isolated and marginalized

12. I usually enjoy thinking about the plusses and minuses of alternative approaches to solving a problem:

    A. very true for me-describes me perfectly
    B. somewhat true of me
    C. somewhat false for me
    D. absolutely false for me-doesn't describe me at all

13. When I have participated in team activities in the past and found that other group members performed better than I have, I most often

    A. examined the skills and strategies that made them so successful
    B. made a last-gasp attempt to measure up
    C. tried to reconfigure the team members so that I wouldn't end up looking bad
    D. resented the easier set of circumstances that made such success possible

14. In the past, when I failed to adequately learn a skill, concept or body of knowledge, ttc failure was most often the result of

    A. other peoples' interference with my approach to learning or solving the problem
    B. poor instruction
    C. having too little time to adequately study and practice
    D. a study plan that aimed too high, without learning the basics first

15. My energy is usually highest when

    A. I work as part of a collaborative team
    B. I work completely on my own
    C. I work mostly on my own, with input from others when I ask for it
    D. I work with ongoing evaluations from superiors

16. My own work standards are

    A. usually completely different from those of others
    B. usually in tune with those of others
    C. always frustratingly more demanding than those of others
    D. sometimes different from others, but easily adapted to fit the group

17. In the past, when I have worked with a group on a task for which I had little experience, I have most often

    A. asked questions and contributed as much as I was able
    B. tried to alter the parameters of the task in order to suit my own abilities
    C. asked for direction and hoped for clear guidance
    D. I don't recall being in this situation.

18. How much do you agree with the following statement: "Unless I am assigned to a team that is made up of people just like myself, the team is not likely to succeed."

    A. Strongly agree   B. Agree somewhat
    C. Disagree somewhat   D. Strongly disagree

19. I am _____ giving other people feedback on their work because _____ .

    A. very comfortable; I usually know more about what it takes to succeed than they do
    B. comfortable; it is a normal and useful part of teamwork
    C. uncomfortable; I don't usually have anything to add
    D. very uncomfortable; I'm afraid I will be resented or rejected

20. In my career, I have changed jobs

    A. only through promotion   B. once or twice
    C. on the average, every few years   D. never

21. In the past, whenever I've been unable to achieve all that I set out to do in a given time period, I have

    A. tried to figure out where I came up short, and devised new strategies
    B. looked for ways to redefine "success"
    C. felt angry or hopeless
    D. I have never failed to achieve what I've set out to do.

22. Other people have _____ referred to me as an over-achiever.

    A. always   B. often   C. occasionally   D. never

23. When it comes to competitiveness, I am

    A. much more competitive than others
    B. slightly more competitive than others
    C. about as competitive as others
    D. generally less competitive than others

24. In the past, when I have achieved an important goal, I have

   A. not made a big deal of it, as it is only one small step toward an ultimate goal
   B. often gone back and tried to imagine how it could have been achieved mere successfully
   C. enjoyed the feeling of satisfaction for a while, before moving on to another goal
   D. tried to make the feeling of accomplishment last for as long as I could

25. My first impressions of people

   A. are almost always dead-on
   B. usually give an incomplete perception that evolves over time
   C. are often wrong, to my delight
   D. are often wrong, to my disappointment

26. When assigned a task, I believe

   A. success is imperative, and I'll do anything to achieve it
   B. success is important, and I focus on doing my best
   C. my investment in the success of the task correlates to my opinion of the task's importance
   D. my investment in the success of the task correlates to my opinion of the task's achievability

27. When trying to evaluate whether I have succeeded on a certain task, I rely mostly on

   A. my own gut feeling
   B. the opinions of peers
   C. a list of objective criteria
   D. people who fill leadership positions and are in a position to judge

28. If I fail to do something well,

   A. it usually isn't my fault
   B. it's probably time to give someone else a chance
   C. I'll look for feedback, reflect on it, and approach it differently another time
   D. I'll redouble my efforts, and won't give up until I succeed

29. At work or in school, when somebody has stood up to me or disagreed with me, I have tended to

   A. make a mental note that the person is an enemy who can't be trusted
   B. react angrily and heatedly, and then tried to make amends afterward
   C. listen carefully and assume that the person's opinion deserves respect
   D. apologize and try to soothe the person

30. In the past, when an assigned task has been altered during the course of my work, my reaction has usually been to

   A. adapt my strategy to fit the new circumstances
   B. wish that the people who first assigned it could make up their minds
   C. wonder what I've been doing wrong
   D. This has never happened to me

31. When times get tough, I usually

    A. become emotionally fragile or volatile
    B. feel more stressed, but make the effort to meet demands
    C. become depressed and find it more difficult to work
    D. tend to engage in unhealthy behaviors such as overeating or getting less sleep

32. I second-guess my decisions

    A. almost never
    B. when there is evidence to suggest that another way might be better
    C. when I feel poorly about myself or my performance
    D. constantly, always mindful of the different available courses of action

33. When I engage in an activity that requires moderate physical exertion, I usually

    A. push myself to ratchet up the physical demands of the activity
    B. feel challenged and energized
    C. come up with ways to make it less strenuous
    D. feel winded and depleted

34. If it were up to me, my success on a certain task would be defined by

    A. myself alone
    B. a set of fair and objective criteria
    C. my friends
    D. the strictest standards available

35. When I have been assigned to work in a group in the past, I have usually

    A. insisted on a leadership position
    B. been asked to assume a leadership position
    C. participated as an equal, and deferred to others when their opinions merited it
    D. been frozen out of decision-making by the more aggressive group members

36. When my regular work schedule changes, I most often

    A. try to stick with my proven formula for success
    B. feel angry and resentful at the whimsy of outside forces
    C. laugh it off as the result of a bureaucracy that often works against logic
    D. try to go with the flow and produce results

37. If somebody tries to talk me out of a decision, I am most likely to

    A. tell them they are wasting their time
    B. say I agree with them to minimize conflict, and then stick to my original plan
    C. try to figure out where they are coming from
    D. ask what I can do to make them happy

38. When I find a task to be unpleasant, but necessary, 38.__

    A. it is usually difficult to motivate myself to work on the task
    B. I try to pass it on to someone who will enjoy it more
    C. I am able to motivate myself to complete the task satisfactorily
    D. I place the task low on my priorities list

39. It seems as if it is _____ case that some people find what I say to be rude or offensive. 39.__

    A. always
    B. often
    C. sometimes
    D. never

40. When I have finished a particular task, I usually find that the time it took to complete was 40.__

    A. about what I had expected and planned for
    B. more than I had expected and planned for
    C. less than I had expected and planned for
    D. other more or less than I had planned for, with no consistent means of predicting either

41. When I undertake a task with several different parts, I usually 41.__

    A. tackle the easiest work first
    B. start organizing the different parts into categories that I can prioritize
    C. start working on them in no particular order it all has to get done anyway
    D. have a difficult time deciding which part to do first

42. When I am assigned a new project, I'm usually 42.__

    A. a little apprehensive about adding to my workload
    B. hopeful that it will be more interesting than the drudgery that takes up most of my time
    C. excited to take on something new and different
    D. nervous about whether I'm up to the task

43. On the occasions when I have been in a position to lead others, I have most often tried to lead by 43.__

    A. isolating and marginalizing the weak links
    B. offering appropriate rewards and punishments
    C. trying to inspire confidence and innovation
    D. allowing decisions to be made by other group members

44. My own academic career has been one characterized by 44.__

    A. achievement beyond even my own expectations
    B. hard work
    C. success without having to try very hard
    D. bitter disappointment in those charged with the task of educating me

45. I believe that when a group composed of talented people fails to achieve an assigned task, it is usually the case that

    A. A the group failed to appoint a leader who could have directed their talents toward a result
    B. the group probably didn't do as good a job at communicating as they could have
    C. some group members were working harder than others
    D. the people who assigned the task had unrealistic expectations

45.____

46. I feel that whatever success I have achieved in life has been attributable largely to

    A. myself alone
    B. hard work and the support of others
    C. the fact that tasks were clearly defined and not too difficult
    D. D. pure luck

46.____

47. In my academic career, I have tended to focus the most energy on course work that

    A. allowed me to express my creativity
    B. I knew would later help to advance my career
    C. challenged me to think in new and different ways
    D. involved memorization and repetition

47.____

48. I usually get a physical workout _____ a week.

    A. 0-1   B. 2-3   C. 3-5   D. 5-7

48.____

49. Of the following, my favorite academic subjects could be most accurately described as

    A. the empirical subjects, such as math and science
    B. expressive and creative subjects such as art
    C. subjects that involved a lot of reading, such as history and English literature
    D. entirely dependent on how the subjects were taught, and in what kind of environment

49.____

50. Of the following, the information sources I tend to trust the most are

    A. network television news programs
    B. Internet blogs
    C. professional and scholarly journals, such as *Scientific American*
    D. other print media such as newspapers and magazines

50.____

Biodata Inventory
Key to Exercises

Note: In a biographical inventory, which asks for factual data, there are no right or wrong answers. It may also be true that for a particular question, more than one answer reflects a trait or viewpoint that might qualify one as a special agent: there is no single type of person or personality type that is acceptable. At the same time, there are some qualities or experiences that would probably suggest that a person is less than an ideal candidate. Generally, you are likely to be considered "qualified" if your answers tend to reveal the skills and abilities that the Biodata Inventory is designed to look for:

- *Ability to Organize, Plan, and Prioritize*
- *Ability to Maintain a Positive Image*
- *Ability to Evaluate Information and Make Judgment Decisions*
- *Initiative and Motivation*
- *Ability to Adapt to Changing Situations*
- *Physical Requirements*

The following responses are the ones most indicative of these skills and abilities:

1. No choice here is better than the others; all describe a problem.
2. D
3. D
4. C
5. A or C

6. No answer is inherently better than the others; candidate suitability will probably depend on the task at hand.
7. A or B
8. D
9. A
10. B or D

11. B
12. A or B
13. A
14. D
15. A

16. D
17. A
18. C or D
19. B
20. None is "right," but choice C is the least desirable, labeling you as one who can't stick with a job.

21. A
22. None is "right," but choice D is the least desirable—it's better to have over-achieved at least once or twice.
23. None is "right," but choice D is the least desirable.
24. C
25. B

Biodata Inventory
Key to Exercises (continued)

26. B
27. C
28. C
29. C
30. A

31. B
32. B
33. B
34. B
35. B or C

36. D
37. C
38. C
39. D
40. A

41. B
42. C
43. C
44. B
45. B

46. B
47. C
48. D
49. None is the "right" answer, but A or C are the best choices.
50. C

PROBLEM SENSITIVITY

This section of the exam measures your ability to choose the course of action that should be taken <u>first</u> in critical situations.

<u>Sample Questions</u>

1. What should an officer do <u>first</u> when investigating an incident?

    A. Write a report of the incident.
    B. Inform other police officers of the incident.
    C. Proceed to the scene of the incident.
    D. Interview witnesses.

1.____

Getting the correct information to the emergency medical personnel is extremely important. It is suggested that you, the police officer, make the call if possible, or assign the task to a person who appears calm. If you are alone at the accident scene, do not leave the victim until breathing is restored, all bleeding has been stopped, the victim is no longer in danger of further injury, and all precautions have been taken against shock. When the emergency medical personnel arrive, brief them as to what happened to the victim, the type of first aid you have administered, and the physical status of the victim.

2. When the emergency medical personnel arrives at the accident scene, you <u>first</u> should tell them:

    A. how long the victim's breathing has been restored.
    B. how long the bleeding has been stopped.
    C. that the victim appeared to be going into shock.
    D. the type of first aid you administered.

2.____

KEY (CORRECT ANSWERS)

1. C
2. D

POLICE PROCEDURES & INFORMATION

Police Officers must be able to understand information and follow specified police procedures. One portion of the exam will test your ability to remember the information presented in this booklet. You are to assume that the police procedures presented here are the procedures that must be followed. The procedures and information to be memorized are:

>Hospital Cases
>Use of Police Radio
>Responsibilities of Police Officers at Crime Scenes
>Transporting Prisoners
>Reporting Vehicular Accidents
>Job Specification for Police Officer Trainee

Carefully learn these police procedures. If there are any words in these procedures you do not understand, look them up in a dictionary. You will NOT have these materials in front of you when you take the test. It is important to learn carefully this information or you will not be able to answer the questions on this section of the test.

Hospital Cases

Police personnel may be assigned to or encounter a hospital case. These cases will be considered emergencies unless a doctor or other medically trained person states otherwise. Hospital cases will be transported to the nearest hospital. In the case of a patient needing specialized care not available at the nearest hospital, a patrol supervisor will be contacted and will make the final decision.

Whenever possible, such as in cases where a stretcher is not needed, hospital cases will be transported by patrol car instead of by patrol wagon. In the case of life-threatening situations, the City Paramedic Unit will be notified immediately. The paramedics will assume the care and transportation of the patient. Police officers will direct traffic and assist paramedics as required.

Use of Police Radio

The purpose of police radio is to receive calls from the general public and dispatch unit, and to aid and inform police personnel in the field. Police dispatchers can give out assignments, relay information, and dispatch supervisors when requested or needed by field officers. Dispatchers cannot make command decisions but can relay the information to the proper command personnel. Police dispatchers also will broadcast information of general interest to police such as names of wanted and missing persons, and information on crimes. In addition, they will assign an identification number to each incident for which an officer is to file a report. This number will be recorded in the proper block on the Incident Report (82-7) and on all subsequent reports resulting from the original incident.

Dispatchers will make assignments by broadcasting the vehicle number, location of assignment and reason (e.g., "214, 2200 Connecticut Avenue, possible child abuse"). Each assignment will be repeated at least three times. If a unit is in-service and does not acknowledge an assignment, the dispatcher will record this and the officer will be required to submit a written memo stating the reason he/she did not respond. Disciplinary action may result.

Units will respond to dispatchers by stating their vehicle number and "Okay" if they can respond to the call. If not, they will state their vehicle number and the reason they are not available. Then the dispatcher may assign another officer. Patrol officers will notify police radio upon arrival at the scene by stating the vehicle number and "on scene." Officers will again notify police radio at the completion of the assignment by stating the vehicle number and "available."

All uniformed officers will remain in radio range at all times unless they are out-of-service or there is a shortage of hand-held units. Officers who will be out of radio range will report to the dispatcher their vehicle number, location, and reason for being out of range (e.g., "214, 2414 Down Drive, no portable unit") and will report back in as soon as they have radio access.

When an officer wishes to contact the dispatcher in a non-emergency situation, he/she will wait for a break in communications and state the vehicle number. The officer will wait for dispatcher acknowledgement (i.e., "214 go ahead") before proceeding. The officer will acknowledge information and assignments by stating vehicle number and "Okay."

In emergency situations, the officer will state his/her vehicle number and "emergency." These calls take precedence and all other transmissions will stop until the emergency call is ended. Emergency calls include: assist officer calls, reports of crimes-in-progress, car accidents involving serious injury, riotous situations, and life-endangering situations.

Responsibilities of Police Officers at Crime Scenes

The first officer on the scene is responsible for protecting the scene and telling the police dispatcher to send the necessary assistance. The officer also will take responsibility for the following:

1. Give first aid to the injured and make arrangements for transportation of the injured immediately. The officer should try to outline the position of the body before removal.

2. Question victim(s), if possible, to find out what happened. Notify police radio so information can be broadcast.

3. Detain all persons at the scene and try to prevent conversations among witnesses.

4. Do not let <u>anyone</u> touch or move anything at the scene or enter the crime scene except:

    A. Those transporting the injured.
    B. Personnel from the investigative unit and crime lab unit. I.D. <u>must</u> be displayed on outer garment.
    C. Police officers guarding the scene.
    D. An object such as a motor vehicle at the scene may be moved if it is a danger to public safety. Before moving it, outline its position and why and when moved. Give this information to the chief investigator on the scene.

5. Maintain a log of the names and badge numbers of all persons entering the scene and the reason for entering.

6. <u>No</u> other personnel, including supervisors not involved in the investigation, are allowed on the crime scene.

Transporting Prisoners

All persons will be searched by the arresting officer in accordance with procedures in section 11.07 of the Patrol Officer's Manual.

All prisoners will be taken to the district station by patrol wagon. If no wagons are available, prisoners will be transported in a patrol car after the officers receive permission from their sergeant. Two officers must be present in the car. The prisoner will sit in the rear seat behind the passenger side and the second officer will sit behind the driver.

All prisoners will be handcuffed behind their backs.

Prisoners should be kept in the rear seat of the patrol car while waiting for the wagon. Officers riding in the wagon will search the prisoner again in accordance with section 11.07 of the Patrol Officer's Manual.

After prisoners have been handed over to other authorities, officers will check their vehicles for contraband or weapons left behind or hidden by the prisoner. Officers should check behind and under seats. In patrol wagons, officers also should check the canvas stretchers and blankets if so equipped. Officers should exercise caution in case razor blades or other dangerous and exposed materials have been left behind.

Reporting Vehicular Accidents

The following procedures will be followed by police officers responding to or observing a vehicular accident:

1. Check to see if there are any injured people who require hospital treatment. If so, use police radio to request transportation.

2. Obtain operator's license(s), registration card(s), and insurance card(s) from the operator(s).

3. Fill out Incident Report for <u>all</u> accidents.

4. If the accident is reportable, also fill out a Police Accident Report. Reportable accidents are those in which any of the following occur:

    A. There is death or injury.
    B. Any vehicle is so damaged that it cannot be driven from the scene of the accident without further damage or danger, and towing is required.
    C. There is any damage to state or local government property or vehicles.
    D. The operator involved leaves the scene of the accident.
    E. It is believed that the operator involved is under the influence of drugs or alcohol.

5. Give operator(s) involved the report number of the completed Police Accident Form.

6. Give each operator an officer's business card containing the officer's rank, name, district of assignment, badge number, and district phone number.

7. Request police radio to send an officer from the Accident Investigation Unit in all cases where there has been fatal or potentially fatal injuries, or a local or state government vehicle is involved.

Note: The job specifications are not official with respect to the position for which you are applying. They are included to test your ability to read, understand, and recall information.

Job Specification for Police Officer Trainee

Nature of Work:

This work applies to entry and training level positions in law enforcement. The officer is trained in all aspects of law enforcement. Often, considerable public contact is involved, therefore, the officer is required to exercise the immediate practical judgment necessary to cope with unusual or emergency situations. The officer is expected to place emphasis on courteous explanation and personal persuasiveness in routinely seeking the compliance of others in obeying the laws. However, situations arise in which the officer must restrain and/or arrest persons threatening the security of the public.

Performance of the work is guided by written procedures. The officer receives close supervision from a higher level police officer. Officers in the trainee class normally do not hold supervisory positions.

Examples of Work:

Patrols assigned areas.
Searches for missing persons.
Compiles data, keeps records, and prepares written reports on enforcement activities.
Enforces federal, state, and local laws.
Issues warnings or summonses and arrests those apprehended for violations.
Investigates accidents and criminal acts.
Presents evidence and gives testimony in court.
Renders emergency first aid.
Gives motorists directions and assistance.
Attends formal training courses.

Required Knowledge and Abilities:

Introductory knowledge of criminal, civil, and traffic laws; and, knowledge of the care and use of firearms.

Ability to handle firearms safely, to comprehend oral and written instructions; to write narrative reports; to meet situations requiring tact, understanding, and good judgment; to detect situations imperiling security and safety; to remember names and faces; to learn.

Minimum Qualifications:

Education: Graduation from high school or possession of a State high school equivalence certificate.

License: A valid Motor Vehicle Operator license.

Conditions of Employment:

1. Candidates will be given a medical examination to determine physical ability to perform the job. This examination may include strength and agility tests. Good vision is required.

2. Due to provisions in the Retirement System Law, candidates aged 70 or over will not be appointed.

3. Duties necessitate being outdoors in all types of weather, standing and walking, or in assigned vehicles.

4. Due to the nature and condition of the work, a criminal conviction record may be a bar to employment. Candidates who have a conviction record will not be prevented from taking the test. If an investigation determines that a criminal conviction record is job-related, the candidate will not be selected and the Department of Personnel will authorize the passing over of such names on the eligible lists as provided by State law.

5. Persons appointed to the position of police officer may be required to be present for duty on Saturdays, Sundays, and holidays. Officers in this position may be assigned to any one of three shifts on a permanent or rotating basis and are required to report to work when called in during emergencies.

6. Demonstration of practical knowledge and proficiency in the safe use and care of firearms may be required of applicants prior to appointment or upon completion of the Police Training Commission course.

7. Prior to appointment being made permanent, a person appointed to a position of police officer trainee must have successfully completed, within the first year of employment, a training course approved by the Police Training Commission. Candidates must, therefore, be able to meet the minimum standards as determined by the Police Training Commission.

8. Candidates receiving a passing rating on all parts of the test will be interviewed before appointment. Also, candidates are subject to investigation by the State Police in order to establish eligibility to be commissioned to make arrests and to obtain a gun permit.

9. Persons appointed to this position may be required to have a telephone in their residence so that they may be contacted at any time.

Sample Questions

The following question is based on "Responsibilities of Police Officers at Crime Scenes."

1. You are the first officer on the scene. Your sergeant, who is not part of the investigation, wants to enter the crime scene. You should:

    A. let him enter.
    B. let him enter but caution him not to move or touch anything.
    C. let him enter and record his name and badge number in the log.
    D. not let him enter.

The following question is based on "Reporting Vehicular Accidents."

2. You arrive at the scene of an accident at the intersection of Apple Street and Orange Avenue. The owner of a badly damaged car tells you she saw a man in a van run into her parked car. You should:

    A. use police radio to broadcast the description of the van.
    B. fill out an Incident Report and a Police Accident Report.
    C. put a tag on the car with the name of the owner and the date of the accident.
    D. question witnesses to verify the car owner's account of the accident.

KEY (CORRECT ANSWERS)

1. D

2. B

EXERCISING JUDGMENT

Another part of the test measures your ability to put information into a meaningful order. No special knowledge is required. It is a question of using good judgment and common sense. In the following format, Roman numerals are used (I = one, II = two, III = three, and IV = four).

Sample Questions

1. A police officer is arresting a suspect. In what order should the officer do the following?
    I. Search the suspect.
    II. Inform the suspect of the intent to arrest him/her and of his/her constitutional rights.
    III. Specify the charges or reason for arrest.
    IV. Identify himself/herself.

    A. IV, II, III, I
    B. II, IV, III, I
    C. III, IV, I, II
    D. IV, I, III, II

2. A police officer has arrived at the scene of a crime and is about to conduct a preliminary investigation. In what order should the officer do the following?
    I. Arrange for searching the scene and collecting evidence.
    II. Locate, detain, and identify witnesses.
    III. Render aid to the injured.
    IV. Get a description of the suspect.

    A. IV, III, II, I
    B. III, IV, II, I
    C. II, III, IV, I
    D. I, III, II, IV

KEY (CORRECT ANSWERS)

1. A
2. B

LAW ENFORCEMENT METHODS AND PRACTICES

These questions test for knowledge of accepted police methods and practices and/or their application to situations in the police field. The questions are a sampling of the various knowledge that police personnel may be required to possess in the course of their day-to-day work-related activities.

TEST TASK: You will be presented with situations in which you must apply knowledge of accepted police methods and practices in order to answer the questions correctly.

SAMPLE QUESTION:

A police officer should have a detailed knowledge of all legitimate business and activity in his patrol area. Which one of the following is the most important reason why the officer should have this knowledge?
- A. The officer will become acquainted with and know the businessmen through a set patrol routine.
- B. The officer will know the unusual or out of the ordinary and it can be investigated.
- C. The officer will know who to notify in case of an emergency.
- D. The officer will know who to call on if he needs assistance

The correct answer to this sample question is B.

SOLUTION:

Choice A is not correct. Patrol should generally be performed in a random manner. A set patrol routine is predictable and unacceptable.

Choice B is the correct answer to this question. Most events which are of interest to police are those that are unusual. The ability to recognize these allows officers to focus their attention where it is most likely to be needed.

Choice C is not correct. Notifications of emergencies should be made through the department's dispatching personnel.

Choice D is not correct. Assistance should be obtained through department dispatching personnel, not extra-departmental channels.

EXAMINATION SECTION

TEST 1

DIRECTIONS: Each question or incomplete statement is followed by several suggested answers or completions. Select the one that BEST answers the question or completes the statement. *PRINT THE LETTER OF THE CORRECT ANSWER IN THE SPACE AT THE RIGHT.*

1. Which of the following events would typically cause the GREATEST amount of stress in a person's life?
   A. A major change in financial status
   B. Vacation
   C. Pregnancy
   D. Marital separation

   1.____

2. A local shopping center has experienced a recent rash of shoplifting. Officer Jones is patrolling the mall parking lot frequently.
   Which situation below should Officer Jones regard as MOST suspicious?
   A. A man running out a store entrance with a shopping bag from the store under his arm
   B. A car parked for a long time near the front entrance of the store
   C. A woman loading a pile of clothes, some with plastic security tags still attached, into the trunk of her car
   D. A young man walking around looking in through the windows of various parked cars

   2.____

3. An officer is faced with the responsibility of telling a woman her husband has been murdered. While the officers should phrase the news as gently as possible, he or she should also demonstrate empathy nonverbally.
   The BEST way to do this is to
   A. stand with arms crossed
   B. hold the woman closely
   C. maintain eye contact
   D. tell the woman you understand her pain

   3.____

4. Cognitive symptoms of anxiety include
   A. rapid heart rate
   B. feelings of fear of helplessness
   C. poor social functioning
   D. euphoria

   4.____

5. Which of the following is MOST likely to help a person to improve her attitude?
   A. Avoiding people who make her feel bad about herself
   B. Learning to become more goal-oriented
   C. Learning to look more clearly at her own faults
   D. Taking charge of an unruly situation

   5.____

6. A suspect has been handcuffed, but refuses to take a seat in the patrol car after several requests.
   The arresting officer should
   A. tap the suspect behind the knees with the baton, just hard enough so that the suspect's legs will fold and he can be inserted into the car
   B. tighten the handcuffs until the pain compel compliance
   C. try to frighten the suspect with threats
   D. inform the suspect of the consequences for resisting arrest

7. Each of the following is likely to be a cause of stress on the job, EXCEPT
   A. work overload
   B. differences in organizational and personal values
   C. a narrowly-defined role
   D. time pressures

8. In communicating with people, especially in stressful or high-conflict situations, nonverbal communication is
   A. more important than the verbal message
   B. less important than the verbal message
   C. universal across all cultures
   D. typically contradictory to the verbal message

9. Problem-oriented police work does NOT
   A. help officers get to the roots of a crime problem
   B. offer a proactive model for policing
   C. focus on responding to calls for service
   D. have any impact on preventing or reducing crime

10. The difference between assertiveness and aggressiveness is that
    A. assertiveness is not potentially harmful to others
    B. aggressiveness involves strangers
    C. aggressiveness has to do with achieving goals
    D. assertiveness is always negative

11. As an officer and his partner arrive to investigate a reported domestic disturbance, the husband and wife are still arguing. In the presence of the officers, each spouse makes a verbal threat of physical harm against the other. In resolving this conflict, the FINAL step that should be taken by the officers is to
    A. indicate the consequences if this behavior continues
    B. empathize with each of the spouses
    C. present the spouses with problem-solving strategies
    D. describe the behaviors that appeared to cause the disturbance

12. Elements of community policing include
    I. the police   II. the business community
    III. the media   IV. religious institutions
    The CORRECT ANSWER IS:
    A. I, II   B. I, II, III   C. I, III   D. I, II, III, IV

13. In a grocery store parking lot, a pair of officers arrest both the buyer and seller   13.____
in an alleged drug transaction in a grocery store parking lot After the suspects
have been handcuffed and placed in a patrol car, one of the officers notices a
wad of bills on the ground where the transaction took place. The officer
pockets the money and decides to keep it, telling herself that the money is
"dirty" and that she has more of a right to it than either of the criminal suspects.
Legally, the officer has committed a crime; ethically, she has committed a(n)
    A. rationalization   B. kickback   C. stereotyping   D. deviance

14. Probably the MOST effective way to deal with on-the-job stress is to   14.____
    A. find alternative employment
    B. take early retirement
    C. participate in a personal wellness program
    D. acquire assertiveness skills that will help confront the people responsible
       for the stress

Questions 15-16.

DIRECTIONS: Questions 15 and 16 deal with the following situation.

A pharmacist has complained to the police department that several drug addicts in his neighborhood have been attempting to obtain drugs legally, usually by passing fake prescriptions.

15. Which of the following people should arouse the MOST suspicion when   15.____
    approaching the prescription counter?
    A. A middle-aged woman who appears homeless and is poorly groomed
    B. A young African-American male in a hooded sweatshirt on a hot day
    C. A man in his thirties who glances around furtively and brings a large
       amount of nonprescription items to the counter for purchase
    D. None of the above should be regarded as suspicious on the basis of their
       appearance alone

16. After refusing to fill several prescriptions, the pharmacist describes or gives   16.____
    each of the prescriptions to an investigating officer.
    Which of the following MOST warrants investigation?
    A. A written investigation that is covered with several coffee rings
    B. A prescription written on a Post-It note
    C. A written prescription for pain killers with a date indicating it was written
       more than a week ago
    D. A prescription that is phoned in by a doctor

17. An individual's personality, whether normal or deviant, will ALWAYS   17.____
    A. refer to the person's deep inner self, rather than just superficial aspects
    B. involve unique characteristics that are all different from another person's
    C. be a product of social and cultural environments, with no biological
       foundation
    D. be organized into patterns that are observable and measurable to some
       degree

18. Change in a person's life that is due to personal growth is almost always
    A. negative   B. dramatic   C. positive   D. minor

19. Residents in an urban neighborhood have complained of a recent increase in gang-related graffiti in their community.
    Which of the following should be regarded as MOST suspicious by an officer on patrol?
    A. One young man walking down the street and flashing gang signs at passing cars
    B. A pair of teenagers riding their bicycles in a tenement parking lot late at night
    C. A group of teenagers hanging out in a convenience store parking lot, leaning against a wall that is covered with graffiti
    D. A group of teenagers hanging out in a convenience store parking lot. One of the teenagers has a spray paint can.

20. Common symptoms of stress include each of the following EXCEPT
    A. digestive problem   B. sluggishness
    C. sleep problems   D. emotional instability

21. The general goal of community policing is
    A. a lower overall crime rate
    B. conviction of criminals who are caught in the community
    C. fewer violent crimes
    D. a higher quality of life in the community

22. In most settings, the simplest and most effective method of stopping sexual harassment is to
    A. threaten the person with legal or administrative consequences
    B. ignore it
    C. avoid the person as much as possible
    D. ask or tell the person to stop

23. Of the following types of crime, the one MOST likely to have a widespread impact on a victims community is
    A. hate or bias crime   B. workplace violence
    C. theft   D. sexual assault

24. Functional roles of the police include:
    I. Crime prevention   II. Order maintenance
    III. Public service   IV. Criminal prosecution
    The CORRECT answer is:
    A. I only   B. I, II   C. I, II, III   D. I, II, III, IV

25. A pre-existing thought or belief that people have about members of a given group—whether the belief is positive, negative, or neutral—is
    A. ethnocentrism   B. a stereotype
    C. self-centeredness   D. discrimination

KEY (CORRECT ANSWERS)

1.	D		11.	A
2.	C		12.	D
3.	C		13.	A
4.	B		14.	C
5.	B		15.	D
6.	D		16.	B
7.	C		17.	D
8.	A		18.	B
9.	C		19.	D
10.	A		20.	B

21. D
22. D
23. A
24. C
25. B

TEST 2

DIRECTIONS: Each question or incomplete statement is followed by several suggested answers or completions. Select the one that BEST answers the question or completes the statement. *PRINT THE LETTER OF THE CORRECT ANSWER IN THE SPACE AT THE RIGHT.*

1. Role expectations for police officers generally
   A. are consistent across the country, with a strong focus on peacekeeping
   B. change from community to community, depending on the local culture
   C. direct them to be more lenient with juvenile offenders
   D. direct them to be self-reliant in both preventing and investigating crime

2. Officer Shinjo takes a complaint from a woman who says she is being stalked by a man who is a classmate in one of her night business courses. The man has sent her unwanted gifts and left numerous unanswered telephone messages, but she did not become concerned until last night, when she noticed the man following her home from class. She asks Officer Shinjo what to do about the situation.
   At least part of Officer Shinjo's advice to the woman should include the suggestion that she
   A. immediately apply for a restraining order
   B. create a logbook to document each of the stalking incidents in as much detail as possible
   C. answer one of the man's telephone calls and try to explain that the unwanted attention is making her uncomfortable
   D. call the man herself and threaten legal action if he doesn't stop bothering her

3. Which of the following is an element of self-direction?
   A. Knowing when to seek help from others
   B. Being able to get from one geographic location to another without a map
   C. Establishing and reaching both short- and long-term goals
   D. Adopting healthier lifestyle habits

4. Each of the following factors is typically associated with ethnicity, EXCEPT
   A. culture   B. language
   C. economic status   D. physical characteristics

5. Among the communication skills necessary for effective communication with people, the foundation upon which all others are based is considered to be
   A. confrontation   B. authoritativeness
   C. attending behavior D. observation

6. Which of the following offers the BEST definition of the word "ethics"?
   A. An individual's means of obtaining what he wants from and for other people in a society
   B. Standards of conduct that express a society's concept of right and wrong

C. A formal code of conduct that delineates a strict set of rules and framework for punishment
D. Morality and the consequences of behaviors

7. Which of the following is a measurement of a rate?　　　　7._____
   A. The ratio of the number of new African-American arrestees for drug-related crimes in the 35-49 age bracket during a specific year, compared to the number of African-Americans in the same age group in the entire community
   B. The number of white females, aged 18-25, who are arrested each year on child endangerment charges
   C. The percentage change in the number of property crimes in a given year, compared to the previous year
   D. The ratio of the number of persons currently under prosecution for violent crimes to the number of people, aged 14-55, in the entire community

8. In recent weeks, several patrons at a local restaurant have had their cars broken　　8._____
   into by having a window smashed in, and then having valuable items taken from the car. Officer Jackson is patrolling the restaurant parking lot.
   Which situation below should she regard as MOST suspicious?
   A. A young man in a hooded sweatshirt walking around the parking lot at lunchtime, carrying a long, heavy flashlight
   B. A car parked so as to partially block other cars from exiting the parking lot
   C. A man's voice raised in anger coming from the parking lot
   D. Several young men leaning against the outside of the parking lot fence in the early evening, bouncing a basketball and apparently waiting for the arrival of another person

9. Among the skills important to effective communication with people, the MOST　　9._____
   complex and difficult to master are those that help to
   A. encourage　　B. confront　　C. influence　　D. summarize

10. The FIRST step in dealing with an alcohol or drug addiction is to　　10._____
    A. admit there is a problem
    B. talk to a counselor or close friend
    C. stop taking the drug or drinking alcohol
    D. join a support group or enter a rehabilitation center

11. Key elements of police professionalism include:　　11._____
    I. an advanced education
    II. a clearly stated code of ethics
    III. accountability through peer review
    IV. demonstrated understanding of the field's core body of knowledge
    The CORRECT answer is:
    A. I, II　　　B. I, III, IV　　　C. II, III, IV　　　D. I, II, III, IV

12. A factor that makes a police officer susceptible to corruption is that the officer
    A. is typically different from most members of society
    B. can be sure that if a suspect is arrested, the suspect will be prosecuted and punished
    C. is usually better off financially than most of the people she interacts with in carrying out her duties
    D. has the professional discretion not to enforce the law

13. In resolving an ethical dilemma, a police officer's FIRST step should generally be to
    A. identify the ethical issues that are in conflict
    B. identify the people and organizations likely to be affected by the decision
    C. consult with colleagues and appropriate experts
    D. examine the reasons in favor of and opposed to each possible course of action

14. During a lengthy interview with a witness, an officer decides to use "reflection of meaning" strategies in order to clarify the information he's being given.
    This strategy would involve each of the following EXCEPT
    A. trying to paraphrase longer statements offered by the witness
    B. closing with a check on the witness's words, such as "So do I understand this correctly?"
    C. beginning sentences with phrases such as "You mean....." or "Sounds as if you saw....."
    D. offering an interpretation of the witness's words

15. Officer McGee is meeting with several community members to determine a course of action for reducing gang-related activities in the area.
    Each of the following is a guideline to be used by an officer in building a constructive relationship with community members, EXCEPT
    A. viewing community members as equals
    B. adopting a completely neutral tone of voice when speaking with people
    C. using a shared vocabulary of easily understood, nonoffensive words
    D. asking for the input of community members before making any suggestions

16. In solving a complex problem, the FIRST step is always to
    A. develop a plan
    B. gather information
    C. define the problem
    D. envision contingencies

17. Role conflict can occur when an officer encounters two sets of expectations that are inconsistent with each other. Role strain can occur when an officer's role is limited by what he or she is authorized to do.
    The MAIN difference between these two is that role
    A. conflict is relatively rare among police officers
    B. conflict can be resolved; role strain cannot
    C. strain creates stressful situations for officers
    D. strain has a greater influence on the officer's exercise of discretion

18. Generally, police community relations differs from public relations in that they
    A. consider the needs of the community first
    B. are much more successful in reducing social problems
    C. are without inherent spheres of interest
    D. encourage two-way communications

19. Factors that place a man at risk as a potential batterer include each of the following, EXCEPT
    A. poverty
    B. drug or alcohol use
    C. 30-45 years of age
    D. witnessing spousal abuse between parents

20. The four major categories of commonly abused substances include
    A. stimulants   B. alcohol   C. nicotine   D. caffeine

21. After receiving their monthly assistance payments from the local social services agency, some members of the homeless community immediately use the money to carry out drug transactions.
    In his patrol of the area around the agency, which situation below should Officer Garcia regard as MOST suspicious?
    A. A group of several homeless people who meet every day in a local park, where they sit together for about three hours and then move on
    B. A homeless woman who walks up and down the entire length of a busy city street all day long, endlessly smoking cigarettes
    C. An abandoned car that sits on a privately-owned lot and is used as a sleeping place by several homeless people throughout the day
    D. A single man remaining in the same area for several hours at a time, during which many homeless people approach him and greet him with handshakes

22. The MOST significant factor that requires police to perform functions other than law enforcement is
    A. greater public trust relative to other agencies or institutions
    B. a broader resource base
    C. round-the-clock availability
    D. the level of police interaction with community members

23. A "minority" group is a group that is discriminated against on the basis of
    A. physical or cultural characteristics
    B. the size of the group relative to the majority
    C. race
    D. the group's degree of conformity to the norms of the majority

24. An officer is talking with a resident of a high-crime urban neighborhood about a recent increase in drug-related activities. Because of the active police presence in the area, some residents are suspicious of the police.
    Each of the following nonverbal cues is a likely indicator of distrust on the part of a listener, EXCEPT

A. holding arms crossed over one's chest
B. steady eye contact
C. clenched jaw
D. shoulders angled away from speaker

25. Personality characteristics necessary for the successful performance of police duties include
   I. dependent style in problem-solving
   II. emotional expressiveness in interpersonal communication
   III. cohesiveness in group performance
   IV. emotional restraint
   The CORRECT answer is:
   A. I, III   B. I, II, IV   C. II, III, IV   D. I, II, III, IV

KEY (CORRECT ANSWERS)

1.	B		11.	D
2.	B		12.	D
3.	C		13.	A
4.	C		14.	D
5.	C		15.	B
6.	B		16.	C
7.	B		17.	B
8.	A		18.	D
9.	C		19.	C
10.	A		20.	A

21. D
22. C
23. A
24. B
25. C

EXAMINATION SECTION
TEST 1

DIRECTIONS: Each question or incomplete statement is followed by several suggested answers or completions. Select the one that BEST answers the question or completes the statement. *PRINT THE LETTER OF THE CORRECT ANSWER IN THE SPACE AT THE RIGHT.*

1. Officer Hayes has arrived at the scene of an automobile accident to find the two drivers arguing heatedly in the middle of the intersection, where their two cars remain entangled by their front bumpers. Traffic has backed up on all four sides of the intersection. As Officer Hayes approaches, the two drivers each begin to tell their side of the story at the same time. As they grow more agitated and begin to call each other names, one of the drivers threatens the other with physical harm.
Officer Hayes' FIRST action should be to
    A. ask each driver to stand on an opposite corner of the intersection and wait for him to begin documenting the accident
    B. call a tow truck to clear the accident from the intersection
    C. arrest the driver who made the threat
    D. ask the drivers to pull their cars out of the intersection and off to the side of the road

2. Probably the MOST important thing a police officer can do to build and strengthen a trusting relationship with community members is to
    A. patrol the area often and conspicuously
    B. listen to them in a respectful and nonjudgmental way
    C. make sure people understand his background and qualifications
    D. establish clear, reachable goals for improving the community

3. Which of the following is NOT a factor that should influence an officer's exercise of discretion?
    A. Clear statutes and protocols
    B. Informal expectations of legislatures and the public
    C. Use of force
    D. Limited resources

4. The term for the policing style which emphasizes order maintenance is _____ style.
    A. service   B. coercive   C. watchman   D. legalistic

5. Officer Torres, a community service law enforcement officer, approaches the home of recent Vietnamese immigrants to speak to several community members gathered there. He notices several pairs of shoes on the front porch.

It is reasonable for Officer Torres too assume that
- A. the people in the home are superstitious
- B. the house must have some religious significance
- C. if he removes his own shoes before entering, it will be perceived as a sign of respect
- D. the homeowners are having their carpets cleaned

6. Ethical issues are
   - A. usually a problem only in individual behaviors
   - B. relevant to all aspects of police work
   - C. usually referred to a board or committee for decision-making
   - D. the same as legal issues

7. In using the "reflection of meaning" technique in a client interview, a social worker should do each of the following, EXCEPT
   - A. begin with a sentence stem such as "You mean..." or "Sounds like you believe..."
   - B. offer an interpretation of the client's words
   - C. add paraphrasing of longer client statements
   - D. close with a "check-out" such as, "Am I hearing you right?"

8. A police officer is speaking with a victim who is hearing-impaired. The police officer should try to do each of the following, EXCEPT
   - A. speak slowly and clearly
   - B. gradually increase the volume of his voice
   - C. face the victim squarely
   - D. reduce or eliminate any background or ambient noise

9. An officer is interviewing a witness who is a recent immigrant from China. In general, the officer should avoid
   - A. verbal tracking or requests for clarification
   - B. open-ended questions
   - C. sustained eye contact
   - D. attentive body language

10. Which of the following statements about rape is FALSE?
    - A. The use of alcohol and drugs can reduce sexual inhibitions.
    - B. Rape is a crime of violence.
    - C. Rape is a crime that can only be committed against women.
    - D. It is not a sustainable legal charge if the partner has already consented to sex in the past.

11. A person's individual code of ethics is typically determined by each of the following factors, EXCEPT
    - A. reason
    - B. religion
    - C. emotion
    - D. law

12. Officer Long, new to the urban precinct where he is assigned patrol, has received a pair of complaints from two customers about the owner of a local convenience store, who works the cash register on most days. According to one customer, the owner became angry and ordered her out of the store after she had asked the price of a certain item. The other customer claims that on another occasion, the owner pulled a handgun from behind the counter and trained it on him as he walked slowly out of the store with his hands up. Each of the customers has lived in the neighborhood for many years and has never before seen or heard of any strange behavior on the owner's part.
In investigating these complaints, Officer Long should suspect that
    A. the owner should be considered armed and dangerous and any entry into the store should be made with weapons drawn
    B. the cause of the problem is most likely the onset of a serious psychological disturbance
    C. the customers may have reasons to be untruthful about the convenience store owner
    D. the store owner has probably experienced a recent trauma, such as a robber attempt or a personal loss

13. Typical signs and symptoms of stress include
    I. weakened immune system
    II. prolonged, vivid daydreams
    III. insomnia
    IV. depression
    The CORRECT answer is:
    A. I only B. I, III, IV C. III, IV D. I, II, III, IV

14. Other than solid, ethical police work, an officer's BEST defense against a lawsuit or complaint is usually
    A. detailed case records
    B. a capable advocate
    C. a vigorous counterclaim against the plaintiff
    D. the testimony of professional character witnesses

15. Assertive people
    A. avoid stating feelings, opinions, or desires
    B. appear passive, but behave aggressively
    C. state their views and needs directly
    D. appear aggressive, but behave passively

16. In the non-verbal communication process, meaning is MOST commonly provided by
    A. body language
    B. touch
    C. tone of voice
    D. context

17. The MOST obvious practical benefit that deviance has on a society is the
    A. advancement of the status quo
    B. vindication of new laws
    C. inducement to reach cultural goals
    D. promotion of social unity

18. What is the term for policing that focuses on providing a wider and more thorough array of social services to defeat the social problems that cause crime?
    A. Reflecting policing
    B. Order maintenance
    C. Social engineering
    D. Holistic policing

19. The term "active listening" MOSTLY refers to a person's ability to
    A. both listen and accomplish other tasks at the same time
    B. take an active role in determining which information is provided by the speaker
    C. concentrate on what is being said
    D. indicate with numerous physical cues that he/she is listening

20. Police officers in any jurisdiction are MOST likely to receive calls about
    A. threats
    B. suspicious persons
    C. petty theft or property crime
    D. disturbances, such as family arguments

21. Which of the following is NOT a physiological explanation for rape?
    A. Uncontrollable sex drive
    B. Lack of available partners
    C. Reaction to repressed desires
    D. Consequence of the natural selection process

22. Which of the following is an element of self-discipline?
    A. Establishing and reaching short-term goals
    B. Establishing and reaching long-term goals
    C. Taking an honest look at one's lifestyle and making conscious changes toward improvement
    D. Taking an honest look at one's personality and revealing traits, both good and bad, to others

23. Most of the events in a person's life are the result of
    A. chance events
    B. a sense of intuition
    C. individual choices and decisions
    D. the decisions of one's parents or other authority figures

24. Which of the following is the MOST effective way for a department to limit the discretion exercised by police officers?
    A. Open and flexible departmental directives
    B. Close supervision by departmental management
    C. Broadening role definitions for officers
    D. Statutory protection from civil liability lawsuits

25. Police officers who demonstrate critical thinking skills are also more likely to demonstrate each of the following, EXCEPT
    A. the ability to empathize
    B. the tendency to criticize
    C. self-awareness
    D. reflective thinking

25._____

KEY (CORRECT ANSWERS)

1. A
2. B
3. A
4. C
5. C

6. B
7. B
8. B
9. C
10. D

11. D
12. D
13. B
14. A
15. C

16. A
17. D
18. D
19. C
20. D

21. C
22. C
23. C
24. B
25. B

TEST 2

DIRECTIONS: Each question or incomplete statement is followed by several suggested answers or completions. Select the one that BEST answers the question or completes the statement. *PRINT THE LETTER OF THE CORRECT ANSWER IN THE SPACE AT THE RIGHT.*

1. Officer Park responds to a domestic disturbance call to find a mother and her two young children huddled together in the living room, all of them crying. The mother explains that her husband is no longer there; he flew into a fit of rage and then stormed out to join his friends for a night of drinking.
   Officer Park's FIRST action would MOST likely be to
   A. determine the location of the husband
   B. contact the appropriate social services agency to arrange a consultation
   C. try to calm the family down and ask the mother to explain what happened
   D. refer the mother to a local battered-spouse shelter

   1.____

2. Most commonly, the reason for crimes involving stranger violence is
   A. anger   B. retaliation   C. hate   D. robbery

   2.____

3. For a police officer, "burst stress" is MOST likely to be caused by
   A. a shootout   B. financial troubles
   C. departmental politics   D. substance abuse

   3.____

4. The MOST significant factor in whether a person achieves success in his/her personal life, school, and career is
   A. intelligence   B. a positive attitude
   C. existing financial resources   D. innate ability

   4.____

5. Typically, a professional code of ethics
   A. embodies a broad picture of expected moral conduct
   B. is voluntary
   C. provides specific guidance for performance in situations
   D. are decided by objective ethicists outside of the profession

   5.____

6. Components recognized by contemporary society as elements of sexual harassment include
   I. abuse of power   II. immature behavior
   III. sexual desire   IV. hormonal imbalance
   The CORRECT answer is:
   A. I only   B. I, III   C. II, III   D. I, II, III, IV

   6.____

7. The phrase "substance abuse" is typically defined as
   A. an addiction to an illegal substance
   B. the continued use of a psychoactive substance even after it creates problems in a person's life
   C. the overuse of an illegal substance
   D. a situation in which a person craves a drug and organizes his or her life around obtaining it

   7.____

8. The humanist perspective of behavior holds that people who commit crimes or otherwise act badly are
   A. willfully disregarding societal norms
   B. reacting to the deprivation of basic needs
   C. suffering from a psychological illness
   D. experiencing a moral lapse

8.____

9. Which of the following is NOT involved in the process of empathic listening?
   A. Actually hearing exactly what the other person is saying
   B. Searching for the "hidden meanings" behind statements
   C. Listening without judgment
   D. Communicating that you're hearing what the other person is saying, both verbally and nonverbally

9.____

10. Which of the following is NOT a component in developing a stress-resistant lifestyle?
    A. Finding leisure time
    B. Eating nutritious foods
    C. Getting enough sleep
    D. Seeking financial independence

10.____

11. Which of the following was NOT a factor that led to the expansion of a community policing model?
    A. Information obtained at a crime scene during a preliminary investigation was the most important factor determining the probability of an arrest.
    B. Police response times typically had little to do with the probability of making an arrest.
    C. Traditional "preventive patrols" generally failed to reduce crime.
    D. People who knew police officers personally often tried to take advantage of them.

11.____

12. Most of the correspondence in a pyramid scheme that has defrauded several elderly victims has been traced to a post office box in a rural area.
    Probably the simplest and most efficient way of arresting the suspect(s) in this case would be to
    A. use an elderly man as a "victim" to lure the suspects into an attempt to defraud him
    B. address a letter to the post office box asking the user to come in for questioning
    C. check Postal Service records to see who is leasing the post office box
    D. physically observe the post office box for a while, to see who is using it

12.____

13. The process of hiring a police officer typically involves each of the following, EXCEPT
    A. technical preparation
    B. medical examination
    C. background checks
    D. physical ability test

13.____

14. The MOST common form of rape is _____ rape.
    A. stranger
    B. acquaintance
    C. sadistic
    D. spousal

14.____

15. Officer Stevens and his partner respond to a domestic disturbance call involving a father and his teenage daughter. As the officers arrive at their home, the two are still arguing heatedly, but when the officers enter, the daughter retreats to the kitchen, where she continues crying. The father explains that his wife, the daughter's mother, died last year, and the daughter's behavior and school performance have suffered as a result. The father is afraid that the daughter is falling in with the wrong crowd, and may be getting involved with drugs. He is afraid for her and doesn't know what to do.
Within the scope of his police role, the MOST appropriate action for Officer Stevens to take in this case would be to
    A. warn both the father and the daughter of the potential consequences of conviction on a charge of disturbing the peace
    B. refer the father and the daughter to a social services or counseling agency
    C. inform the daughter of the drug statutes that may apply in her case as a way to influence her choices
    D. question the daughter about her feelings surrounding the death of her mother

16. During an interview, a suspect confesses to the rape of a co-worker that occurred in the office after the rest of the employees had left for the day. The suspect says he was tormented by the seductive behavior of the co-worker until he could no longer stand it. He was himself a victim, he says.
In this case, the suspect is making use of the psychological defense mechanism known as
    A. projection   B. regression   C. denial   D. sublimation

17. Which of the following is NOT a good stress-reduction strategy?
    A. Spend some time each day doing absolutely nothing
    B. Become more assertive
    C. Develop a hobby
    D. Have a sense of humor

18. The term for the policing style which emphasizes problem-solving is _____ style.
    A. watchman   B. order maintenance
    C. service   D. legalistic

19. According to current rules and statutes, any employer
    A. may inquire as to a job applicant's age or date of birth
    B. may keep on file information regarding an employee's race, color, religion, sex, or national origin
    C. may refuse employment to someone without a car
    D. must give a woman who has taken time off for maternity leave her same job and salary when she is read to return to work

20. During a conversation with the mother of a teenage boy who has been arrested twice for shoplifting, an officer attempts to be an active listener as the mother explains why she thinks the boy is having so much trouble.
    Being an active listener includes each of the following strategies, EXCEPT
    A. putting the speaker at ease
    B. interrupting with questions to clarify meaning
    C. summarizing the speaker's major ideas and feelings
    D. withholding criticism

21. Which of the following is NOT a characteristic of the typical poverty-class family?
    A. Female-headed, single-parent families
    B. Unwed parents
    C. Isolated from neighbors and relatives
    D. High divorce rates

22. When speaking with community members about improving the quality of life in the neighborhood, an officer should look for signs of social desirability bias among the people with whom he's talking.
    Social desirability bias often causes people to
    A. judge other people based on their social role rather than inner character
    B. attribute their successes to skill while blaming external factors for failures
    C. modify their interactions or behaviors based on what they think is acceptable to others
    D. contend for leadership positions

23. For a number of reasons, Officer Stone thinks a fellow officer might have a drinking problem, and decides to talk to her about it. The officer says she doesn't have a drinking problem; she doesn't even take a drink until after it gets dark.
    Her answer indicates that she
    A. doesn't have a drinking problem
    B. is probably a social drinker
    C. drinks more during the winter months
    D. is in denial

24. Factors which shape the police role include each of the following, EXCEPT
    A. individual goals   B. role expectations
    C. role acquisition   D. multiple-role phenomenon

25. "Deviance" is a social term denoting
    A. any violation of norms
    B. any serious violation of norms
    C. a type of nonconforming behavior recognizable in all cultures
    D. a specific set of crime statistics

KEY (CORRECT ANSWERS)

1.	C	11.	D
2.	D	12.	D
3.	A	13.	A
4.	B	14.	B
5.	A	15.	B
6.	A	16.	A
7.	B	17.	A
8.	B	18.	C
9.	B	19.	B
10.	D	20.	B

21. C
22. C
23. D
24. A
25. A

EXAMINATION SECTION
TEST 1

DIRECTIONS: Each question or incomplete statement is followed by several suggested answers or completions. Select the one that BEST answers the question or completes the statement. *PRINT THE LETTER OF THE CORRECT ANSWER IN THE SPACE AT THE RIGHT.*

1. An indictment is a

    A. formal charge
    B. overdue payment
    C. bill of particulars relating to a dispute
    D. felony

2. In a trial, a hostile witness is a(n) _____ witness.

    A. controversial   B. unfriendly
    C. combative   D. evasive

3. Which of the following was an event from 1999 that may reduce the number of guns in this country?

    A. The passage of a strict gun law in Congress
    B. Gun shows were restricted by Congress
    C. The Colt Corporation restricted the sale of its guns
    D. An embargo was placed on guns coming into this country

4. In the state, headlights should be used when visibility is equal to a minimum or less than _____ feet.

    A. 500   B. 750   C. 1,000   D. 1,250

5. You are required to dim your headlights when an approaching vehicle is within _____ feet of your vehicle.

    A. 500   B. 400   C. 300   D. 200

6. *Some features of the arrangement of contents in the following pages may perplex some readers.*
   The word *perplex*, as used in the above sentence, means MOST NEARLY

    A. interest   B. enlighten
    C. turnoff   D. confuse

7. Hearsay evidence means

    A. false evidence
    B. evidence that needs to be verified
    C. it is generally not admissible in court
    D. the person testifying is unsure of its truth

Questions 8-9.

DIRECTIONS: Questions 8 and 9 refer to the following paragraph.

The variations in report writing range from such picayune details as using A.M. or a.m. to more substantive issues as the inclusion or omission of a report summary in the first paragraph.

8. In the above paragraph, the word *picayune* means MOST NEARLY

    A. grammatic
    B. debatable
    C. trivial
    D. tendentious

9. In the above paragraph, the word *substantive* means MOST NEARLY

    A. cursory
    B. meaningless
    C. critical
    D. substantial

10. In accordance with the driver's manual issued by the state, you must report an accident when damage is _____ or more.

    A. $500
    B. $1,000
    C. $1,500
    D. $2,000

11. It is easier to pass a heavy truck on a highway

    A. when the roadway is level
    B. when going uphill
    C. when going downhill
    D. on a concrete pavement

12. In most states, motorcyclists are required to use

    A. headlights and taillights only after sundown
    B. headlights and taillights at all times
    C. taillights only during daylight hours
    D. headlights only during daylight hours

13. DNA refers to

    A. a person who dies upon arriving at a hospital
    B. genetic material
    C. a chemical reaction
    D. a powerful drug

14. An odometer measures the _____ an automobile.

    A. speed of
    B. velocity of
    C. distance traveled by
    D. revolutions per second of the engine of

15. *Profiling has recently become a controversial issue in police work.*
    Profiling, as used in the above sentence, relates to paying special attention to

    A. a recognizable class of people
    B. people of low income

C. people who exceed the speed limits
D. the class of people who drive expensive cars

16. Most highways have a minimum speed of _____ MPH. 16._____

    A. 40   B. 35   C. 30   D. 25

17. The lowest automobile accident rate occurs in the _____ year age group. 17._____

    A. 20 to 35   B. 35 to 50   C. 50 to 65   D. 65 to 80

18. *Writing is characterized as narrative description, exposition, and argument.* 18._____
    Exposition, as used in the above sentence, means MOST NEARLY

    A. describing the circumstances of the situation
    B. the explanation of a piece of information
    C. explaining your conclusions
    D. giving the pros and cons of a conclusion

19. A report states that the latent prints have been sent to the laboratory. The word *latent*, as 19._____
    used in the above statement, means MOST NEARLY

    A. missing   B. visible   C. hidden   D. damaged

20. After being *acquitted* in the first trial, O.J. Simpson faced a second trial. The second trial 20._____
    was not double jeopardy because

    A. evidence was withheld from the jury
    B. he was tried on different criminal charges
    C. the second trial was a civil trial
    D. the first trial was against the weight of the evidence

21. To *loiter* means MOST NEARLY to 21._____

    A. gather in a group of five or more
    B. create suspicion of wrongdoing while hanging around
    C. obstruct pedestrian movement
    D. linger in an aimless way

22. The minimum automobile insurance required for property camage in New York State is 22._____

    A. $3,000   B. $5,000   C. $10,000   D. $20,000

23. The maximum speed limit in a village or town is usually _____ MPH. 23._____

    A. 20   B. 25   C. 30   D. 40

24. The purpose of the *two second rule* in driving is to 24._____

    A. give you enough time to stop if there is a traffic signal ahead
    B. give you enough clearance to cut into another lane when passing a car
    C. keep enough room between your vehicle and the one ahead
    D. provide enough room when entering a highway

25. In most states, you may be arrested for driving with a blood alcohol content of _____ percent or more.

    A. .05   B. .10   C. .15   D. .20

25.____

KEY (CORRECT ANSWERS)

1. A	11. B
2. B	12. B
3. C	13. B
4. C	14. C
5. A	15. A
6. D	16. A
7. C	17. B
8. C	18. B
9. D	19. C
10. B	20. C

21. D
22. B
23. C
24. C
25. B

TEST 2

DIRECTIONS: Each question or incomplete statement is followed by several suggested answers or completions. Select the one that BEST answers the question or completes the statement. *PRINT THE LETTER OF THE CORRECT ANSWER IN THE SPACE AT THE RIGHT.*

1. A yellow sign showing two children in black indicates a school crossing. The shape of the sign is a   1.____

   A. square   B. rectangle   C. hexagon   D. pentagon

2. Personal vehicles driven by volunteer firefighters responding to alarms are allowed to display _____ lights.   2.____

   A. blue   B. green   C. red   D. amber

3. The color amber is closest to   3.____

   A. green   B. yellow   C. purple   D. blue

4. Larceny in the legal sense means   4.____

   A. the unlawful taking away of another person's property without his consent
   B. overcharging another person who is making a purchase
   C. deceiving another person as to the value of an item he wishes to purchase
   D. adding a service charge to an agreed price to an item that is purchased

5. A misdemeanor in law refers to   5.____

   A. a financial dispute between two litigants
   B. a minor offense
   C. a burglary where a small amount of goods was stolen
   D. unruly behavior in public

6. An overt act means MOST NEARLY a(n)   6.____

   A. foolish act   B. act done publicly
   C. illegal act   D. outrageous act

7. A defense lawyer works for a client *pro bono*. This means he   7.____

   A. gets paid only if he wins the case
   B. gets paid a fixed fee
   C. works for free
   D. represents his client at half his usual fee

8. Corpus delicti refers to the   8.____

   A. missing person   B. murderer
   C. scene of the crime   D. dead victim

9. The shape of a stop sign is   9.____

   A. triangular   B. square
   C. six-sided   D. eight-sided

10. Service signs are _____ with white letters and symbols.

    A. blue   B. green   C. yellow   D. red

11. Destination signs are _____ with white letters and symbols.

    A. blue   B. green   C. yellow   D. red

12. According to the driver's manual, you are prohibited from passing if you cannot safely return to the right lane before any approaching vehicle comes within _____ feet of your car.

    A. 100   B. 150   C. 200   D. 250

13. When parking near a hydrant, you must be clear of the hydrant a minimum distance of _____ feet.

    A. 5   B. 10   C. 15   D. 20

14. When parking your vehicle between two parked vehicles, you must park a maximum of _____ inches from the curb.

    A. 12   B. 15   C. 18   D. 21

15. In order to insure approval, the framers of the Constitution agreed to add a series of amendments after approval to protect people's rights.
    The number of amendments that were added is

    A. six   B. eight   C. ten   D. twelve

16. The amendment number that insures a person's right to bear arms is

    A. one   B. two   C. three   D. five

17. The amendment number that prevents a person from incriminating himself is

    A. one   B. three   C. five   D. seven

18. The right of a person to be secure in his house, and against unreasonable search is amendment number

    A. two   B. four   C. six   D. eight

19. The right of people to assemble peaceably is amendment number

    A. one   B. two   C. three   D. four

20. 90 kilometers per hour is equivalent to _____ MPH.

    A. 40   B. 45   C. 50   D. 55

21. A commercial driver's license is required if the vehicle being driven has a gross weight rating of equal to or more than _____ pounds.

    A. 24,000   B. 26,000   C. 28,000   D. 30,000

22. One kilogram is equivalent to _____ pounds.

    A. 2.2   B. 2.4   C. 2.6   D. 2.8

23. Failing to stop for a school bus in New York State is worth _____ points on your license.   23._____
    A. 3 B. 4 C. 5 D. 6

24. In the state, the minimum liability insurance required against the death of one person is   24._____
    A. $30,000 B. $50,000 C. $100,000 D. $150,000

25. Before a person is arrested, he is read a statement by the arresting officer. The name associated with this procedure is   25._____
    A. Megan B. Zenger C. Scott D. Miranda

KEY (CORRECT ANSWERS)

1.	D	11.	B
2.	A	12.	C
3.	B	13.	C
4.	A	14.	A
5.	B	15.	C
6.	B	16.	B
7.	C	17.	C
8.	D	18.	B
9.	D	19.	A
10.	A	20.	D

21. B
22. A
23. C
24. B
25. D

TEST 3

DIRECTIONS: Each question or incomplete statement is followed by several suggested answers or completions. Select the one that BEST answers the question or completes the statement. *PRINT THE LETTER OF THE CORRECT ANSWER IN THE SPACE AT THE RIGHT.*

1. In legal terms, a deposition is

   A. a statement made by a person in open court
   B. a statement under oath, but not in open court
   C. the testimony made by a defendant under oath in open court
   D. a statement under oath that is mainly hearsay

   1.____

2. In an automobile accident, first check to see if the injured person is breathing. If not, apply

   A. MPR   B. IBR   C. FHR   D. CPR

   2.____

3. Hazard vehicles, such as snow plows and tow trucks, display _____ -colored lights.

   A. blue   B. green   C. amber   D. red

   3.____

4. The hand signal shown at the right indicates
   A. caution because there is an obstruction ahead
   B. a right turn
   C. a left turn
   D. a stop

   4.____

5. A felony is a

   A. crime only where someone is murdered
   B. major crime
   C. crime only where someone is injured
   D. crime only where major physical damage occurs

   5.____

6. *Embezzlement* means MOST NEARLY

   A. deceiving   B. the hiding of funds
   C. stealing   D. investing illegally

   6.____

7. The writer should be wary of using an entire paragraph for information, while necessary is not really of great importance.
   The word *wary* in the above sentence means MOST NEARLY

   A. uncertain   B. cautious
   C. certain   D. serious

   7.____

8. Hearsay evidence is evidence that

   A. is usually admissible in court
   B. can be inferred from preceding evidence
   C. is based on what another person said out of court
   D. is implied in the testimony of a witness

   8.____

9. *Excessive bail shall not be required* is amendment number

   A. two   B. four   C. six   D. eight

10. The writ of habeas corpus is used to

    A. insure a defendant receives a fair trial
    B. insure a defendant's Fifth Amendment rights
    C. reduce or eliminate bail
    D. prevent a person from being detained illegally

11. The number of justices in the United States Supreme Court is

    A. 6   B. 7   C. 8   D. 9

12. The *blue wall* refers to law enforcement officers who

    A. do not publicly condemn fellow officers regardless of facts
    B. set up roadblocks
    C. support their superiors
    D. do their utmost to improve their image

13. The difference between burglary and robbery is

    A. burglary is breaking into a building to commit theft, while robbery is the use of violence in taking property from a person
    B. the money value taken in a burglary is less than $10,000, whereas in a robbery the money value taken is more than $10,000
    C. burglary takes place at night, whereas robbery takes place in the daytime
    D. burglary takes place indoors, whereas robbery takes place outdoors

14. The Federal government announced new guidelines relating to automobiles. These standards relate to

    A. automobile weight   B. gas mileage requirements
    C. car infant seats   D. bumper heights

15. General Motors was involved in a famous lawsuit relating to the Chevy Corvair based on

    A. its crashworthiness
    B. faulty design of the brake system
    C. failure of the transmissions
    D. location of the gas tanks

16. State legislatures are considering restrictions on the use of cellular phones while driving an automobile. The main argument for the restrictions is that

    A. driving with one hand is hazardous
    B. conversations on the phone are a distraction
    C. cellular phones interfere with the ignition system
    D. the driver is unlikely to hear sirens or hornblowing

17. *Much of their business involves the unpredictable and the bizarre.*
    The word *bizarre*, as used in the above statement, means MOST NEARLY

    A. weird   B. routine
    C. complicated   D. life-threatening

18. *The federal government seized 145 metric tons of cocaine coming into the United States from South America.*
    A metric ton is equal to _____ pounds.

    A. 1,800 B. 2,000 C. 2,200 D. 2,400

19. A kilogram is most nearly _____ pounds.

    A. 2.0 B. 2.2 C. 2.4 D. 2.6

20. A narcotic drug used in medicine, but less habit-forming than morphine, is

    A. cocaine B. methadone C. LSD D. heroin

21. Of the following, the one that is a hazard for the large recreational vehicles is

    A. their inability to meet the emission requirements
    B. their bumper height above the ground does not match the height of the bumpers on the smaller-sized vehicles
    C. because the driver is high above the ground, his ability to see his surroundings is impaired
    D. because of the high center of gravity of the recreational vehicles, they become unstable at high speeds

22. State inspection procedures on emissions focus on

    A. hydrocarbons and CO_2
    B. CO and CO_2
    C. SO_2 and CO
    D. hydrocarbons and CO

23. *In order to bring a case before a Grand Jury, the prosecutor must present a prima facie case of guilt before the Grand Jury.*
    Prima facie in the above statement means MOST NEARLY

    A. overwhelming evidence to convict
    B. sufficient to convict unless rebutted by the defense
    C. possibly sufficient to convict by an objective jury
    D. with additional evidence would be sufficient to convict

24. The KKK was denied a permit to hold a parade in New York City. The Klan sued in court claiming a violation of their rights under the _____ Amendment.

    A. First B. Third C. Fifth D. Eighth

25. In a jury trial for a felony, a jury of twelve must have

    A. a majority decision
    B. 9 members finding the defendant guilty
    C. 11 members finding the defendant guilty
    D. a unanimous finding of guilt

KEY (CORRECT ANSWERS)

1. B
2. D
3. C
4. D
5. B

6. C
7. B
8. C
9. D
10. D

11. D
12. A
13. A
14. C
15. D

16. B
17. A
18. C
19. B
20. B

21. B
22. D
23. B
24. A
25. D

TEST 4

DIRECTIONS: Each question or incomplete statement is followed by several suggested answers or completions. Select the one that BEST answers the question or completes the statement. *PRINT THE LETTER OF THE CORRECT ANSWER IN THE SPACE AT THE RIGHT.*

1. State law defines a juvenile as _____ years of age or less. 1.___
    A. 15 B. 16 C. 17 D. 18

2. A writ of habeas corpus is an order to 2.___
    A. dismiss charges against a detained person
    B. reduce the charges against a detained person
    C. have a detained person confront his accusors
    D. have a detained person brought before a court

3. A person is brought into a police station to face charges. The person brought in when interrogated refuses to tell more than his name and address. 3.___
    In the face of his silence, the proper course to be followed by the interviewer is to
    A. remind the detainee that he is guilty of obstruction of justice
    B. stop the interrogation
    C. remind the detainee that his unwillingness to cooperate will result in high bail
    D. tell the interviewee he is required to cooperate with the police

4. *The implication in most discussions on police discretion is that it is the police administrator who should undertake to spell out policies and rules.* 4.___
    In the above statement, the word *discretion* means MOST NEARLY
    A. the power to judge or act
    B. behavior
    C. competence
    D. ability to reach a conclusion

5. A nickname for amphetamine is 5.___
    A. ice B. pot C. downer D. grass

6. A nickname for cocaine is 6.___
    A. speed   B. red devils
    C. snow   D. Mary Jane

7. A nickname for marijuana is 7.___
    A. ice B. downer C. snow D. grass

8. A nickname for barbiturates is 8.___
    A. angel dust   B. quaaludes
    C. meth   D. downers

9. Of the following, the most widely used drug is

   A. LSD   B. crack   C. marijuana   D. cocaine

10. Crack is related to

    A. angel dust
    B. quaaludes
    C. LSD
    D. cocaine

11. The police department is changing the type of ammunition they use. The new bullets will have a softer head. The main reason for this change is that

    A. it will not ricochet if it hits a wall
    B. it will cause less injury to a person struck by the bullet
    C. the bullet is less expensive
    D. it will be easier to recover

12. Of the following weapons, the one that is of the semiautomatic type is the

    A. Colt revolver
    B. 45
    C. AK-47
    D. Springfield rifle

13. A *Saturday Night Special* is a

    A. semi-automatic gun
    B. small, cheaply made weapon
    C. gun used for hunting
    D. difficult gun to conceal

14. One inch is equal to _____ centimeters.

    A. 2.54   B. 2.64   C. 2.74   D. 2.84

15. A gun control bill was passed in Congress that was named after President Reagan's press secretary who was shot in an attack on the President. The name of the bill was the _____ bill.

    A. McClure
    B. Brady
    C. Volkmer
    D. Everett Koop

16. In New York City, if you are caught carrying a concealed gun for which you do not have a permit, you can be jailed for a maximum of _____ months.

    A. 3   B. 6   C. 9   D. 12

17. The Federal Firearm License Law is designed to ensure that individuals who obtain licenses have a legitimate reason for doing so and to deny guns to

    A. people who carry large amounts of money on their person
    B. people who have a criminal record
    C. senior citizens
    D. people under 22 years old

18. According to government studies, the number of guns in the United States is over _____ million.

    A. one hundred
    B. one hundred and twenty
    C. one hundred and fifty
    D. two hundred

19. According to statistics, when a woman is killed with a gun, it is LEAST likely to be by

A. her husband
B. a relative
C. a stranger
D. a friend

20. Federal law states that a person is prohibited from buying a gun who is under the age of   20.___

    A. sixteen
    B. eighteen
    C. twenty
    D. twenty-two

21. Of the following countries in South America, the one that is the largest exporter of drugs into the United States is   21.___

    A. Columbia
    B. Venezuela
    C. Chile
    D. Argentina

22. Of the following, the state in the United States that allows citizens to carry concealed guns is   22.___

    A. Arizona
    B. New Mexico
    C. Texas
    D. Oklahoma

23. A bullet has a diameter of 9 mm. Its diameter, in inches, is MOST NEARLY _____ inch.   23.___

    A. 1/4   B. 3/8   C. 1/2   D. 5/8

24. The repeal of the amendment to the Constitution barring the manufacture and selling of whiskey occurred under the administration of President   24.___

    A. Roosevelt   B. Hoover   C. Truman   D. Coolidge

25. The shrub from which cocaine is derived is   25.___

    A. cacao   B. hemp   C. liana   D. coca

KEY (CORRECT ANSWERS)

1. D
2. D
3. B
4. A
5. A

6. C
7. D
8. D
9. C
10. D

11. A
12. C
13. B
14. A
15. B

16. D
17. B
18. D
19. C
20. B

21. A
22. C
23. B
24. A
25. D

EXAMINATION SECTION
TEST 1

DIRECTIONS: This section contains descriptions of problem situations. Each problem situation has four alternative actions that might be taken to deal with the problem. You are to make two judgments for each problem.

First, decide which alternative you would MOST LIKELY choose in response to the problem. It might not be exactly what you would do in that situation, but it should be the alternative that comes closest to what you would actually do. Record your answers on the answer sheet by writing the appropriate letter next to the prompt for MOST LIKELY.

Second, decide which alternative you would be LEAST LIKELY to choose in that situation. Write the letter of that alternative next to the prompt for LEAST LIKELY.

1. You realize that an error has been made in the documentation of evidence for a case. The amount of the cash reported seized at the scene is now significantly less than when it was originally recorded. You would
    A. go back and talk to everyone who was involved in the chain of custody
    B. immediately tell a supervisor about the problem
    C. consider it a clerical error and try to conceal the discrepancy while you try to figure out how it happened but tell a supervisor if you cannot figure out what happened
    D. consider that the mistake was made when the evidence was seized, and alter the log to reflect the existing amount

    Most likely:_____ Least likely:_____

2. You are assigned to lead a search for evidence that may have been deposited somewhere within a large tract of woods. The recovery of this evidence is critical to the prosecution of the suspect in the crime. For this task, you are MOST likely to lead by
    A. blazing a trail for others to follow
    B. helping people choose the best course of action
    C. punishing mistakes
    D. appealing to shared goals and values

    Most likely:_____ Least likely:_____

3. Your partner, who has become your oldest and dearest friend, recently admitted to you that he removed something from the evidence room that might suggest the innocence of a suspect whom he knew without a doubt to be guilty. Your supervisor has discovered that the evidence is missing, and your partner asks you to say that you forgot to log the evidence in. You know that this would easily resolve the situation. You would
    A. not go along with the idea to say the mistake was yours, and tell the supervisor what happened
    B. not go along with the idea, but would say nothing about your partner's admission

C. not go along with the idea, and encourage your partner to own up to what he did
D. go along with your partner; he broke the rules but his intentions were good

Most likely:_____ Least likely:_____

4. You are having a telephone conversation with a supervisor who is leaving a confidential message to another agent in your office about facts pertaining to an important case. You are on your cellphone, in a public area, surrounded by many unfamiliar people. In order to verify that you have correctly taken the message, you
   A. read the message back to the supervisor
   B. ask the supervisor to call you back later
   C. explain that you will call back when you can find a more private location
   D. ask the supervisor to repeat the message

Most likely:_____ Least likely:_____

5. You're in a conversation with someone who has difficulty finding the proper words to say. You
   A. wait for the person to finish, and then offer a restatement of what you think she was trying to say
   B. gladly interrupt and supply the words for her
   C. wait for her to finish, and then ask a series of clarifying questions
   D. interrupt and ask that she take some time to think about it before speaking

Most likely:_____ Least likely:_____

6. You are meeting with several other law enforcement officials and community members to determine a course of action for reducing drug trafficking in the area. In order to build a constructive relationship with officials and community members, you
   A. assure the group that you are an expert who has a long record of experience in these matters, and tell them how the problem can be solved
   B. advise them that the solution to the problem can be solved
   C. ask for input from representatives from each group before making suggestions
   D. adopt a completely neutral tone of voice when addressing group members

Most likely:_____ Least likely:_____

7. When working in a group, someone raises a question that you've already given a lot of thought. You're not sure, however, about how the question should best be answered. You decide to
   A. speak up, briefly explaining the different alternatives that occurred to you
   B. wait for somebody to mention something that has already occurred to you, and then voice your agreement
   C. advise the group that this is a thorny problem that probably can't be solved
   D. keep quiet and listen to the group's discussion, offering feedback when you think it's appropriate

Most likely:_____ Least likely:_____

8. Completely by accident, you notice a significant error in a colleague's report. The report is about to be released to key decision-makers, and you have absolutely no responsibility for the report. You would MOST likely
    A. spread the word about the error to the colleague's co-workers, in the hope that the information makes its way to the report's author
    B. take a mental note of the error and mention it if anyone asks
    C. keep quiet—it's not your responsibility and you don't want to create friction
    D. find the person who wrote the report and point out the mistake

    Most likely:_____ Least likely:_____

9. A detective who is often nasty to you and your colleagues has compiled an impressive record of success in her investigations; nearly all have led to arrests, and every one of those arrests has ended in conviction. In going over one of the detective's reports, you notice that she has neglected to properly document the chain of custody for a piece of evidence. You aren't that familiar with the case, and don't know how important it is to the case. You have a feeling that the detective will be angry if you point out her mistake. You
    A. do nothing and let her deal with the consequences
    B. pull her aside and tell her about the mistake
    C. tell her you noticed a mistake in her report, and ask her if she is interested in knowing what it is
    D. inform her supervisor and her partner about the mistake

    Most likely:_____ Least likely:_____

10. A crime was recently committed. You believe that, among the following, the MOST useful interview subject would probably be a(n)
    A. informant   B. victim   C. suspect   D. witness

    Most likely:_____ Least likely:_____

11. In order to complete a certain task, you need to ask a favor of a colleague whom you don't know very well. The BEST way to do this would be to
    A. ask the colleague briefly for assistance, stating your reasons for asking
    B. ask the colleague and offer to do something for him in return
    C. tell the colleague there will be many intangible rewards associated with his cooperation
    D. explain that one of the ways the colleague can gain favor with his superiors is to cooperate with you

    Most likely:_____ Least likely:_____

12. A team composed of you and your colleagues encounters a problem similar to one you have encountered when working within another team in the past. Together, you and your team come up with a solution that has the potential for success, even though it is significantly different from the one that worked for you in the past. Your reaction to this new solution is to

A. feel good about the team's originality and go along for the ride on this new plan
B. be concerned about the possibility of failure with the new solution, but accept that there may be more than one way to solve the problem
C. tell them there is a proven way to succeed in solving this problem, and insist that they adopt your solution
D. tell colleagues you're uneasy with the unknowns and variables involved in this new solution, and then urge them to go with your proven success

Most likely:_____ Least likely:_____

13. You have become so proficient at the documentation/paperwork part of your job that you actually now have some time to spare during work hours. With this extra time, you decide to
    A. take initiative and propose a new project to the supervisor
    B. see your supervisor and tell him or her you are ready for more work
    C. take care of some personal errands that you have been unable to do because of work
    D. take some of the pressure off existing work and take more time to complete existing tasks

    Most likely:_____ Least likely:_____

14. Your investigative team is having a disagreement about strategy that has become a heated debate, with members divided nearly equally between two strategic choices. You think both choices have some merit, and don't feel strongly one way or the other about which is selected. You
    A. take the side of the group that contains more of your friends and associates
    B. calmly wait for them to work out their differences
    C. try to figure out which side is more likely to win the argument before taking sides
    D. calmly point out the benefits of both plans and suggest a compromise

    Most likely:_____ Least likely:_____

15. You turn the corner at the office one day and spot an agent altering the evidence log, which has been left unattended. Later, you look and see that the entry was for an amount of an illicit substance, and the new entry appears to match the amount that exists in the evidence room. You are not sure how much of the substance was initially collected. You would
    A. ask the agent to return the missing evidence and tell him/her that if you see it happen again you will tell your supervisor
    B. tell the agent you saw him making the change, and ask him why it was necessary
    C. let the matter drop; you don't know that anything untoward occurred, and bringing it up will only result in bad feelings
    D. tell other colleagues and try to confront the agent as a group to try to deal with the problem on your own

    Most likely:_____ Least likely:_____

16. In developing a plan for investigating a crime spree that has taken place on both sides of the state line, a team encounters problems in how to coordinate the input of federal and state resources. The FIRST step in solving this problem would be to
    A. gather information
    B. define the problem as completely as possible
    C. envision contingencies
    D. develop a plan for solving the problem

    Most likely:_____ Least likely:_____

17. Because your work unit has recently become severely understaffed, you are asked to perform a task that you believe is far beneath the skills and capabilities associated with your position. You respond to this request by
    A. performing the task slowly or inadequately before resuming your more important work, in order to insure that you won't be asked again
    B. doing what is asked, but asking a supervisor to make sure these tasks are evenly distributed among co-workers until the unit can be fully staffed
    C. refusing it on the grounds of professional integrity
    D. complying cheerfully and accepting the task as part of a new expanded job description

    Most likely:_____ Least likely:_____

18. Your supervisor has decided to transfer you to an unfamiliar department as part of an agency restructuring of your organization. The department is in the same building and there will be no changes in compensation or benefits. Your reaction is to be
    A. thrilled at the opportunity to push yourself and learn new skills
    B. not to mind the transfer, because it is likely to teach you something new
    C. entirely neutral, since you won't have to relocate or take a pay cut
    D. disappointed that you will have to change your regular routine

    Most likely:_____ Least likely:_____

19. Your investigative team has developed a plan for investigating a series of violent crimes that have occurred in the tri-state area. In developing the plan, your team must balance the need to conduct the investigation "by the book" meticulously gathering and documenting a body of evidence and testimony, with the need to catch the criminal before another person becomes a victim. The plan, in attempting to balance these concerns, includes a few procedures that involve certain risks. The team should attempt to minimize the consequences of risk-taking by
    A. keeping the focus on capturing the suspect as soon as possible, and dealing with the consequences as they come
    B. reworking the plan to avoid risk whenever possible
    C. setting aside emotional concerns about victims and assembling an airtight case
    D. planning ahead and preparing for each outcome

    Most likely:_____ Least likely:_____

20. An informant has come forward to offer information about a crime. You believe it is important to understand the informant's motivation for coming forward, so you ask him about this
    A. when he least expects it
    B. after he has given an account, but before you have asked any questions
    C. at the conclusion of the interview
    D. at the beginning of the interview

    Most likely:_____ Least likely:_____

21. You are faced with a problem that, try as you might, you're unable to solve. You
    A. ask your most trusted associate
    B. ask for input from several people who you know will have different viewpoints
    C. drop it, hope that it won't become a significant concern, and move on to another task
    D. shift your focus to another problem for a while before giving this problem a fresh look

    Most likely:_____ Least likely:_____

22. You are interviewing several witnesses to a particularly violent crime that was committed recently. One of the witnesses, an older woman, is so upset that she can barely speak coherently. Her testimony does not seem to make much sense, especially when compared to that of others. In continuing to interview her, you make a mental note to document her emotional state when you write up the interview, because strong emotional responses are likely to affect a person's
    A. prior knowledge   B. intelligence
    C. perceptions of current reality   D. reflexes

    Most likely:_____ Least likely:_____

23. An informant in an ongoing investigation tells you that he resents having to work with you because you have adopted a superior attitude with him and made work unpleasant. The informant is working on the investigation as a condition of a prior court plea. Your BEST response would be to
    A. tell the informant that you are not interested in his opinion of you; he is required to cooperate on the case
    B. try to find out why the offender cannot work with you and tell him that his work is important to the case
    C. consider the informant as rebellious, and inform the court that the terms of his sentencing have been violated
    D. apologize to the offender and tell him you have been under a lot of strain

    Most likely:_____ Least likely:_____

24. Within a few days, you will meet with supervisors for a scheduled work evaluation. For the review, you will
    A. take the evaluation as it comes and improvise your responses
    B. prepare a list of your accomplishments, skills, and ideas for how to contribute more to the organization

C. assume that your performance will be criticized, and prepare for the attack
D. undertake a little reflection on your failures and successes, but nothing elaborate

Most likely:_____   Least likely:_____

25. You and your partner are in the middle of a very heated argument about the conduct of an investigation. You normally like your partner and get along very well with her, but you are so furious that you are about to say something very nasty that you know will hurt her feelings. Your MOST likely reaction would be to
    A. walk away immediately without saying a word
    B. say what is on your mind and sort it out later
    C. say that you are too angry to talk right now and give yourself time to calm down
    D. leave the room while mumbling the comment in a low voice

Most likely:_____   Least likely:_____

26. In casual conversation, a person asks you for information about your work as an FBI agent. You should
    A. explain that you are not supposed to talk about your responsibilities to outsiders
    B. refer the person to the public relations department
    C. speak vaguely and give out as few facts as possible
    D. be frank and tell the person as much factual information as you can about your general responsibilities

Most likely:_____   Least likely:_____

27. In the field, you are in an isolated and rural area and find yourself in a situation with circumstances you have never encountered before. You would be MOST likely to use your own judgment
    A. when existing policy and rules appear to be unfair in their application
    B. when immediate action is necessary and the rules do not cover the situation
    C. only if a superior is present
    D. whenever a situation is not covered by established rules

Most likely:_____   Least likely:_____

28. One of your colleagues has gone on vacation and his mother, an elderly woman who lives in another state, has filed a complaint with your office; she thinks she may have been defrauded via an e-mail scam. The case has been assigned to Agent Broom, who works in your office. Your colleague phones you from his vacation and asks if you can find out more about her case. Your reaction is to
    A. simply refuse to answer your colleague's questions
    B. find the case file and tell the colleague what he wants to know
    C. speak to your supervisor, explain the situation and ask for the information that your colleague wants
    D. ask the mother if she gives permission for you to find out more from Agent Broom

Most likely:_____   Least likely:_____

29. When working with team members, you offer what you think is a well-reasoned solution to a problem. Your team members reject it out of hand, saying that it could never work. In a later meeting with mid-level administrators, your supervisor makes the same suggestion. You
    A. say nothing to the supervisor, but later make sure your team members understand that they should be more deferential to your judgment
    B. make sure the supervisor knows you suggested the same solution, but were ignored
    C. feel vindicated by the supervisor's concurrence, but don't feel the need to say anything
    D. demand an apology from your team members for being so closed-minded

    Most likely:_____ Least likely:_____

30. After your partner conducts an interview with an informant, the informant emerges from the interrogation room with some swelling around his right eye. You are pretty sure the swelling was not present when the informant entered the room. You
    A. do nothing; you can't be certain your partner did anything wrong
    B. immediately report the partner's abuse to a supervisor
    C. ask other agents in the office if anything like this has ever happened before
    D. confront your partner and ask what happened

    Most likely:_____ Least likely:_____

31. You and another agent in your unit do not get along, to put it mildly. The problem is, you and she have been assigned to direct an investigation together, and in order to have a good outcome, the two of you need to get along. You
    A. realize the destructive potential for run-ins with her, and quietly get yourself assigned to another case
    B. make an effort to be civil, but if she isn't returning the favor, try to keep a low profile and get the work done
    C. take this as a personal challenge and make it your mission to win her over
    D. try to get your supervisors to understand the seriousness of the friction between you, and ask that they reassign her to another case

    Most likely:_____ Least likely:_____

32. At the end of a busy day at work, you accidentally send an e-mail containing an attachment with some confidential case file information to the wrong person. Which of the following would be the BEST thing to do?
    A. Forget what happened and send the e-mail to the correct person
    B. Leave the office for the day and deal with it tomorrow
    C. Explain to your supervisor what has happened and let her handle the issue
    D. Immediately send another e-mail to the 'wrong' person explaining your mistake

    Most likely:_____ Least likely:_____

33. A crime has just been committed at a bank, and you arrive at the scene first, before any local law enforcement personnel. Before the police arrive, a handful of bank officials arrive and ask to enter the crime scene. You would
    A. request their cooperation in remaining outside the scene until the area can be properly secured
    B. keep them out by any means necessary
    C. tell them to take it up with the police when they arrive
    D. defer to their wishes

    Most likely:_____ Least likely:_____

34. You are interviewing the victim of a crime that was committed only about an hour ago. During the course of the interview you try to
    A. maintain a calm and steady demeanor
    B. make sure at least one other agent is present before beginning
    C. get the facts by any means necessary
    D. keep the victim away from others who are familiar to him/her

    Most likely:_____ Least likely:_____

35. You inherit a large sum of money, and your financial advisor suggests two types of investments. In the first, you invest a moderate, set amount each year, and receive a modest guaranteed payoff at the end of the investment period. The second choice includes a much larger investment (most of your inheritance), but also has a larger potential payoff, with the possibility of losing all your money in an economic downturn. Which type of investment would you choose?
    A. A combination of the two
    B. The first type of investment
    C. The second type of investment
    D. Neither. You wouldn't risk your savings on investments.

    Most likely:_____ Least likely:_____

36. You and your partner are working on a complex project that demands a great deal of effort from both of you. Your partner is frequently absent as a result of burnout and stress from his personal problems. You do not know much about the circumstances, nor have you known him for long. Your partner contributes very little to the project, and, as a result, you are putting in an excessive amount of overtime in order to keep the project moving ahead. You feel that your health may begin to suffer if you continue to work this many hours. You handle this situation by
    A. raising the issue with your supervisor and request additional help to ensure that the project is completed on schedule
    B. offering to help your partner deal with his personal problems
    C. continuing to put in overtime to keep the project moving ahead
    D. meeting with your partner to request that he does his share of the work

    Most likely:_____ Least likely:_____

37. For the first time, you are assigned the lead on a case. You oversee a team of about five people. Your supervisor has assigned you a fairly clear-cut case, and in the end, despite a few logistical and technical problems, you and your team wrap things up fairly quickly. After a speedy conviction, you meet with a group of three supervisors, who congratulate you on your success. They then launch a critique of your leadership of the case that, while pointing out your strengths as a leader, can only be interpreted as somewhat unfavorable, given the team's logistical and technical problems. Most likely, your reaction is to feel that
    A. it probably would not be a good idea for you to assume leadership of a more difficult case in the future
    B. you should keep this critique in mind the next time you take charge of a team
    C. the bottom line is that the case resulted in a conviction, and this is the only measure that really matters
    D. the members of your team really let you down with their mistakes

    Most likely:_____ Least likely:_____

38. You and another agent are conducting an investigation together. You have noticed that the other agent is taking some shortcuts as he collects evidence and obtains statements from the victims and witnesses. These shortcuts are reducing the quality of the investigation. You would MOST likely
    A. point out to the trooper the impact his shortcuts will have on the traffic investigation
    B. notify your supervisor of the shortcuts being taken by the other agent
    C. go back and redo those aspects of the investigation on which the agent has taken shortcuts
    D. ignore the agent's work performance, since it is not your responsibility to monitor his performance

    Most likely:_____ Least likely:_____

39. During a meeting, you and a group of supervisors are discussing your performance on a recently completed project. Using a list of objective criteria, the supervisors explain where you performed most successfully. They then shift their focus to areas in which your performance fell short of the standards. Your reaction is to
    A. launch a vigorous defense of your performance and explain why you think the standards are not appropriate in your case
    B. listen carefully, ask for clarification when necessary, and then discuss with them why these shortcomings occurred
    C. tell them you are very sorry and promise to do better in the future
    D. explain that you did your best and are skeptical that any of them could have done better, given the circumstances

    Most likely:_____ Least likely:_____

40. While you are conducting an investigation at a crime scene, a citizen walks past you and makes a demeaning and derogatory comment about your law enforcement responsibilities. You would MOST likely

A. ask the person to come back and explain why he made such a comment
B. ask the person to show you some identification, so that you can take his name down in case of further trouble
C. ignore the comment and continue with your work
D. confront the individual and demand an apology for the comment

Most likely:_____ Least likely:_____

41. You are working on a case under the direct supervision of a regional supervisor. In your opinion, she has her mind set on a plan that is mediocre, uninspired, and likely to meet only a minimal set of objectives. She is happy with having finally made a decision, wants to finalize, and makes a point of telling you not to try to talk her out of her plan. You think the plan is a waste of resources and perhaps even a mistake, even though most of your colleagues have already told you to let it go. How would you deal with the situation?
    A. Quietly work to get transferred to another project
    B. Tell the supervisor that she is making a mistake, and try to convince her to change her mind
    C. Resist the temptation to try changing her mind
    D. Ask if she is certain she doesn't want to think it over one last time

    Most likely:_____ Least likely:_____

42. When interviewing a potential witness, you notice that she has a tendency to wander off the subject and talk about herself and her family for expended intervals. When you ask her where she was at about noon the day before yesterday, she launches into a long description of her normal daily routine. You respond by
    A. telling her sternly that your time is limited and you would like her to stick to answering your questions
    B. waiting for a pauses in her speech during which you can politely steer the conversation back toward her whereabouts yesterday at noon
    C. cutting her off and repeating the question, as if she hadn't been speaking at all
    D. letting her "talk herself out" and then repeating the question, this time in a more closed-ended format

    Most likely:_____ Least likely:_____

43. You are the leader of an investigative team, and wonder about the role of praise in the team's success. As the leader, your philosophy about praise is that it
    A. can improve performance if it is given when it is most appropriate
    B. should almost always be withheld in order to make team members understand there is always room for improvement
    C. should be given sparely, and reserved for truly exceptional achievements
    D. should be given to team members even, and perhaps especially, when they perform poorly, in order to boost their self-esteem

    Most likely:_____ Least likely:_____

44. You are assigned to an investigation with Agent Stark, who is known to be somewhat inattentive to detail. His mistakes or omissions have resulted in at least one case dismissal that you know of. Throughout the course of the investigation, you
    A. make it a point to be involved in every aspect of the investigation, accompanying Agent Stark on every interview, and insisting on collaboration in written work
    B. leave Agent Stark mostly alone, and then go back and make corrections to his work and documentation when they are necessary
    C. work to block Agent Stark's access to important witnesses, evidence, and case files, thereby minimizing the harm he is likely to do
    D. document every one of Agent Stark's missteps and report them to your superiors as they occur, in order to avoid jeopardizing the case

    Most likely:_____ Least likely:_____

45. An interview has strayed far beyond what you had intended. To redirect the subject's response, you say
    A. "I'm interested in what you were saying a few minutes ago. Can you tell me more about it?"
    B. "Why are we talking about this?"
    C. "Let me ask the rest of the questions I need answered, then we can talk."
    D. "This is interesting, but it isn't related to the business of this interview."

    Most likely:_____ Least likely:_____

46. You have been asked to recruit a new detective to come work for your regional office. She is an up-and-coming star with a lot of potential, and you and your supervisor both feel she would be a good fit for your office. Unfortunately, despite your best efforts, she ends up seeking and receiving an assignment elsewhere. You later find out through your supervisor that you came off as seeming a little too aggressive and desperate. Your supervisor offers you some suggestions for how to handle this situation if it ever comes up again. Your reaction is to think that
    A. putting you in charge of the detective's recruitment was a terrible idea to begin with
    B. the detective's choice was her own loss; you made it clear that your office had the most to offer
    C. you wish there was some way you could make it up to your supervisor
    D. maybe you did come on too strong and should re-examine your methods

    Most likely:_____ Least likely:_____

47. You have become aware that a colleague, who is nearing retirement and now working only part-time for the bureau, has been using office phone and tax facilities to run his own private investigation business. You think that he may have been warned about this once before and that he promised to stop. You have just found a fax for his business placed in your mailbox by mistake. You would MOST likely
    A. Put the fax in your colleague's mailbox without saying anything to anyone
    B. Politely inform your colleague that you will tell your supervisor the next time you catch him using agency resources for his own private business.

C. Put the fax in your supervisor's mailbox without saying anything to anyone
D. Give the fax to your co-worker and remind her that office equipment is not supposed to be used for personal use.

48. You are working on a case with a detective in another regional office who has, once again, rescheduled your meeting appointment at the last minute. Apparently, he left a last-minute message for you this time, but you didn't get it because you were already on your way. This is not the first time you have canceled prior engagements to accommodate his schedule. Each time you have been inconvenienced and very irritated, but this is a very important case and he is a good detective when he is at work. How do you react to this person?
    A. Tell the detective it is disrespectful and inconvenient when he makes last-minute changes to your schedule
    B. Don't let on that you are irritated, but ask the detective to give you longer notice the next time he has to cancel.
    C. Maintain a cold professionalism when rescheduling the appointment
    D. Don't let on that you are irritated, but make a point to subject the detective to a few last-minute cancellations of his own, so he'll know how it feels

    Most likely:_____ Least likely:_____

49. A pharmacist has complained to the police department that several drug addicts in his neighborhood have been attempting to obtain drugs illegally, often by passing fake prescriptions. Based only on this information during a stakeout of the prescription counter, you would be MOST likely to find suspicious
    A. a young African-American male in a hooded sweatshirt on a hot day
    B. a woman in her thirties who glances around furtively and brings a large amount of nonprescription items to the counter for purchase
    C. a middle-aged man who appears homeless and is poorly groomed
    D. none of the above should be regarded as suspicious on the basis of their appearance alone

    Most likely:_____ Least likely:_____

50. At a work meeting, your supervisor mentions an interesting new assignment that has not been assigned yet. It sounds like something you could handle, though it would be demanding. You
    A. grow increasingly nervous about the possibility that you would be assigned the job
    B. immediately volunteer to handle the project yourself
    C. tell the supervisor that you would be willing to take it on, but ask if it might be possible to delegate some of your current workload
    D. tell the supervisor that you would be willing to take it on, but only if you receive a raise in pay

    Most likely:_____ Least likely:_____

SITUATIONAL JUDGMENT
KEY TO EXERCISES

NOTE: While a few situations in the examination have one choice that is clearly better or worse than the others, some have two or even three choices that would be equally as good or bad as the rest. The key that follows should be taken as a rough guideline and not a definitive formula for success on the test. The answers below reflect the fact that the situational judgment test is designed to measure your:
- Ability to Organize, Plan, and Prioritize
- Ability to Relate Effectively with Others
- Ability to Maintain a Positive Image
- Ability to Evaluate Information and Make Judgment Decisions
- Ability to Adapt to Changing Situations Integrity

1. Most Likely: B; Least Likely: D
2. Most Likely: D, Least Likely: C
3. Most Likely: A or C; Least Likely: D
4. Most Likely: D; Least Likely: A
5. Most Likely: A or C; Least Likely: D

6. Most Likely: C; Least Likely; A or B
7. Most Likely: A; Least Likely: C
8. Most Likely: D; Least Likely: C
9. Most Likely: B; Least Likely: A
10. Most Likely: D; Least Likely: C

11. Most Likely: A; Least Likely: D
12. Most Likely: B; Least Likely: C
13. Most Likely: B; Least Likely: C or D
14. Most Likely: D; Least Likely: A, B, or C
15. Most Likely: B; Least Likely: A

16. Most Likely: B; Least Likely: A, C, or D
17. Most Likely: B; Least Likely: C
18. Most Likely: B; Least Likely: D
19. Most Likely: D; Least Likely: A, B, or C
20. Most Likely: C; Least Likely: A, B, or D

21. Most Likely: B; Least Likely: C
22. Most Likely: C; Least Likely: A, B, or D
23. Most Likely: B; Least Likely: C
24. Most Likely: B; Least Likely: C
25. Most Likely: C; Least Likely: B

15 (#1)

26. Most Likely: D; Least Likely: A
27. Most Likely: B; Least Likely: D
28. Most Likely: C; Least Likely: A
29. Most Likely: C; Least Likely: D
30. Most Likely: D; Least Likely: A

31. Most Likely: C; Least Likely: A or D
32. Most Likely: C; Least Likely: A
33. Most Likely: A; Least Likely: B, C, or D
34. Most Likely: A; Least Likely: C or D
35. Most Likely: A; Least Likely: D

36. Most Likely: A; Least Likely: C
37. Most Likely: B; Least Likely: A, C, or D
38. Most Likely: A; Least Likely: D
39. Most Likely: B; Least Likely: C or D
40. Most Likely: C; Least Likely: A, B, or D

41. Most Likely: D; Least Likely: A
42. Most Likely: B; Least Likely: A
43. Most Likely: A; Least Likely: B or D
44. Most Likely: A; Least Likely: C
45. Most Likely: A; Least Likely: B

46. Most Likely: D; Least Likely: A or B
47. Most Likely: D; Least Likely: A
48. Most Likely: B; Least Likely: D
49. Most Likely: D; Least Likely: A, B, or C
50. Most Likely: C; Least Likely: A or D

EVALUATING INFORMATION AND EVIDENCE
EXAMINATION SECTION
TEST 1

DIRECTIONS: Each question or incomplete statement is followed by several suggested answers or completions. Select the one that BEST answers the question or completes the statement. *PRINT THE LETTER OF THE CORRECT ANSWER IN THE SPACE AT THE RIGHT.*

Question 1-4.

DIRECTIONS: Questions 1 through 4 measure your ability (1) to determine whether statements from witnesses say essentially the same thing and (2) to determine the evidence needed to make it reasonably certain that a particular conclusion is true.
To do well in this part of the test, you do NOT have to have a working knowledge of police procedures and techniques or to have any more familiarity with crimes and criminal behavior than that acquired from reading newspapers, listening to radio, or watching TV. In order to do well in this part, you must read carefully and reason closely. Sloppy reading or sloppy reasoning will lead to a low score.

1. In which of the following do the two statements made say essentially the same thing in two different ways?
   I. All members of the pro-x group are free from persecution.
      No person that is persecuted is a member of the pro-x group.
   II. Some responsible employees of the police department are not supervisors.
      Some police department supervisors are not responsible employees.
   The CORRECT answer is:
   A. I only
   B. II only
   C. Both I and II
   D. Neither I nor II

1.____

2. In which the following do the two statements made say essentially the same thing in two different ways?
   I. All Nassau County police officers weigh less than 225 pounds.
      No police officer weighs more than 225 pounds.
   II. No police officer is an alcoholic.
      No alcoholic is a police officer.
   The CORRECT answer is:
   A. I only
   B. II only
   C. Both I and II
   D. Neither I nor II

2.____

3. Summary of Evidence Collected to Date: All pimps in the precinct own pink-colored cars and carry knives.
   Prematurely Drawn Conclusion: Any person in the precinct who carries a knife is a pimp.

3.____

Which one of the following additional pieces of evidence, if any, would make it *reasonably certain* that the conclusion drawn is TRUE?
- A. Each person who carries a knife owns a pink-colored car.
- B. All persons who own pink-colored cars pimp.
- C. No one who carries a knife has a vocation other than pimping.
- D. None of the above

4. Summary of Evidence Collected to Date: 4.____
   a. Some of the robbery suspects have served time as convicted felons.
   b. Some of the robbery suspects are female.
   Prematurely Drawn Conclusion: Some of the female suspects have never served time as convicted felons.
   Which one of the following additional pieces of evidence, if any, would make it *reasonably certain* that the conclusion drawn is TRUE?
   - A. The number of female suspects is the same as the number of robber suspects who have served time as convicted felons.
   - B. The number of female suspects is smaller than the number of convicted felons.
   - C. The number of suspects that have served time is smaller than the number of suspects that have been convicted of a felony.
   - D. None of the above

Questions 5-8.

DIRECTIONS: Questions 5 through 8 measure your ability to orient yourself within a given section of a town, neighborhood, or particular area. Each of the questions describes a starting point and a destination. Assume that you are driving a patrol car in the area shown on the map accompanying the questions. Use the map as a basis for choosing the shortest way to get from one point to another without breaking the law.

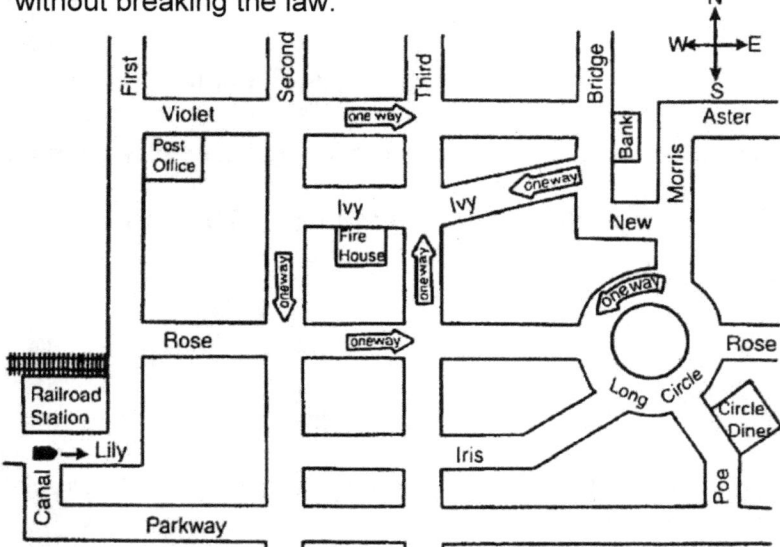

A street marked one way is one-way for the full length, even when there are breaks or jogs in the street. EXCEPTION: A street that does not have the same name over the full length.

5. A patrol car at the train station is sent to the bank to investigate a robbery. 5.____
   The SHORTEST way to get there without breaking any traffic laws is to go
   A. east on Lily, north on First, east on Rose, north on Third, and east on Ivy to bank
   B. east on Lily, north on First, east on Violet, and south on Bridge to bank
   C. south on Canal, east on Parkway, north on Poe, around Long Circle to Morris, west on New, and north on Bridge to bank
   D. south on Canal, east on Parkway, north on Third, and east on Ivy to bank

6. At the bank, the patrol car receives a call to hurry to the post office. 6.____
   The SHORTEST way to get there without breaking any traffic laws is to go
   A. west on Ivy, south on Second, west on Rose, and north on First to post office
   B. west on Ivy, south on Second, west on Rose, and south on First to post office
   C. south on Bridge, east on New, south on Morris, around Long Circle, south on Poe, west on Parkway, north on Canal, east on Lily, and north on First to post office
   D. north on Bridge, west on Violet, and south on First to post office

7. On leaving the post office, the police officers decide to go to the Circle Diner. 7.____
   The SHORTEST way to get there without breaking any traffic laws is to go
   A. south on First, left on Rose, right on Second, left on Parkway, and right on Poe to diner
   B. south on First, left on Rose, around Long Circle, and right on Poe to diner
   C. south on First, left on Rose, right on Second, right on Iris, around Long Circle, and left on Poe to diner
   D. west on Violet, right on Bridge, right on new, right on Morris, around Long Circle, and left on Poe to diner

8. During lunch break, a fire siren sounds and the police officers rush to their patrol 8.____
   car and head to the firehouse.
   The SHORTEST way to get there without breaking any traffic laws is to go
   A. north on Poe, around Long Circle, west on Iris, north on Third, and west on Ivy to firehouse
   B. north on Poe, around Long Circle,, north on Morris, west on New, north on Bridge, and west on Ivy to firehouse
   C. north on Poe, around Long Circle, west on Rose, north on Third, and west on Ivy to firehouse
   D. south on Poe, west on Parkway, north on Third, and east on Ivy to firehouse

Questions 9-13.

DIRECTIONS: Questions 9 through 13 measure your ability to understand written descriptions of events. Each question presents you with a description of an accident, a crime, or an event and asks you which of four drawings BEST represent it.

4 (#1)

In the drawings, the following symbols are used (these symbols and their meanings will be repeated in the test):

A moving vehicle is represented by this symbol: (front) ◁▭ (rear)

A parked vehicle is represented by this symbol: (front) ◀▬ (rear)

A pedestrian or a bicyclist is represented by this symbol: •

The path and direction of travel of a vehicle or pedestrian is indicated by a solid line: ⟶

EXCEPTION: The path and direction of travel of each vehicle or person directly involved in a collision from the point of impact is indicated by a dotted line: ---➤

9. A driver pulling out from between two parked cars on Magic is struck by a vehicle heading east which turns left onto Maple and flees.
Which of the following depicts the accident?   9.____

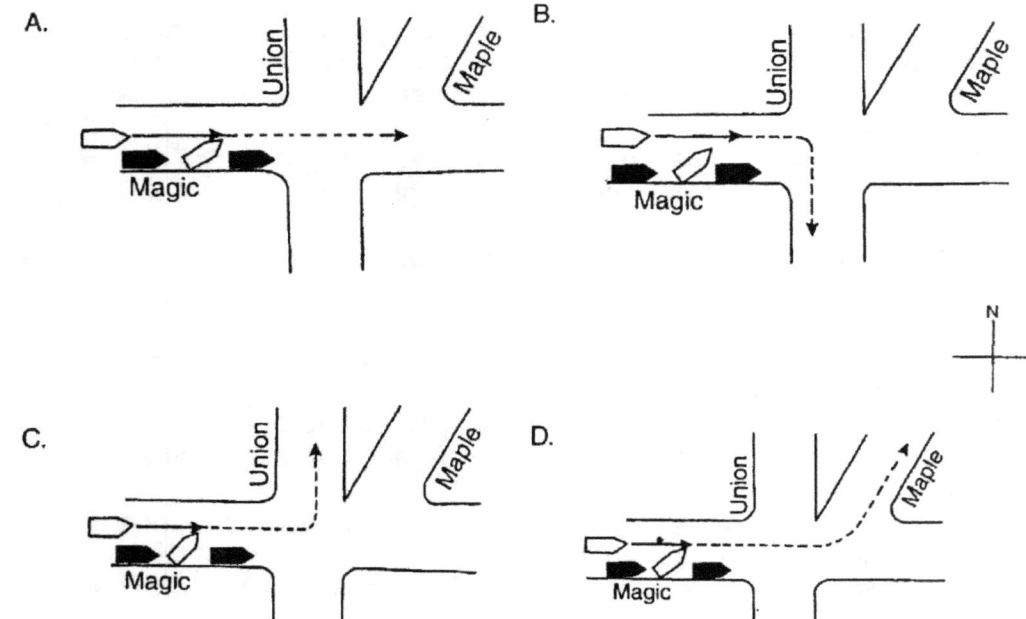

10. As Mr. Jones is driving south on Side St., he falls asleep at the wheel. His car goes out of control and sideswipes an oncoming car, goes through an intersection, and hits a pedestrian on the southeast corner of Main Street. Which of the following depicts the accident?

10.____

A.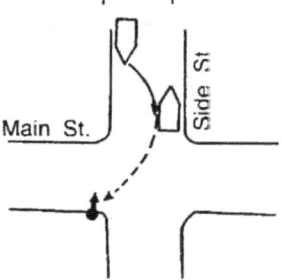

B.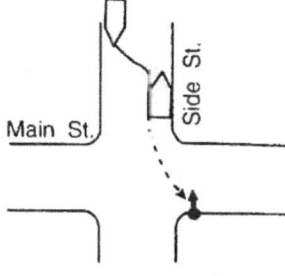

C.

D.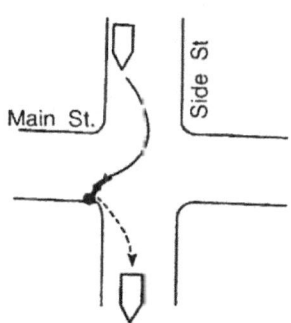

11. A car traveling south on Baltic skids through a red light at the intersection of Baltic and Atlantic, sideswipes a car stopped for a light in the northbound lane, skids 180 degrees, and stops on the west sidewalk of Baltic. Which of the following depicts the accident?

11.____

A.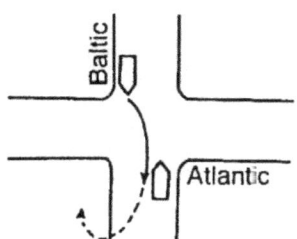

B.

C.

D.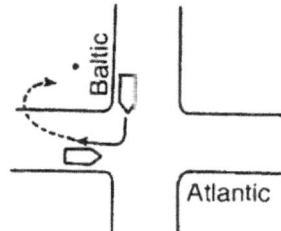

12. When found, the right front end of an automobile was smashed and bent   12.____
    around a post, and the hood was buckled.
    Which of the following cars on a service lot is the car described?

    A.    B.

    C.    D.

13. An open floor safe with its door bet out of shape was found at the scene. It was   13.____
    empty. An electric drill and several envelopes and papers were found on the
    floor near the safe.
    Which of the following shows the scene described?

    A.    B.

    C.    D.

Questions 14-16.

DIRECTIONS: In Questions 14 through 16, you are to pick the word or phrase CLOSEST in meaning to the word or phrase printed in capital letters.

14. HAZARDOUS   14.____
    A. uncertain   B. threatening   C. difficult   D. dangerous

15. NEGLIGENT
    A. careless   B. fearless   C. ruthless   D. useless

16. PROVOKE
    A. accuse   B. arouse   C. insist   D. suspend

Questions 17-20.

DIRECTIONS: Questions 17 through 20 measure your ability to do arithmetic related to police work. Each question presents a separate arithmetic problem to be solved.

17. To the nearest hour, how long can a specialized police vehicle with a 40-gallon fuel tank be on the road before heading for a service facility, assuming that the vehicle consumes 8 gallons per hour and must head for a service facility when there are only 8 gallons in the tank?
    A. 3   B. 4   C. 5   D. None of the above

18. A man with a history of vagrancy was found dead under a bridge with the following U.S. currency in a band around his belly:
    7 $5 bills, 3 $10 bills, 11 $20 bills, 9 $50 bills, 4 $100 bills
    What is the TOTAL amount of the money that was found in the band?
    A. $1,015   B. $1,135   C. $2,719   D. None of the above

19. X is 110 dimes; Y is 1,111 pennies.
    Which of the following statements about the values of X and Y above is TRUE?
    A. X is greater than Y.
    B. Y is greater than X.
    C. x equals Y.
    D. The relationship of X to Y cannot be determined from the information given.

20. Which of the following individuals drinking hard liquor in a bar was 21 years old at the time of the incident?
    A. One born August 26, 1989. Date of incident is March 17, 2010.
    B. One born January 6, 1989. Date of incident is New Year's Eve 2009.
    C. One born 3/17/89. Date of incident is 2/14/10
    D. None of the above

KEY (CORRECT ANSWERS)

1.	A	11.	C
2.	B	12.	D
3.	C	13.	B
4.	D	14.	D
5.	B	15.	A
6.	C	16.	B
7.	B	17.	B
8.	B	18.	B
9.	D	19.	B
10.	B	20.	D

EVALUATING INFORMATION AND EVIDENCE
EXAMINATION SECTION
TEST 1

DIRECTIONS: Each question or incomplete statement is followed by several suggested answers or completions. Select the one that BEST answers the question or completes the statement. *PRINT THE LETTER OF THE CORRECT ANSWER IN THE SPACE AT THE RIGHT.*

Questions 1-9.

DIRECTIONS: Questions 1 through 9 measure your ability to (1) determine whether statements from witnesses say essentially the same thing and (2) determine the evidence needed to make it reasonably certain that a particular conclusion is true.

1. Which of the following pairs of statements say essentially the same thing in two different ways?
   I. Some employees at the water department have fully vested pensions.
      At least one employee at the water department has a pension that is not fully vested.
   II. All swans are white birds.
      A bird that is not white is not a swan.
   The CORRECT answer is:
   A. I only   B. I and II   C. II only   D. Neither I nor II

2. Which of the following pairs of statements say essentially the same thing in two different ways?
   I. If you live in Humboldt County, your property taxes are high.
      If your property taxes are high, you live in Humboldt County.
   II. All the Hutchinsons live in Lindsborg.
      At least some Hutchinsons do not live in Lindsborg.
   The CORRECT answer is;
   A. I only   B. I and II   C. II only   D. Neither I nor II

3. Which of the following pairs of statements say essentially the same thing in two different ways?
   I. Although Spike is a friendly dog, he is also one of the most unpopular dogs on the block.
      Although Spike is one of the most unpopular dogs on the block, he is a friendly dog.
   II. Everyone in Precinct 19 is taller than Officer Banks.
      Nobody in Precinct 19 is shorter than Officer Banks.
   The CORRECT answer is:
   A. I only   B. I and II   C. II only   D. Neither I nor II

4. Which of the following pairs of statements say essentially the same thing in two different ways?
   I. On Friday, every officer in Precinct 1 is assigned parking duty or crowd control, or both.
      If a Precinct 1 officer has been assigned neither parking duty nor crowd control, it is not Friday.
   II. Because the farmer mowed the hay fields today, his house will have mice tomorrow.
      Whenever the farmer mows his hay fields, his house has mice the next day.
   The CORRECT answer is:
   A. I only   B. I and II   C. II only   D. Neither I nor II

5. Summary of Evidence Collected to Date:
   I. Fishing in the Little Pony River is against the law.
      Captain Rick caught an 8-inch trout and ate it for dinner.
   Prematurely Drawn Conclusion: Captain Rick broke the law.
   Which of the following pieces of evidence, if any, would make it reasonably certain that the conclusion drawn is true?
   A. Captain Rick caught his trout in the Little Pony River.
   B. There is no size limit on trout mentioned in the law.
   C. A trout is a species of fish.
   D. None of the above

6. Summary of Evidence Collected to Date:
   I. Some of the doctors in the ICU have been sued for malpractice.
   II. Some of the doctors in the ICU are pediatricians.
   Prematurely Drawn Conclusion: Some of the pediatricians in the ICU have never been sued for malpractice.
   Which of the following pieces of evidence, if any, would make it reasonably certain that the conclusion drawn is true?
   A. The number of pediatricians in the ICU is the same as the number of doctors who have been sued for malpractice.
   B. The number of pediatricians in the ICU is smaller than the number of doctors who have been sued for malpractice.
   C. The number of ICU doctors who have been sued for malpractice is smaller than the number who are pediatricians.
   D. None of the above

7. Summary of Evidence Collected to Date:
   I. Along Paseo Boulevard, there are five convenience stores.
   II. EZ-GO is east of Pop-a-Shop.
   III. Kwik-E-Mart is west of Bob's Market.
   IV. The Nightwatch is between EZ-GO and Kwik-E-Mart.
   Prematurely Drawn Conclusion: Pop-a-Shop is the westernmost convenience store on Paseo Boulevard.

Which of the following pieces of evidence, if any, would make it reasonably certain that the conclusion drawn is true?
- A. Bob's Market is the easternmost convenience store on Paseo.
- B. Kwik-E-Mart is the second store from the west.
- C. The Nightwatch is west of the EZ-GO.
- D. None of the above

8. Summary of Evidence Collected to Date:
Stark drove home from work at 70 miles an hour and wasn't breaking the law.
Prematurely Drawn Conclusion: Stark was either on an interstate highway or in the state of Montana.
Which of the following pieces of evidence, if any, would make it reasonably certain that the conclusion drawn is true?
- A. There are no interstate highways in Montana.
- B. Montana is the only state that allows a speed of 70 miles an hour on roads other than interstate highways.
- C. Most states don't allow speed of 70 miles an hour on state highways.
- D. None of the above

9. Summary of Evidence Collected to Date:
I. Margaret, owner of MetroWoman magazine, signed a contract with each of her salespeople promising an automatic $200 bonus to any employee who sells more than 60 subscriptions in a calendar month.
II. Lynn sold 82 subscriptions to MetroWoman in the month of December.
Prematurely Drawn Conclusion: Lynn received a $20 bonus.
Which of the following pieces of evidence, if any, would make it reasonably certain that the conclusion is true?
- A. Lynn is a salesperson.
- B. Lynn works for Margaret.
- C. Margaret offered only $200 regardless of the number of subscriptions sold.
- D. None of the above

Questions 10-14.

DIRECTIONS: Questions 10 through 14 refer to Map #3 and measure your ability to orient yourself within a given section of town, neighborhood or particular area. Each of the questions describes a starting point and a destination. Assume that you are driving a car in the area shown on the map accompanying the questions. Use the map as a basis for the shortest way to get from one point to another without breaking the law.
On the map, a street marked by arrows, or by arrows and the words "One Way," indicates one-way travel and should be assumed to be one-way for the entire length, even when there are breaks or jogs in the street. EXCEPTION: A street that does not have the same name over the full length.

4 (#1)

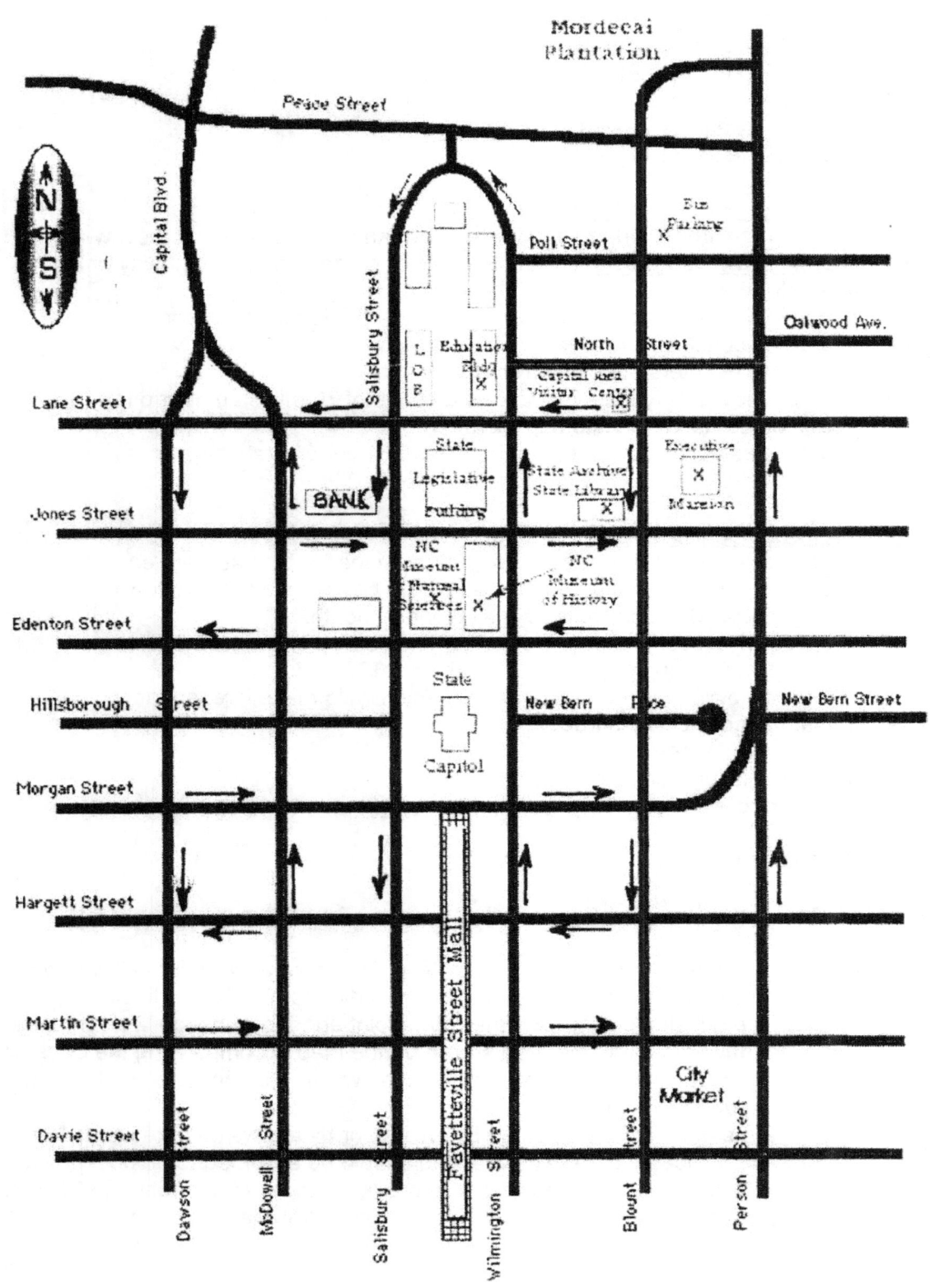

5 (#1)

10. The SHORTEST legal way from the south end of the Fayetteville Street Mall, at Davie Street, to the city of Raleigh Municipal Building is
    A. west on Davie, north on McDowell
    B. west on Davie, north on Dawson
    C. east on Davie, north on Wilmington, west on Morgan
    D. east on Davie, north on Wilmington, west on Hargett

10.____

11. The SHORTEST legal way from the City Market to the Education Building is
    A. north on Blount, west on North
    B. north on Person, west on Lane
    C. north on Blount, west on Lane
    D. west on Martin, north on Wilmington

11.____

12. The SHORTEST legal way from the Education Building to the State Capitol is
    A. south on Wilmington
    B. north on Wilmington, west on Peace, south on Capitol, bear west to go south on Dawson, and east on Morgan
    C. west on Lane, south on Salisbury
    D. each on North, south on Blount, west on Edenton

12.____

13. The SHORTEST legal way from the State Capitol to Peace College is
    A. north on Wilmington, jog north, east on Peace
    B. east on Morgan, north on Person, west on Peace
    C. west on Edenton, north on McDowell, north on Capitol Blvd., east on Peace
    D. east on Morgan, north on Blount, west on Peace

13.____

14. The SHORTEST legal way from the State Legislative Building to the City Market is
    A. south on Wilmington, east on Martin
    B. east on Jones, south on Blount
    C. south on Salisbury, east on Davie
    D. east on Lane, south on Blount

14.____

Questions 15-19.

DIRECTIONS: Questions 15 through 19 refer to Figure #3, on the following page, and measure your ability to understand written descriptions of events. Each question presents a description of an accident or event and asks you which of the following five drawings in Figure #3 BEST represents it.
In the drawings, the following symbols are used:
Moving vehicle ⌂   Non-moving vehicle ▲
Pedestrian or bicyclist •
The path and direction of travel of a vehicle or pedestrian is indicated by a solid line.
The path and direction of travel of each vehicle or pedestrian directly involved in a collision from the point of impact is indicated by a dotted line.

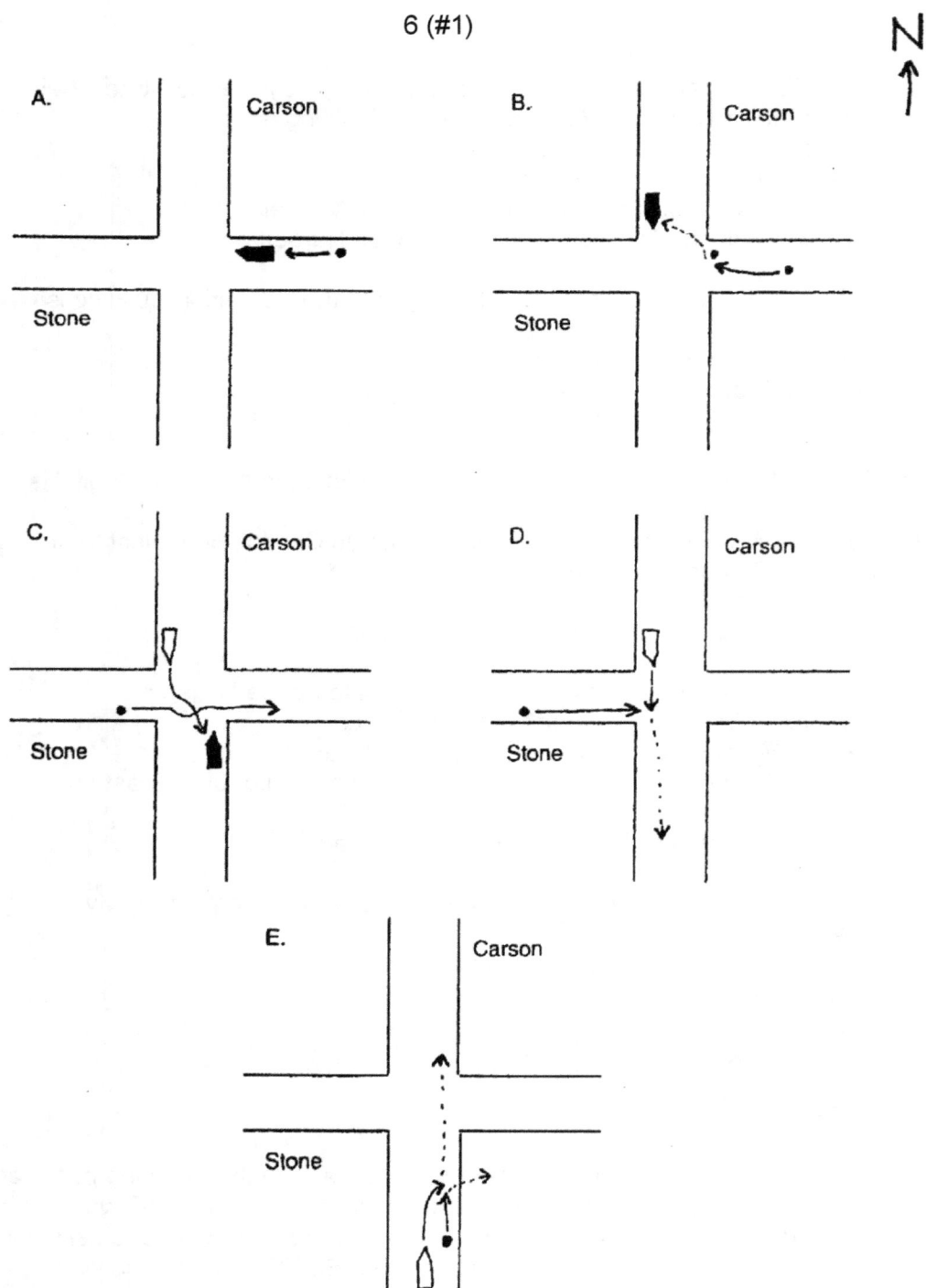

In the space at the right, print the letter of the drawing that BEST fit the descriptions written below.

15. A driver headed north on Carson veers to the right and strikes a bicyclist who is also headed north. The bicyclist is thrown from the road. The driver flees north on Carson.

15.____

16. A driver heading south on Carson runs the stop sign and barely misses colliding with an eastbound cyclist. The cyclist swerves to avoid the collision and continues traveling east. The driver swerves to avoid the collision and strikes a car parked in the northbound lane on Carson.

16.____

17. A bicyclist heading west on Stone collides with a pedestrian in the crosswalk, then veers through the intersection and collides with the front of a car parked in the southbound lane on Carson.

17.____

18. A driver traveling south on Carson runs over a bicyclist who has run the stop sign, and then flees south on Carson.

18.____

19. A bicyclist heading west on Stone collides with the rear of a car parked in the westbound lane.

19.____

Questions 20-22.

DIRECTIONS: In Questions 20 through 22, choose the word or phrase CLOSEST in meaning to the word or phrase printed in capital letters.

20. INSOLVENT
    A. bankrupt   B. vagrant   C. hazardous   D. illegal

20.____

21. TENANT
    A. laborer   B. occupant   C. owner   D. creditor

21.____

22. INFRACTION
    A. portion   B. violation   C. remark   D. detour

22.____

Questions 23-25.

DIRECTIONS: Questions 23 through 25 measure your ability to do fieldwork-related arithmetic. Each question presents a separate arithmetic problem for you to solve.

23. Officer Jones has served on the police force longer than Smith. Smith has served longer than Moore. Moore has served less time than Jones, and Park has served longer than Jones.
    Which officer has served the LONGEST on the police force?
    A. Jones   B. Smith   C. Moore   D. Park

23.____

24. A car wash has raised the price of an outside-only wash from $4 to $5. The car wash applies the same percentage increase to its inside-and-out wash, which was $10.
    What is the new cost of the inside-and-out wash?
    A. $8   B. $11   C. $12.50   D. $15

24.____

25. Ron and James, college students, make $10 an hour working at the restaurant. 25._____
Ron works 13 hours a week and James works 20 hours a week.
To make the same amount that Ron earns in a year, James would work about _____ weeks.

   A. 18   B. 27   C. 34   D. 45

KEY (CORRECT ANSWERS)

1.	C	11.	B
2.	D	12.	C
3.	B	13.	A
4.	B	14.	B
5.	A	15.	E
6.	D	16.	C
7.	B	17.	B
8.	B	18.	D
9.	B	19.	A
10.	A	20.	A

21. B
22. B
23. D
24. C
25. C

9 (#1)

SOLUTIONS TO QUESTIONS 1-9

P implies Q = original statement

Not Q implies not P = contrapositive of the original statement. A statement and its contrapositive are logically equivalent.

Q implies P = converse of the original statement

Not P implies not Q = inverse of the original statement. The converse and inverse of an original statement are logically equivalent.

P implies Q = Not P or Q.

1. The CORRECT answer is C.
   Item I is wrong because "some employees" means "at least one employee" and possibly "all employees." If it is true that all employees have fully vested pensions, then the second statement is false. Item II is correct because the second statement is the contrapositive of the first statement.

2. The CORRECT answer is D.
   Item I is wrong because the converse of a statement does not necessarily follow from the original statement. Item II is wrong because statement I implies that there are no Hutchinson family members who live outside Lindsborg.

3. The CORRECT answer is B. Item I is correct because it is composed of the same two compound statements that are simply mentioned in a different order. Item II is correct because if each person is taller than Officer Banks, then there is no person in that precinct who can possibly be shorter than Officer Banks.

4. The CORRECT answer is B.
   Item I is correct because the second statement is the contrapositive of the first statement. Item II is correct because each statement indicates that mowing the hay fields on a particular day leads to the presence of mice the next day.

5. The CORRECT answer is A.
   If Captain Rick caught his trout in the Little Pony River, then we can conclude that he was fishing there. Since statement I says that fishing in the Little Pony Rive is against the law, we conclude that Captain Rick broke the law.

6. The CORRECT answer is D.
   The number of doctors in each group whether the same or not, has no bearing on the conclusion. There is nothing in evidence to suggest that the group of doctors sued for malpractice overlaps with the group of doctors that are pediatricians.

7. The CORRECT answer is B.
   If we are given that Kwik-E-Mart is the second store from the west, then the order of stores from west to east, is Pop-a-Shop, Kwik-E-Mart, Nightwatch, EZ-GO, and Bob's Market.

8. The CORRECT answer is B.
We are given that Stark drove at 70 miles per hour and didn't break the law. If we also know that Montana is the only state that allows a speed of 70 miles per hour, then we can conclude that Stark must have been driving in Montana or else was driving on some interstate.

9. The CORRECT answer is B.
The only additional piece of information needed is that Lynn works for Margaret. This will guarantee that Lynn receives the promised $200 bonus.

TEST 2

DIRECTIONS: Each question or incomplete statement is followed by several suggested answers or completions. Select the one that BEST answers the question or completes the statement. *PRINT THE LETTER OF THE CORRECT ANSWER IN THE SPACE AT THE RIGHT.*

Questions 1-9.

DIRECTIONS: Questions 1 through 9 measure your ability to (1) determine whether statements from witnesses say essentially the same thing and (2) determine the evidence needed to make it reasonably certain that a particular conclusion is true.
To do well on this part of the test, you do NOT have to have a working knowledge of police procedures and techniques. Nor do you have to have any more familiarity with criminals and criminal behavior than that acquired from reading newspapers, listening to radio or watching TV. To do well in this part, you must read and reason carefully.

1. Which of the following pairs of statements say essentially the same thing in two different ways?   1.____
   I. All of the teachers at Slater Middle School are intelligent, but some are irrational thinkers.
   Although some teachers at Slater Middle School are irrational thinkers, all of them are intelligent.
   II. Nobody has no friends.
   Everybody has at least one friend.
   The CORRECT answer is:
   A. I only   B. I and II   C. II only   D. Neither I nor II

2. Which of the following pairs of statements say essentially the same thing in two different ways?   2.____
   I. Although bananas taste good to most people, they are also a healthy food.
   Bananas are a healthy food, but most people eat them because they taste good.
   II. If Dr. Jones is in, we should call at the office.
   Either Dr. Jones is in, or we should not call at the office.
   The CORRECT answer is:
   A. I only   B. I and II   C. II only   D. Neither I nor II

3. Which of the following pairs of statements say essentially the same thing in two different ways?   3.____
   I. Some millworker work two shifts.
   If someone works only one shift, he is probably not a millworker.
   II. If a letter carrier clocks in at nine, he can finish his route by the end of the day.
   If a letter carrier does not clock in at nine, he cannot finish his route by the end of the day.
   The CORRECT answer is:
   A. I only   B. I and II   C. II only   D. Neither I nor II

4. Which of the following pairs of statements say essentially the same thing in two different ways?
   I. If a member of the swim team attends every practice, he will compete in the next meet.
   Either a swim team member will compete in the next meet, or he did not attend every practice.
   II. All the engineers in the drafting department who wear glasses know how to use AutoCAD.
   If an engineer wears glasses, he will know how to use AutoCAD.
   The CORRECT answer is:
   A. I only   B. I and II   C. II only   D. Neither I nor II

5. Summary of Evidence Collected to Date:
   All of the parents who attend the weekly parenting seminars are high school graduates.
   Prematurely Drawn Conclusion: Some parents who attend the weekly parenting seminars have been convicted of child abuse.
   Which of the following pieces of evidence, if any, would make it reasonably certain that the conclusion drawn is true?
   A. Those convicted of child abuse are often high school graduates.
   B. Some high school graduates have been convicted of child abuse.
   C. There is no correlation between education level and the incidence of child abuse.
   D. None of the above

6. Summary of Evidence Collected to Date:
   I. Mr. Cantwell promised to vote for new school buses if he was reelected to the board.
   II. If the new school buses are approved by the school board, then Mr. Cantwell was not reelected to the board.
   Prematurely Drawn Conclusion: Approval of the new school buses was defeated in spite of Mr. Cantwell's vote.
   Which of the following pieces of evidence, if any, would make it reasonably certain that the conclusion drawn is true?
   A. Mr. Cantwell decided not to run for reelection.
   B. Mr. Cantwell was reelected to the board.
   C. Mr. Cantwell changed his mind and voted against the new buses.
   D. None of the above

7. Summary of Evidence Collected to Date:
   I. The station employs three detectives: Francis, Jackson, and Stern. One of the detectives is a lieutenant, one is a sergeant, and one is a major.
   II. Francis is not a lieutenant.
   Prematurely Drawn Conclusion: Jackson is a lieutenant.
   Which of the following pieces of evidence, if any, would make it reasonably certain that the conclusion drawn is true?
   A. Stern is not a sergeant.   B. Stern is a major.
   C. Francis is a major.   E. None of the above

8. Summary of Evidence Collected to Date:
   I. In the office building, every survival kit that contains a gas mask also contains anthrax vaccine.
   II. Some of the kits containing water purification tablets also contain anthrax vaccine.
   Prematurely Drawn Conclusion: If the survival kit near the typists' pool contains a gas mask, it does not contain water purification tablets.
   Which of the following pieces of evidence, if any, would make it reasonably certain that the conclusion drawn is true?
   A. Some survival kits contain all three items.
   B. The survival kit near the typists' pool contains anthrax vaccine.
   C. The survival kit near the typists' pool contains only two of these items.
   D. None of the above

9. Summary of Evidence Collected to Date:
   The shrink-wrap mechanism is designed to shut itself off if the heating coil temperature drops below 400 during the twin cycle.
   Prematurely Drawn Conclusion: If the machine was operating the twin cycle on Monday, it was not operating properly.
   Which of the following pieces of evidence, if any, would make it reasonably certain that the conclusion drawn is true?
   A. On Monday, the heating coil temperature reached 450.
   B. When the machine performs functions other than the twin cycle, the heating coil temperature sometimes drops below 400.
   C. The shrink-wrap mechanism did not shut itself off on Monday.
   D. None of the above

Questions 10-14.

DIRECTIONS: Questions 10 through 14 refer to Map #3 and measure your ability to orient yourself within a given section of town, neighborhood or particular area. Each of the questions describes a starting point and a destination. Assume that you are driving a car in the area shown on the map accompanying the questions. Use the map as a basis for the shortest way to get from one point to another without breaking the law.
On the map, a street marked by arrows, or by arrows and the words "One Way," indicates one-way travel and should be assumed to be one-way for the entire length, even when there are breaks or jogs in the street. EXCEPTION: A street that does not have the same name over the full length.

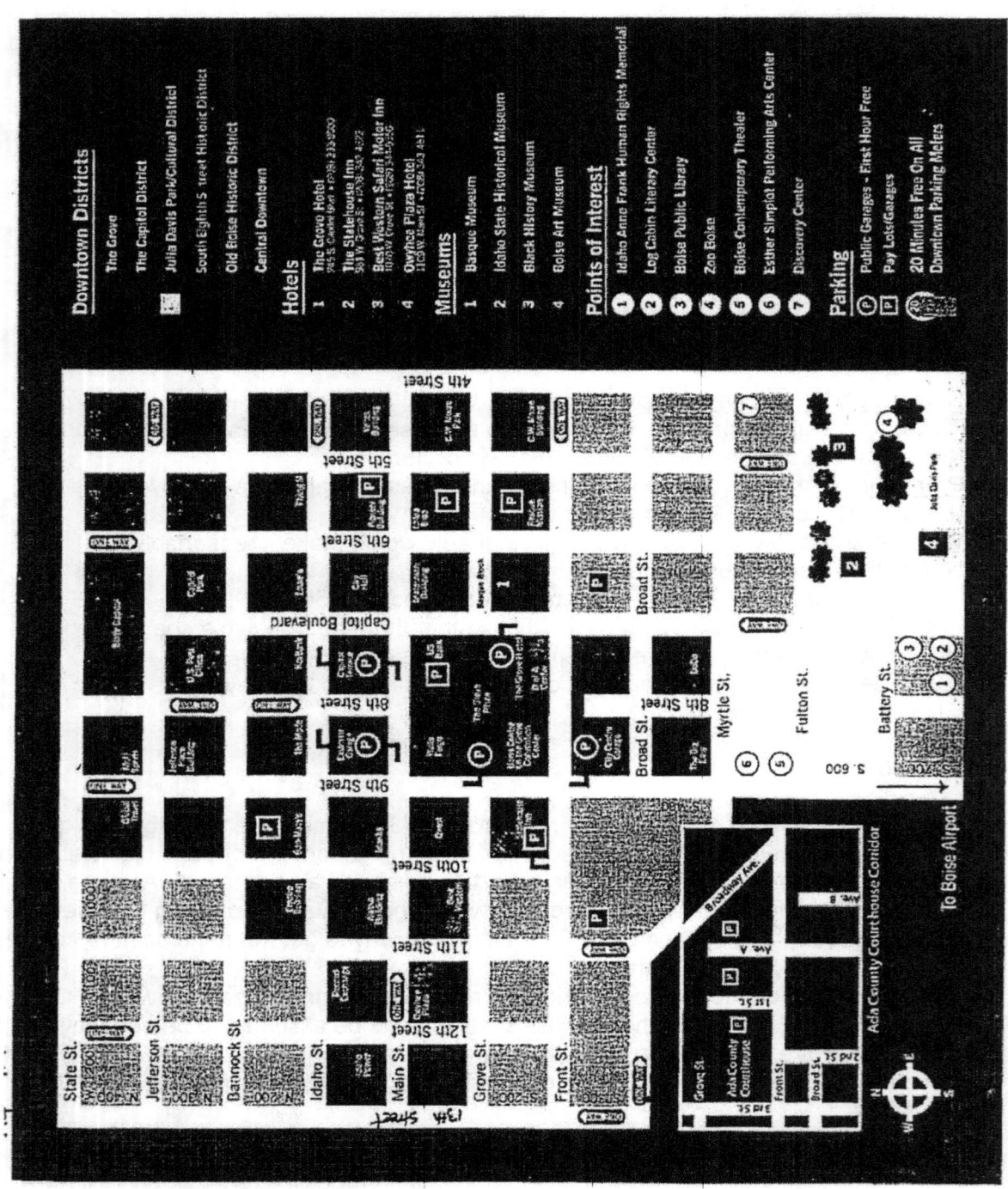

10. The SHORTEST legal way from the State Capitol to Idaho Power is
    A. south on Capitol Blvd., west on Main, north on 12th
    B. south on 8th, west on Main
    C. west on Jefferson, south on 12th
    D. south on Capitol Blvd., west on Front, north on 12th

11. The SHORTEST legal way from the Jefferson Place Building to the Statesman Building is
    A. east on Jefferson, south on Capitol Blvd.
    B. south on 8th, east on Main
    C. east on Jefferson, south on 4th, west on Main
    D. south on 9th, east on Main

    11.____

12. The SHORTEST legal way from Julia Davis Park to Owyhee Plaza Hotel is
    A. north on 5th, west on Front, north on 11th
    B. north on 6th, west on Main
    C. west on Battery, north on 9th, west on Front, north on Main
    D. north on 5th, west on Front, north on 13th, east on Main

    12.____

13. The SHORTEST legal way from the Big Easy to City Hall is
    A. north on 9th, east on Main
    B. east on Myrtle, north on Capitol Blvd.
    C. north on 9th, east on Idaho
    D. east on Myrtle, north on 6th

    13.____

14. The SHORTEST legal way from the Boise Contemporary Theater to the Pioneer Building is
    A. north on 9th, east on Main
    B. north on 9th, east on Myrtle, north on 6th
    C. east on Fulton, north on Capitol Blvd., east on Main
    D. east on Fulton, north on 6th

    14.____

Questions 15-19.

DIRECTIONS: Questions 15 through 19 refer to Figure #3, on the following page, and measure your ability to understand written descriptions of events. Each question presents a description of an accident or event and asks you which of the following five drawings in Figure #3 BEST represents it.
In the drawings, the following symbols are used:
Moving vehicle ◊   Non-moving vehicle ▲
Pedestrian or bicyclist •
The path and direction of travel of a vehicle or pedestrian is indicated by a solid line.
The path and direction of travel of each vehicle or pedestrian directly involved in a collision from the point of impact is indicated by a dotted line.

In the space at the right, print the letter of the drawing that BEST fit the descriptions written below.

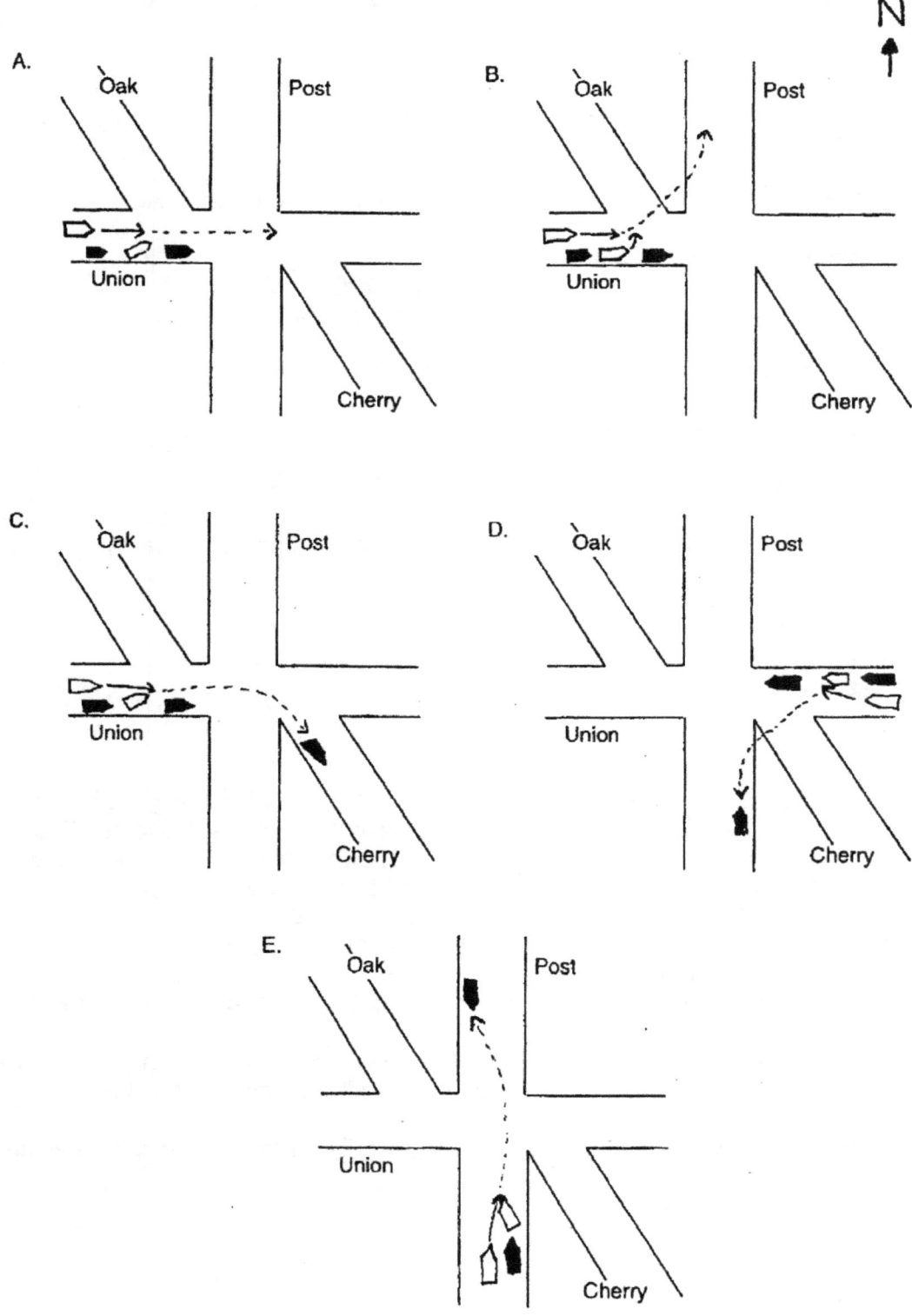

15. A driver headed east on Union strikes a car that is pulling out from between two parked cars, and then continues east.

16. A driver headed north on Post strikes a car that is pulling out from in front of a parked car, then veers into the oncoming lane and collides head-on with a car that is parked in the southbound lane of Post.

17. A driver headed east on Union strikes a car that is pulling out from two parked cars, travels through the intersection, and makes a sudden right turn onto Cherry, where he strikes a parked car in the rear.

18. A driver headed west on Union strikes a car that is pulling out from between two parked cars, and then swerves to the left. He cuts the corner and travels over the sidewalk at the intersection of Cherry and Post, and then strikes a car that is parked in the northbound lane on Post.

19. A driver headed east on Union strikes a car that is pulling out from between two parked cars, and then swerves to the left. He cuts the corner and travels over the sidewalk at the intersection of Oak and Post, and then flees north on Post.

Questions 20-22.

DIRECTIONS: In Questions 20 through 22, choose the word or phrase CLOSEST in meaning to the word or phrase printed in capital letters.

20. TITLE
    A. danger   B. ownership   C. description   D. treatise

21. REVOKE
    A. cancel   B. imagine   C. solicit   D. cause

22. BRIEF
    A. summary   B. ruling   C. plea   D. motion

Questions 23-25.

DIRECTIONS: Questions 23 through 25 measure your ability to do fieldwork-related arithmetic. Each question presents a separate arithmetic problem for you to solve.

23. An investigator plans to drive from his home to Los Angeles, a trip of 2,800 miles. His car has a 24-gallon tank and gets 18 miles to the gallon. If he starts out with a full tank of gasoline, what is the FEWEST number of stops he will have to make for gasoline to complete his trip to Los Angeles?
    A. 4   B. 5   C. 6   D. 7

24. A caseworker has 24 home visits to schedule for a week. She will visit three homes on Sunday, and on every day that follows she will visit one more home than she visited on the previous day.
At the end of the day on _____, the caseworker will have completed all of her home visits.
   A. Wednesday   B. Thursday   C. Friday   D. Saturday

24._____

25. Ms. Langhorn takes a cab from her house to the airport. The cab company charges $3.00 to start the meter and $.50 per mile after that. It's 15 miles from Ms. Langhorn's house to the airport.
How much will she have to pay for a cab?
   A. $10.50   B. $11.50   C. $14.00   D. $15.50

25._____

KEY (CORRECT ANSWERS)

1.	B		11.	D
2.	A		12.	A
3.	D		13.	B
4.	B		14.	C
5.	D		15.	A
6.	B		16.	E
7.	B		17.	C
8.	C		18.	D
9.	C		19.	B
10.	C		20.	B

21. A
22. A
23. C
24. B
25. A

SOLUTIONS TO QUESTIONS 1-9

P implies Q = original statement

Not Q implies not P = contrapositive of the original statement. A statement and its contrapositive are logically equivalent.

Q implies P = converse of the original statement

Not P implies not Q = inverse of the original statement. The converse and inverse of an original statement are logically equivalent.

P implies Q = Not P or Q.

1. The CORRECT answer is B.
   For Item I, the irrational thinking teachers at the Middle School belong the group of all Middle School teachers. Since all teachers at the Middle School are intelligent, this includes the subset of irrational thinkers. For item II, if no one person has no friends, this implies that each person must have at least one friend.

2. The CORRECT answer is A.
   In item I, both statements state that (a) bananas are healthy and (b) bananas are eaten mainly because they taste good. In item II, the second statement is not equivalent to the first statement. An equivalent statement to the first statement would be "Either Dr. Jones is not in or we should call at the office."

3. The CORRECT answer is D.
   In item I, given that a person works one shift, we cannot draw any conclusion about whether he/she is a millworker. It is possible that a millworker works one, two, or a number more than two shifts. In item II, the second statement is the inverse of the first statement; they are not logically equivalent.

4. The CORRECT answer is B.
   In item I, any statement in the form "P implies Q" is equivalent to "Not P or Q." In this case, P = A member of the swim team attends practice, and Q = He will compete in the next meet. In item II, "P implies Q" is equivalent to "all P belongs to Q." In this case, P = Engineer wears glasses, and Q = He will know how to use AutoCAD.

5. The CORRECT answer is D. Because the number of high school graduates is so much larger than the number of convicted child abusers, none of the additional pieces of evidence make it reasonably certain that there are convicted abusers within this group of parents.

6. The CORRECT answer is B.
   Statement II is equivalent to "If Mr. Cantwell is reelected to the school board, then school buses are not approved. Statement I assures us that Mr. Cantwell will vote for new school buses. The only logical conclusion is that in spite of Mr. Cantwell's reelection to the board and subsequent vote, approval of the buses was still defeated.

7. The CORRECT answer is B. From Statement II, we conclude that Francis is either a sergeant or a major. If we also know that Stern is a major, we can deduce that Francis is a sergeant. This means that the third person, Jackson, must be a lieutenant.

8. The CORRECT answer is C.
Given that a survival kit contains a gas mask, Statement I assures us that it also contains the anthrax vaccine. If the survival kit near the typist pool only contains two items, than we can conclude that the gas mask in this location cannot contain a third item, namely the anthrax vaccine.

9. The CORRECT answer is C.
The original statement can be written in "P implies Q" form, where P = the heating coil temperature drops below 400 during the twin cycle, and Q = the mechanism shuts itself off. The contrapositive (which must be true) would be "If the mechanism did not shut itself off then the heating coil temperature did not drop below 400." We would then conclude that the temperature was too high and, therefore, the machine did not operate properly.

EVALUATING CONCLUSIONS IN LIGHT OF KNOWN FACTS

EXAMINATION SECTION

TEST 1

DIRECTIONS: Each question or incomplete statement is followed by several suggested answers or completions. Select the one that BEST answers the question or completes the statement. *PRINT THE LETTER OF THE CORRECT ANSWER IN THE SPACE AT THE RIGHT.*

Questions 1-9.

DIRECTIONS: In Questions 1 through 9, you will read a set of facts and a conclusion drawn from them. The conclusion may be valid or invalid, based on the facts. It is your task to determine the validity of the conclusion.
For each question, select the letter before the statement that BEST expresses the relationship between the given facts and the conclusion that has been drawn from them. Your choices are:
    A. The facts prove the conclusion.
    B. The facts disprove the conclusion; or
    C. The facts neither prove nor disprove the conclusion.

1. FACTS: Lauren must use Highway 29 to get to work. Lauren has a meeting today at 9:00 A.M. If she misses the meeting, Lauren will probably lose a major account. Highway 29 is closed all day today for repairs.

   CONCLUSION: Lauren will not be able to get to work.

   A. The facts prove the conclusion
   B. The facts disprove the conclusion.
   C. The facts neither prove nor disprove the conclusion.

2. FACTS: The Tumbleweed Follies, a traveling burlesque show, is looking for a new line dancer. The position requires both singing and dancing skills. If the show cannot fill the position by Friday, it will begin to look for a magician to fill the time slot currently held by the line dancers. Willa, who wants to audition for the line dancing position, can sing, but cannot dance.

   CONCLUSION: Willa is qualified to audition for the part of line dancer.

   A. The facts prove the conclusion.
   B. The facts disprove the conclusion.
   C. The facts neither prove nor disprove the conclusion.

3. FACTS: Terry owns two dogs, Spike and Stan. One of the dogs is short-haired and has blue eyes. One dog as a pink nose. The blue-eyed dog never barks. One of the dogs has white fur on its paws. Sam has long hair.

   CONCLUSION: Spike never barks.

   A. The facts prove the conclusion.
   B. The facts disprove the conclusion.
   C. The facts neither prove nor disprove the conclusion.

3.____

4. FACTS: No science teachers are members of the PTA. Some English teachers are members of the PTA. Some English teachers in the PTA also wear glasses. Every PTA member is required to sit on the dunking stool at the student carnival except for those who wear glasses, who will be exempt. Those who are exempt, however, will have to officiate the hamster races. All of the English teachers in the PTA who do not wear glasses are married.

   CONCLUSION: All the married English teachers in the PTA will set on the dunking stool at the student carnival.

   A. The facts prove the conclusion.
   B. The facts disprove the conclusion.
   C. The facts neither prove nor disprove the conclusion.

4.____

5. FACTS: If the price of fuel is increased and sales remain constant, oil company profits will increase. The price of fuel was increased, and market experts project that sales levels are likely to be maintained.

   CONCLUSION: The price of fuel will increase.

   A. The facts prove the conclusion.
   B. The facts disprove the conclusion.
   C. The facts neither prove nor disprove the conclusion.

5.____

6. FACTS: Some members of the gymnastics team are double-jointed, and some members of the gymnastics team ae also on the lacrosse team. Some double-jointed members of the gymnastics team are also coaches. All gymnastics team members perform floor exercises, except the coaches. All the double-jointed members of the gymnastics team who are not coaches are freshmen.

   CONCLUSION: Some double-jointed freshmen are coaches.

   A. The facts prove the conclusion.
   B. The facts disprove the conclusion.
   C. The facts neither prove nor disprove the conclusion.

6.____

7. FACTS: Each member of the International Society speaks at least one foreign language, but no member speaks more than four foreign languages. Five members speak Spanish; three speak Mandarin; four speak French; four speak German; and five speak a foreign language other than Spanish, Mandarin, French, or German.

   CONCLUSION: The lowest possible number of members in the International Society is eight.

   A. The facts prove the conclusion.
   B. The facts disprove the conclusion.
   C. The facts neither prove nor disprove the conclusion.

8. FACTS: Mary keeps seven cats in her apartment. Only three of the cats will eat the same kind of food. Mary wants to keep at least one extra bag of each kind of food.

   CONCLUSION: The minimum number of bags Mary will need to keep as extra is 7.

   A. The facts prove the conclusion.
   B. The facts disprove the conclusion.
   C. The facts neither prove nor disprove the conclusion.

9. FACTS: In Ed and Marie's exercise group, everyone likes the treadmill or the stationary bicycle, or both, but Ed does not like the stationary bicycle. Marie has not expressed a preference, but spends most of her time on the stationary bicycle.

   CONCLUSION: Everyone in the group who does not like the treadmill likes the stationary bicycle.

   A. The facts prove the conclusion.
   B. The facts disprove the conclusion.
   C. The facts neither prove nor disprove the conclusion.

Questions 10-17.

DIRECTIONS: Questions 10 through 17 are based on the following reading passage. It is not your knowledge of the particular topic that is being tested, but your ability to reason based on what you have read. The passage is likely to detail several proposed courses of action and factors affecting these proposals. The reading passage is followed by a conclusion or outcome based on the facts in the passage, or a description of a decision taken regarding the situation. The conclusion is followed by a number of statements that have a possible connection to the conclusion. For each statement, you are to determine whether:

A. The statement proves the conclusion.
B. The statement supports the conclusion but does not prove it.
C. The statement disproves the conclusion.
D. The statement weakens the conclusion but does not disprove it.
E. The statement has no relevance to the conclusion.

Remember that the conclusion after the passage is to be accepted as the outcome of what actually happened, and that you are being asked to evaluate the impact each statement would have had on the conclusion.

PASSAGE

The Owyhee Mission School District's Board of Directors is hosting a public meeting to debate the merits of the proposed abolition of all bilingual education programs within the district. The group that has made the proposal believes the programs, which teach immigrant children academic subjects in their native language until they have learned English well enough to join mainstream classes, inhibit the ability of students to acquire English quickly and succeed in school and in the larger American society. Such programs, they argue, are also a wasteful drain on the district's already scant resources.

At the meeting, several teachers and parents stand to speak out against the proposal. The purpose of an education, they say, should be to build upon, rather than dismantle, a minority child's language and culture. By teaching children in academic subjects in their native tongues, while simultaneously offering English language instruction, schools can meet the goals of learning English and progressing through academic subjects along with their peers.

Hiram Nguyen, a representative of the parents whose children are currently enrolled in bilingual education, stands at the meeting to express the parents' wishes. The parents have been polled, he says, and are overwhelmingly of the opinion that while language and culture are important to them, they are not things that will disappear from the students' lives if they are no longer taught in the classroom. The most important issue for the parents is whether their children will succeed in school and be competitive in the larger American society. If bilingual education can be demonstrated to do that, then the parents are in favor of continuing it.

At the end of the meeting, a proponent of the plan, Oscar Ramos, stands to clarify some misconceptions about the proposal. It does not call for a "sink or swim" approach, he says, but allows for an interpreter to be present in mainstream classes to explain anything a student finds too complex or confusing.

The last word of the meeting is given to Delia Cruz, a bilingual teacher at one of the district's elementary schools. A student is bound to find anything complex or confusing, she says, if it is spoken in a language he has never heard before. It is more wasteful to place children in classrooms where they don't understand anything, she says, than it is to try to teach them something useful as they are learning the English language.

CONCLUSION: After the meeting, the Owyhee Mission School District's Board of Directors votes to terminate all the district's bilingual education programs at the end of the current academic year, but to maintain the current level of funding to each of the schools that have programs cut.

10. A poll conducted by the *Los Angeles Times* at approximately the same time as the Board's meeting indicated that 75% of the people were opposed to bilingual education; among Latinos, opposition was 84%.
    A. The statement proves the conclusion.
    B. The statement supports the conclusion but does not prove it.
    C. The statement disproves the conclusion.
    D. The statement weakens the conclusion but does not disprove it.
    E. The statement has no relevance to the conclusion.

11. Of all the studies connected on bilingual education programs, 64% indicate that students learned English grammar better in "sink or swim" classes without any special features than they did in bilingual education classes.
    A. The statement proves the conclusion.
    B. The statement supports the conclusion but does not prove it.
    C. The statement disproves the conclusion.
    D. The statement weakens the conclusion but does not disprove it.
    E. The statement has no relevance to the conclusion.

12. In the academic year that begins after the Board's vote, Montgomery Burns Elementary, an Owyhee Mission District school, launches a new bilingual program for the children of Somali immigrants.
    A. The statement proves the conclusion.
    B. The statement supports the conclusion but does not prove it.
    C. The statement disproves the conclusion.
    D. The statement weakens the conclusion but does not disprove it.
    E. The statement has no relevance to the conclusion.

13. In the previous academic year, under severe budget restraints, the Owyhee Mission District cut all physical education, music, and art classes, but its funding for bilingual education classes increased by 18%.
    A. The statement proves the conclusion.
    B. The statement supports the conclusion but does not prove it.
    C. The statement disproves the conclusion.
    D. The statement weakens the conclusion but does not disprove it.
    E. The statement has no relevance to the conclusion.

14. Before the Board votes, a polling consultant conducts randomly sampled assessments of immigrant students who enrolled in Owyhee District schools at a time when they did not speak any English at all. Ten years after graduating from high school, 44% of those who received bilingual education were professionals – doctors, lawyers, educators, engineers, etc. Of those who did not receive bilingual education, 38% were professionals.
    A. The statement proves the conclusion.
    B. The statement supports the conclusion but does not prove it.
    C. The statement disproves the conclusion.
    D. The statement weakens the conclusion but does not disprove it.
    E. The statement has no relevance to the conclusion.

15. Over the past several years, the scores of Owyhee District students have gradually declined, and enrollment numbers have followed as anxious parents transferred their children to other schools or applied for a state-funded voucher program.
    A. The statement proves the conclusion.
    B. The statement supports the conclusion but does not prove it.
    C. The statement disproves the conclusion.
    D. The statement weakens the conclusion but does not disprove it.
    E. The statement has no relevance to the conclusion.

15._____

16. California and Massachusetts, two of the most liberal states in the country, have each passed ballot measures banning bilingual education in public schools.
    A. The statement proves the conclusion.
    B. The statement supports the conclusion but does not prove it.
    C. The statement disproves the conclusion.
    D. The statement weakens the conclusion but does not disprove it.
    E. The statement has no relevance to the conclusion.

16._____

17. In the academic year that begins after the Board's vote, no Owyhee Mission Schools are conducting bilingual instruction.
    A. The statement proves the conclusion.
    B. The statement supports the conclusion but does not prove it.
    C. The statement disproves the conclusion.
    D. The statement weakens the conclusion but does not disprove it.
    E. The statement has no relevance to the conclusion.

17._____

Questions 18-25.

DIRECTIONS: Questions 18 through 25 each provide four factual statements and a conclusion based on these statements. After reading the entire question, you will decide whether:
  A. The conclusion is proved by Statements 1-4;
  B. The conclusion is disproved by Statements 1-4;
  C. The facts are not sufficient to prove or disprove the conclusion.

18. FACTUAL STATEMENTS:
    1) Gear X rotates in a clockwise direction if Switch C is in the OFF position.
    2) Gear X will rotate in a counter-clockwise direction if Switch C is ON.
    3) If Gear X is rotating in a clockwise direction, then Gear Y will not be rotating at all.
    4) Switch C is OFF.

    CONCLUSION: Gear Y is rotating.

    A. The conclusion is proved by Statements 1-4;
    B. The conclusion is disproved by Statements 1-4;
    C. The facts are not sufficient to prove or disprove the conclusion.

18._____

7 (#1)

19. **FACTUAL STATEMENTS:**
    1) Mark is older than Jim but younger than Dan.
    2) Fern is older than Mark but younger than Silas.
    3) Dan is younger than Silas but older than Edward.
    4) Edward is older than Mark but younger than Fern.

    CONCLUSION: Dan is older than Fern.

    A. The conclusion is proved by Statements 1-4;
    B. The conclusion is disproved by Statements 1-4;
    C. The facts are not sufficient to prove or disprove the conclusion.

20. **FACTUAL STATEMENTS:**
    1) Each of Fred's three sofa cushions lies on top of four lost coins.
    2) The cushion on the right covers two pennies and two dimes.
    3) The middle cushion covers two dimes and two quarters.
    4) The cushion on the left covers two nickels and two quarters.

    CONCLUSION: To be guaranteed of retrieving at least one coin of each denomination, and without looking at any of the coins, Frank must take three coins each from under the cushions on the right and the left.

    A. The conclusion is proved by Statements 1-4;
    B. The conclusion is disproved by Statements 1-4;
    C. The facts are not sufficient to prove or disprove the conclusion.

21. **FACTUAL STATEMENTS:**
    1) The door to the hammer mill chamber is locked if light 6 is red.
    2) The door to the hammer mill chamber is locked only when the mill is operating.
    3) If the mill is not operating, light 6 is blue.
    4) The door to the hammer mill chamber is locked.

    CONCLUSION: The mill is in operation.

    A. The conclusion is proved by Statements 1-4;
    B. The conclusion is disproved by Statements 1-4;
    C. The facts are not sufficient to prove or disprove the conclusion.

22. **FACTUAL STATEMENTS:**
    1) In a five-story office building, where each story is occupied by a single professional, Dr. Kane's office is above Dr. Assad's.
    2) Dr. Johnson's office is between Dr. Kane's and Dr. Conlon's.
    3) Dr. Steen's office is between Dr. Conlon's and Dr. Assad's.
    4) Dr. Johnson is on the fourth story.

    CONCLUSION: Dr. Steen occupies the second story.

8 (#1)

    A. The conclusion is proved by Statements 1-4;
    B. The conclusion is disproved by Statements 1-4;
    C. The facts are not sufficient to prove or disprove the conclusion.

23. FACTUAL STATEMENTS: 23.____
    1) On Saturday, farmers Hank, Earl, Roy, and Cletus plowed a total of 520 acres.
    2) Hank plowed twice as many acres as Roy.
    3) Roy plowed half as much as the farmer who plowed the most.
    4) Cletus plowed 160 acres.

    CONCLUSION: Hank plowed 200 acres.
        A. The conclusion is proved by Statements 1-4;
        B. The conclusion is disproved by Statements 1-4;
        C. The facts are not sufficient to prove or disprove the conclusion.

24. FACTUAL STATEMENTS: 24.____
    1) Four travelers – Tina, Jodie, Alex, and Oscar – each traveled to a different island – Aruba, Jamaica, Nevis, and Barbados – but not necessarily respectively.
    2) Tina did not travel as far to Jamaica as Jodie traveled to her island.
    3) Oscar traveled twice as far as Alex, who traveled the same distance as the traveler who went to Aruba.
    4) Oscar went to Barbados.

    CONCLUSION: Oscar traveled the farthest.

        A. The conclusion is proved by Statements 1-4;
        B. The conclusion is disproved by Statements 1-4;
        C. The facts are not sufficient to prove or disprove the conclusion.

25. FACTUAL STATEMENT: 25.____
    1) In the natural history museum, every Native American display that contains pottery also contains beadwork.
    2) Some of the displays containing lodge replicas also contain beadwork.
    3) The display on the Choctaw, a Native American tribe, contains pottery.
    4) The display on the Modoc, a Native American tribe, contains only two of these items.

CONCLUSION: If the Modoc display contains pottery, it does not contain lodge replicas.

    A. The conclusion is proved by Statements 1-4;
    B. The conclusion is disproved by Statements 1-4;
    C. The facts are not sufficient to prove or disprove the conclusion.

KEY (CORRECT ANSWERS)

1.	A	11.	B
2.	B	12.	C
3.	A	13.	B
4.	A	14.	D
5.	C	15.	E
6.	B	16.	E
7.	B	17.	A
8.	B	18.	B
9.	A	19.	C
10.	B	20.	A
21.	A		
22.	A		
23.	C		
24.	A		
25.	A		

TEST 2

DIRECTIONS: Each question or incomplete statement is followed by several suggested answers or completions. Select the one that BEST answers the question or completes the statement. *PRINT THE LETTER OF THE CORRECT ANSWER IN THE SPACE AT THE RIGHT.*

Questions 1-9.

DIRECTIONS: In Questions 1 through 9, you will read a set of facts and a conclusion drawn from them. The conclusion may be valid or invalid, based on the facts. It is your task to determine the validity of the conclusion.
For each question, select the letter before the statement that BEST expresses the relationship between the given facts and the conclusion that has been drawn from them. Your choices are:
   A. The facts prove the conclusion.
   B. The facts disprove the conclusion; or
   C. The facts neither prove nor disprove the conclusion.

1. FACTS: If the maximum allowable income for Medicaid recipients is increased, the number of Medicaid recipients will increase. If the number of Medicaid recipients increases, more funds must be allocated to the Medicaid program, which will require a tax increase. Taxes cannot be approved without the approval of the legislature. The legislature probably will not approve a tax increase.

   CONCLUSION: The maximum allowable income for Medicaid recipients will increase.

   A. The facts prove the conclusion.
   B. The facts disprove the conclusion; or
   C. The facts neither prove nor disprove the conclusion.

2. FACTS: All the dentists on the baseball team are short. Everyone in the dugout is a dentist, but not everyone in the dugout is short. The baseball team is not made up of people of any particular profession.

   CONCLUSION: Some people who are not dentists are in the dugout.

   A. The facts prove the conclusion.
   B. The facts disprove the conclusion; or
   C. The facts neither prove nor disprove the conclusion.

3. FACTS: A taxi company's fleet is divided into two fleets. Fleet One contains cabs A, B, C, and D. Fleet Two contains E, F, G, and H. Each cab is either yellow or green. Five of the cabs are yellow. Cabs A and E are not both yellow. Either Cab C or F, or both, are not yellow. Cabs B and H are either both yellow or both green.

   CONCLUSION: Cab H is green.

A. The facts prove the conclusion.
B. The facts disprove the conclusion; or
C. The facts neither prove nor disprove the conclusion.

4. FACTS: Most people in the skydiving club are not afraid of heights. Everyone in the skydiving club makes three parachute jumps a month.

    CONCLUSION: At least one person who is afraid of heights makes three parachute jumps a month.

    A. The facts prove the conclusion.
    B. The facts disprove the conclusion; or
    C. The facts neither prove nor disprove the conclusion.

    4._____

5. FACTS: If the Board approves the new rule, the agency will move to a new location immediately. If the agency moves, five new supervisors will be immediately appointed. The Board has approved the new proposal.

    CONCLUSION: No new supervisors were appointed.

    A. The facts prove the conclusion.
    B. The facts disprove the conclusion; or
    C. The facts neither prove nor disprove the conclusion.

    5._____

6. FACTS: All the workers at the supermarket chew gum when they sack groceries. Sometimes Lance, a supermarket worker, doesn't chew gum at all when he works. Another supermarket worker, Jenny, chews gum the whole time she is at work.

    CONCLUSION: Jenny always sacks groceries when she is at work.

    6._____

7. FACTS: Lake Lottawatta is bigger than Lake Tacomi. Lake Tacomi and Lake Ottawa are exactly the same size. All lakes in Montana are bigger than Lake Ottawa.

    CONCLUSION: Lake Lottawatta is in Montana.

    A. The facts prove the conclusion.
    B. The facts disprove the conclusion; or
    C. The facts neither prove nor disprove the conclusion.

    7._____

8. FACTS: Two men, Cox and Taylor, are playing poker at a table. Taylor has a pair of aces in his hand. One man is smoking a cigar. One of them has no pairs in his hand and is wearing an eye patch. The man wearing the eye patch is smoking a cigar. One man is bald.

    CONCLUSION: Cox is smoking a cigar.

    8._____

A. The facts prove the conclusion.
B. The facts disprove the conclusion; or
C. The facts neither prove nor disprove the conclusion.

9. FACTS: All Kwakiutls are Wakashan Indians. All Wakashan Indians originated on Vancouver Island. The Nootka also originated on Vancouver Island.

   CONCLUSION: Kwakiutls originated on Vancouver Island.

   A. The facts prove the conclusion.
   B. The facts disprove the conclusion; or
   C. The facts neither prove nor disprove the conclusion.

9.____

Questions 10-17.

DIRECTIONS: Questions 10 through 17 are based on the following reading passage. It is not your knowledge of the particular topic that is being tested, but your ability to reason based on what you have read. The passage is likely to detail several proposed courses of action and factors affecting these proposals. The reading passage is followed by a conclusion or outcome based on the facts in the passage, or a description of a decision taken regarding the situation. The conclusion is followed by a number of statements that have a possible connection to the conclusion. For each statement, you are to determine whether:
A. The statement proves the conclusion.
B. The statement supports the conclusion but does not prove it.
C. The statement disproves the conclusion.
D. The statement weakens the conclusion but does not disprove it.
E. The statement has no relevance to the conclusion.

Remember that the conclusion after the passage is to be accepted as the outcome of what actually happened, and that you are being asked to evaluate the impact each statement would have had on the conclusion.

PASSAGE

The World Wide Web portal and search engine, HipBot, is considering becoming a subscription-only service, locking out nonsubscribers from the content on its web site. HipBot currently relies solely on advertising revenues.

HipBot's content director says that by taking in an annual fee from each customer, the company can both increase profits and provide premium content that no other portal can match.

The marketing director disagrees, saying that there is no guarantee that anyone who now visits the web site for free will agree to pay for the privilege of visiting it again. Most will probably simply use the other major portals. Also, HipBot's advertising clients will not be happy when they learn that the site will be viewed by a more limited number of people.

4 (#2)

CONCLUSION: In January of 2016, the CEO of HipBot decides to keep the portal open to all web users, with some limited "premium content" available to subscribers who don't mind paying a little extra to access it. The company will aim to maintain, or perhaps increase, its advertising revenue.

10. In an independent marketing survey, 62% of respondents said they "strongly agree" with the following statement: "I almost never pay attention to advertisements that appear on the World Wide Web."
    A. The statement proves the conclusion.
    B. The statement supports the conclusion but does not prove it.
    C. The statement disproves the conclusion.
    D. The statement weakens the conclusion but does not disprove it.
    E. The statement has no relevance to the conclusion.

10.____

11. When it learns about the subscription-only debate going on at HipBot, Wernham Hogg Entertainment, one of HipBot's most reliable clients, says it will withdraw its ads and place them on a free web portal if HipBot decides to limit its content to subscribers. Wernham Hogg pays HipBot about $6 million annually – about 12% of HipBot's gross revenues – to run its ads online.
    A. The statement proves the conclusion.
    B. The statement supports the conclusion but does not prove it.
    C. The statement disproves the conclusion.
    D. The statement weakens the conclusion but does not disprove it.
    E. The statement has no relevance to the conclusion.

11.____

12. At the end of the second quarter of FY 2016, after continued stagnant profits, the CEO of HipBot assembles a blue ribbon commission to gather and analyze data on the costs, benefits, and feasibility of adding a limited amount of "premium" content to the HipBot portal.
    A. The statement proves the conclusion.
    B. The statement supports the conclusion but does not prove it.
    C. The statement disproves the conclusion.
    D. The statement weakens the conclusion but does not disprove it.
    E. The statement has no relevance to the conclusion.

12.____

13. In the following fiscal year, Wernham Hogg Entertainment, satisfied with the "hit counts" on HipBot's free web site, spends another $1 million on advertisements that will appear on web pages that are available to HipBot's "premium subscribers.
    A. The statement proves the conclusion.
    B. The statement supports the conclusion but does not prove it.
    C. The statement disproves the conclusion.
    D. The statement weakens the conclusion but does not disprove it.
    E. The statement has no relevance to the conclusion.

13.____

14. HipBot's information technology director reports that the engineers in his department have come up with a feature that will search not only individual web pages, but tie into other web-based search engines, as well, and then comb through all these results to find those most relevant to the user's search.

14.____

A. The statement proves the conclusion.
B. The statement supports the conclusion but does not prove it.
C. The statement disproves the conclusion.
D. The statement weakens the conclusion but does not disprove it.
E. The statement has no relevance to the conclusion.

15. In an independent marketing survey, 79% of respondents said they "strongly agree" with the following statement: "Many web sites are so dominated by advertisements these days that it is increasingly frustrating to find the content I want to read or see."
    A. The statement proves the conclusion.
    B. The statement supports the conclusion but does not prove it.
    C. The statement disproves the conclusion.
    D. The statement weakens the conclusion but does not disprove it.
    E. The statement has no relevance to the conclusion.

15.____

16. After three years of studies at the federal level, the Department of Commerce releases a report suggesting that, in general, the only private "subscriber-only" web sites that do well financially are those with a very specialized user population.
    A. The statement proves the conclusion.
    B. The statement supports the conclusion but does not prove it.
    C. The statement disproves the conclusion.
    D. The statement weakens the conclusion but does not disprove it.
    E. The statement has no relevance to the conclusion.

16.____

17. HipBot's own marketing research indicates that the introduction of premium content has the potential to attract new users to the HipBot portal.
    A. The statement proves the conclusion.
    B. The statement supports the conclusion but does not prove it.
    C. The statement disproves the conclusion.
    D. The statement weakens the conclusion but does not disprove it.
    E. The statement has no relevance to the conclusion.

17.____

Questions 18-25.

DIRECTIONS: Questions 18 through 25 each provide four factual statements and a conclusion based on these statements. After reading the entire question, you will decide whether:
  A. The conclusion is proved by Statements 1-4;
  B. The conclusion is disproved by Statements 1-4;
  C. The facts are not sufficient to prove or disprove the conclusion.

18. FACTUAL STATEMENTS:
    1) If the alarm goes off, Sam will wake up.
    2) If Tandy wakes up before 4:00, Linda will leave the bedroom and sleep on the couch.
    3) If Linda leaves the bedroom, she'll check the alarm to make sure it is working.
    4) The alarm goes off.

    CONCLUSION: Tandy woke up before 4:00.

    A. The conclusion is proved by Statements 1-4;
    B. The conclusion is disproved by Statements 1-4;
    C. The facts are not sufficient to prove or disprove the conclusion.

19. FACTUAL STATEMENTS:
    1) Four brothers are named Earl, John, Gary, and Pete.
    2) Earl and Pete are unmarried.
    3) John is shorter than the youngest of the four.
    4) The oldest brother is married, and is also the tallest.

    CONCLUSION: Pete is the youngest brother.

    A. The conclusion is proved by Statements 1-4;
    B. The conclusion is disproved by Statements 1-4;
    C. The facts are not sufficient to prove or disprove the conclusion.

20. FACTUAL STATEMENTS:
    1) Automobile engines are cooled either by air or by liquid.
    2) If the engine is small and simple enough, air from a belt-driven fan will cool it sufficiently.
    3) Most newer automobile engines are too complicated to be air-cooled.
    4) Air-cooled engines are cheaper and easier to build then liquid-cooled engines.

    CONCLUSION: Most newer automobile engines use liquid coolant.

    A. The conclusion is proved by Statements 1-4;
    B. The conclusion is disproved by Statements 1-4;
    C. The facts are not sufficient to prove or disprove the conclusion.

21. FACTUAL STATEMENTS:
    1) Erica will only file a lawsuit if she is injured while parasailing.
    2) If Rick orders Trip to run a rope test, Trip will check the rigging.
    3) If the rigging does not malfunction, Erica will not be injured.
    4) Rick orders Trip to run a rope test.

CONCLUSION: Erica does not file a lawsuit.

   A. The conclusion is proved by Statements 1-4;
   B. The conclusion is disproved by Statements 1-4;
   C. The facts are not sufficient to prove or disprove the conclusion.

22. FACTUAL STATEMENTS:
   1) On Maple Street, which is four blocks long, Bill's shop is two blocks east of Ken's shop.
   2) Ken's shop is one block west of the only shop on Maple Street with an awning.
   3) Erma's shop is one block west of the easternmost block.
   4) Bill's shop is on the easternmost block.

   CONCLUSION: Bill's shop has an awning.

   A. The conclusion is proved by Statements 1-4;
   B. The conclusion is disproved by Statements 1-4;
   C. The facts are not sufficient to prove or disprove the conclusion.

23. FACTUAL STATEMENTS:
   1) Gear X rotates in a clockwise direction if Switch C is in the OFF position.
   2) Gear X will rotate in a counter-clockwise direction if Switch C is ON.
   3) If Gear X is rotating in a clockwise direction, then Gear Y will not be rotating at all.
   4) Gear Y is rotating.

   CONCLUSION: Gear X is rotating in a counter-clockwise direction.

   A. The conclusion is proved by Statements 1-4;
   B. The conclusion is disproved by Statements 1-4;
   C. The facts are not sufficient to prove or disprove the conclusion.

24. FACTUAL STATEMENTS:
   1) The Republic of Garbanzo's currency system has four basic denominations: the pastor, the noble, the donner, and the rojo.
   2) A pastor is worth 2 nobles.
   3) 2 donners can be exchanged for a rojo.
   4) 3 pastors are equal in value to 2 donners.

   CONCLUSION: The rojo is most valuable.

   A. The conclusion is proved by Statements 1-4;
   B. The conclusion is disproved by Statements 1-4;
   C. The facts are not sufficient to prove or disprove the conclusion.

25. FACTUAL STATEMENTS:
   1) At Prickett's Nursery, the only citrus trees left are either Meyer lemons or Valencia oranges, and every citrus tree left is either a dwarf or a semidwarf.
   2) Half of the semidwarf trees are Meyer lemons.
   3) There are more semidwarf trees left than dwarf trees.
   4) A quarter of the dwarf trees are Valencia oranges.

   CONCLUSION: There are more Valencia oranges left at Prickett's Nursery than Meyer lemons.

   A. The conclusion is proved by Statements 1-4;
   B. The conclusion is disproved by Statements 1-4;
   C. The facts are not sufficient to prove or disprove the conclusion.

25.____

KEY (CORRECT ANSWERS)

1. C
2. B
3. B
4. A
5. B

6. C
7. C
8. A
9. A
10. E

11. B
12. C
13. A
14. E
15. D

16. B
17. B
18. C
19. C
20. A

21. C
22. B
23. C
24. A
25. B

READING COMPREHENSION
UNDERSTANDING AND INTERPRETING WRITTEN MATERIAL

EXAMINATION SECTION
TEST 1

DIRECTIONS: Each question or incomplete statement is followed bpy several suggested answers or completions. Select the one that BEST answers the question or completes the statement. *PRINT THE LETTER OF THE CORRECT ANSWER IN THE SPACE AT THE RIGHT.*

Questions 1-4.

DIRECTIONS: Questions 1 through 4 are to be answered on the basis of the following passage.

It should be emphasized that one goal of law enforcement is the reduction of stress between one population group and another. When no stress exists between populations, law enforcement can deal with other tensions or simply perform traditional police functions. However, when stress between populations does exist, law enforcement, in its efforts to prevent disruptive behavior, becomes committed to reducing that stress (if for no other reason than its responsibility to maintain an orderly environment). The type of stress to be reduced, unlike the tension stemming from social change, is stress generated through intergroup and interracial friction. Of course, all sources of tension are inextricably interrelated, but friction between different populations in the community is of immediate concern to law enforcement.

1. The above passage emphasizes that, during times of stress between groups in the community, it is necessary for the police to attempt to

    A. continue their traditional duties
    B. eliminate tension resulting from social change
    C. reduce intergroup stress
    D. punish disruptive behavior

    1.____

2. Based on the above passage, police concern with tension among groups in a community is MOST likely to stem primarily from their desire to

    A. establish racial justice
    B. prevent violence
    C. protect property
    D. unite the diverse groups

    2.____

3. According to the above passage, enforcers of the law are responsible for

    A. analyzing consequences of population-group hostility
    B. assisting social work activities
    C. creating order in the environment
    D. explaining group behavior

    3.____

4. The factor which produces the tension accompanying social change is

   A. a disorderly environment
   B. disruptive behavior
   C. inter-community hostility
   D. not discussed in the above passage

Questions 5-7.

DIRECTIONS: Questions 5 through 7 are to be answered SOLELY on the basis of the following paragraphs.

Perhaps the most difficult administrative problem of the police records unit is the maintenance of cooperative relationships with the operating units in the department. Unless these relationships are completely accepted by the operating units, some records activities will result in friction. The records system is a tool of the chief administrative officer and the various supervising officers in managing personnel, police operations, and procedures. However, the records unit must constantly check on the records activities of all members of the department if the records system is to serve as a really effective tool for these supervisory officers.

The first step in avoiding conflict between the records and the operating units is to develop definite policies and regulations governing the records system. These regulations should be prepared jointly by the head of the records unit and the heads of the operating units under the leadership of the chief administrative officer of the department. Once the records policies and regulations have been agreed upon, the task is to secure conformity. Theoretically, if a patrolman fails to prepare a report of an investigation, his commanding officer should be notified by the records unit and he, in turn, should take appropriate measures to secure the report. Practically, this line of command must be cut across in the case of such routine matters, or the commanding officer will spend time in keeping the records system going that should be devoted to the other police duties which comprise the major work of the department. However, if the patrolman is persistently negligent, or if a new policy or procedure is being initiated, the records unit must deal through the commanding officer.

5. According to the above passage, the one of the following situations in which the records unit would MOST likely contact a commanding officer of an operating unit is when

   A. a patrolman has expressed disagreement with a records unit policy and suggests a modification of the policy
   B. an important report, which involves more than one operating unit, has been carelessly prepared by a patrolman
   C. the commanding officer of the operating unit devotes little time to police duties which comprise the major work of the department
   D. the records unit has received orders from the chief administrative officer to institute several changes in previous records procedures

6. According to the above paragraph, obtaining agreement as to definite policies, and regulations governing the records system

   A. guarantees the avoidance of conflict between the records and operating divisions
   B. is of lesser importance than the maintenance of cooperative relationships thereafter

C. should precede any active records division efforts to gain compliance with such policies and regulations
D. should be preceded by an evaluation of the extent to which supervisory officers consider the system an effective management tool

7. According to the above passage, conflict between the records division and the operating divisions is MOST likely to result when the

   A. chief administrative officer denies to the records division the authority to check on the records activities of all members of the department
   B. operating divisions are not convinced that their work contacts with the records division are useful and desirable
   C. records division voluntarily attempts to establish productive relationships with operating divisions
   D. operating divisions understand the specific nature i of records division duties

Questions 8-10.

DIRECTIONS: Questions 8 through 10 are to be answered SOLELY on the basis of the following paragraph.

Early in the development of police service, legislators granted powers and authority to policemen beyond their inherent rights as citizens in order that they would be able to act effectively in the discharge of their duties. The law makers also recognized the fact that unless policemen were excused from complete obedience to certain laws and regulations, they would be seriously encumbered in the effective discharge of their duties. The exemptions were specifically provided for by legislative action because of the danger of abuse of power involved in granting blanket privileges and powers. The public, however, has not been so discriminating and has gone well beyond the law in excusing policemen from full obedience to regulatory measures. The liberal interpretation that the public has placed upon the right of police officers to disobey the law has been motivated in part by public confidence in law enforcement and in part by a sincere desire of the public to assist the police in every way in the performance of their duties. Further, the average citizen is not interested in the technicalities of law enforcement nor is he aware of the legal limitations that are placed upon the authority of policemen. It is a regrettable fact that many policemen assume so-called rights of law that either do not exist or that are subject to well-defined legal limitations, because the public generally is unaware of the limitations placed by law upon policemen.

8. According to the above paragraph, the one of the following statements which BEST explains the reason for granting special legal powers to policemen is that such powers are granted

   A. because the exercise of their inherent rights by citizens frequently conflicted with efficient law enforcement
   B. because the public has not been sufficiently vigilant in objecting to blanket grants of power
   C. in order to excuse policemen from full obedience to laws and regulations which they are unable to enforce
   D. in order to remove certain handicaps experienced by policemen in law enforcement operations

9. According to the above paragraph, specific legislative exemptions for policemen from complete obedience to certain laws and regulations

   A. are based largely on so-called rights of law that either do not exist or are misinterpreted by the public
   B. have not been abused by the police even though most individual policemen ignore proper legal limitations
   C. have not provided a fully effective limitation on the exercise of unwarranted police authority
   D. have been misunderstood by the police and the public partly because they are based on unduly technical laws

10. According to the above paragraph, the one of the following statements which BEST explains the liberal attitude of the public toward the special powers of policemen is that the public

    A. believes that the police are justified in disregarding the technicalities of law enforcement and also wants to assist the police in the performance of their duties
    B. feels that the laws restricting police authority are overly strict and also believes that the police are performing their duties in a proper manner
    C. is not aware of the legal restrictions on police authority and also believes that the police are performing their duties in a proper manner
    D. wants to assist the police in the performance of their duties and also feels that the laws on police authority are sufficiently restrictive

Questions 11-12.

DIRECTIONS: Questions 11 and 12 are to be answered SOLELY on the basis of the following paragraph.

The personal conduct of each member of the department is the primary factor in promoting desirable police-community relations. Tact, patience, and courtesy shall be strictly observed under all circumstances. A favorable public attitude toward the police must be earned; it is influenced by the personal conduct and attitude of each member of the force; by his personal integrity and courteous manner; by his respect for due process of law; by his devotion to the principles of justice, fairness, and impartiality.

11. According to the above paragraph, what is the BEST action an officer can take in dealing with people in a neighborhood?

    A. Assist neighborhood residents by doing favors for them
    B. Give special attention to the community leaders in order to be able to control them effectively
    C. Behave in an appropriate manner and give all community members the same just treatment
    D. Prepare a plan detailing what he, the officer, wants to do for the community and submit it for approval

12. As used in the above paragraph, the word impartiality means MOST NEARLY

    A. observant
    B. unbiased
    C. righteousness
    D. honesty

Questions 13-16.

DIRECTIONS: Questions 13 through 16 are to be answered on the basis of the information given in the following passage.

The public often believes that the main job of a uniformed officer is to enforce laws by simply arresting people. In reality, however, many of the situations that an officer deals with do not call for the use of his arrest power. In the first place, an officer spends much of his time preventing crimes from happening, by spotting potential violations or suspicious behavior and taking action to prevent illegal acts. In the second place, many of the situations in which officers are called on for assistance involve elements like personal arguments, husband-wife quarrels, noisy juveniles, or mentally disturbed persons. The majority of these problems do not result in arrests and convictions, and often they do not even involve illegal behavior. In the third place, even in situations where there seems to be good reason to make an arrest, an officer may have to exercise very good judgment. There are times when making an arrest too soon could touch off a riot, or could result in the detention of a minor offender while major offenders escaped, or could cut short the gathering of necessary on-the-scene evidence.

13. The above passage IMPLIES that most citizens

    A. will start to riot if they see an arrest being made
    B. appreciate the work that law enforcement officers do
    C. do not realize that making arrests is only a small part of law enforcement
    D. never call for assistance unless they are involved in a personal argument or a husband-wife quarrel

14. According to the above passage, one way in which law enforcement officers can prevent crimes for happening is by

    A. arresting suspicious characters
    B. letting minor offenders go free
    C. taking action on potential violations
    D. refusing to get involved in husband-wife fights

15. According to the above passage, which of the following statements is NOT true of situations involving mentally disturbed persons?

    A. It is a waste of time to call on law enforcement officers for assistance in such situations.
    B. Such situations may not involve illegal behavior.
    C. Such situations often do not result in arrests.
    D. Citizens often turn to law enforcement officers for help in such situations.

16. The last sentence in the passage mentions *detention of minor offenders.*
    Of the following, which BEST explains the meaning of the word *detention* as used here?

    A. Sentencing someone
    B. Indicting someone
    C. Calling someone before a grand jury
    D. Arresting someone

Questions 17-18.

DIRECTIONS: Questions 17 and 18 are to be answered SOLELY on the basis of the following paragraph.

In order that the police officer can function in a role that is outside the area of his personal prejudices, it is necessary to develop in him a real sense of professionalism. Policing is increasingly recognized as requiring a high degree of technical knowledge and skill. This, however, is only one mark of a profession. Another is the increasing emphasis upon public duty and service to the community. The time has long passed in enlightened police circles when a man became an officer of the law by merely donning a uniform and flashing a star. Training, dedication, and understanding are the cornerstones of modern police science. The police officer must become increasingly aware of the role he plays as a symbol of society's authority - aware that only by examining the relation of his personal sentiments and feelings to his public duties can he achieve true impartiality and neutrality. This is an educational problem in its own right, and it is equal in importance to the acquisition of new information as to the technicalities of crime detection.

17. According to the above paragraph,

    A. the achievement of true neutrality in law enforcement is the most important problem facing the police officer
    B. the emphasis on community service is one of the characteristics of a profession that is being increasingly stressed as a part of police work
    C. the emphasis on the technicalities of crime detection is improper if it detracts from the need of the police to be a symbol of society's authority
    D. technical training is an area of police work which has always received recognition as an important aspect of police science

18. According to the above paragraph,

    A. a consideration of the distinguishing characteristics of other professions leads to the conclusion that police work is not a profession
    B. concern for impartiality in law enforcement has always characterized police administration
    C. the absence of personal prejudice in a police officer determines his effectiveness
    D. the police officer should aim to achieve impartiality by examining his personal sentiments and prejudices, since he serves as a symbol of society's authority

Questions 19-22.

DIRECTIONS: Questions 19 through 22 are to be answered on the basis of the following paragraph.

During actual pursuit of a traffic offender and particularly in speed cases when the operator of the police vehicle is maneuvering for clocking, there is a need for haste so that the clocking may be applied when the motorist is traveling in violation of the speed laws. However, necessary haste cannot include rashness. The pursuit, for whatever purpose, must not be at the expense of the safety of other users of the road. When changing lanes to get ahead, the police operator must do it safely or not at all. Giving proper and clear signals as to his intentions is a must but should not be construed as a guarantee of completing the maneuver safely. He must use good judgment in determining whether his S pass can be made safely. If there is a possibility that the motorist to be passed would be forced to apply his brakes to avoid a collision, the passing should be delayed. Instead, he should be notified by hand signal of the police vehicle operator's intention to pass and directed to reduce speed so that the police vehicle can be driven past safely. In other than emergencies, sudden stops should be avoided. In a situation where law enforcement needs require a sudden reduction in speed, consideration must be given to the vehicles behind to preclude rear-end collisions. A gradual reduction in speed, coupled with a sufficient warning to convey the intention to stop or turn is the preferential course of action. Similarly, if at all possible, the police operator should avoid turning at locations that are clearly unfavorable for turning, such as through safety zones or between stanchions placed to prohibit passage, since such maneuvers increase the probability of an accident.

19. The one of the following which MOST adequately describes the central theme of the paragraph is the _____ motorized traffic offenders.

    A. essentiality of maintaining maximum speed during the pursuit of
    B. danger of passing intervening vehicles while pursuing
    C. precautions to take in the pursuit of
    D. methods of attaining greater speed while pursuing

20. According to the above paragraph, when the operator of a police vehicle is pursuing an offender in the same lane, and approaches another vehicle which is between him and the offender's vehicle, it would be MOST correct to state that the operator of the police vehicle

    A. may attempt to by-pass the vehicle between him and the offender with complete safety so long as he has given proper and clear automatic and hand signals to its operator
    B. may attempt to by-pass the vehicle between him and the offender even if it would be necessary for him to make an S pass to do so
    C. must not attempt to by-pass the vehicle between him and the offender until he has directed its operator to reduce speed
    D. must not attempt to by-pass the vehicle between him and the offender unless he can do so safely without leaving the lane

21. According to the above paragraph, when the operator of a police vehicle notices a motorist driving along and suspects that the motorist may have just violated some traffic law, he MAY

    A. not exceed the posted speed limit except when he is attempting to get into position to clock the offender's speed
    B. travel at whatever speed he deems necessary in order to catch up with and clock the speeding suspect but only as long as both remain in the same lane and the lane remains clear
    C. not exceed the posted speed limit unless he feels certain that the offender has exceeded or can be reasonably expected to exceed the posted speed limit
    D. exceed the posted speed limit in order to apprehend the violator but must never do so if there is any possibility of danger to anyone else using the road

22. A police vehicle is in pursuit of a motorized traffic offender who is attempting to evade capture by alternating between weaving in and out of slower-moving traffic, making sudden stops, and going through safety zones or stanchions placed to prohibit passage.
According to the above paragraph, the operator in pursuit should GENERALLY

   A. follow right behind the offender through all these maneuvers but keep alert for sudden changes in tactics
   B. avoid engaging in such of these maneuvers as he can without increasing the distance between him and the offender
   C. refrain from engaging in driving maneuvers similar to the offender's without duly considering the inherent dangers
   D. anticipate the offender's actions and take the steps necessary to cut him off when he emerges from safety zones

23. Citizens understand in a vague and general way that their civil liberties must be respected by the police, but they do not appreciate that this protection necessarily extends both to those who consider themselves to be law observers and to those who are law violators.
The MOST important deduction to be made from this by a police officer is that

   A. public opinion is uninformed and hence may be disregarded
   B. the basis is laid for serious misunderstanding between the police and the public
   C. the public attitude toward severe arrest procedures depends on the personal character of the arrestee and not the crime charged
   D. the public favors a policy of selective law enforcement

Questions 24-25.

DIRECTIONS: Questions 24 and 25 are to be answered on the basis of the following paragraph.

The most significant improvements in personnel selection procedures can be expected from a program designed to obtain more precise statements of the requirements for a particular position and from the development of procedures that will make it possible to select not just those applicants who are generally best, but those whose abilities and personal characteristics provide the closest fit to the specific job requirement.

24. According to the above paragraph, better personnel selection procedures will result from

   A. simplification of job description
   B. better recruiting procedures
   C. obtaining more detailed experience data from applicants
   D. detailed statements of training and skills required for positions

25. According to the above paragraph, the MOST desirable applicant for a position is

   A. the one who has all the necessary training, even though he lacks the necessary personal characteristics
   B. the one whose abilities and personal characteristics are of the highest order
   C. generally not the same as the best qualified person
   D. the one whose qualifications are most nearly the same as the job requirement

KEY (CORRECT ANSWERS)

1.	C	11.	C
2.	B	12.	B
3.	C	13.	C
4.	D	14.	C
5.	D	15.	A
6.	C	16.	D
7.	B	17.	B
8.	D	18.	D
9.	C	19.	C
10.	C	20.	B

21. D
22. C
23. B
24. D
25. D

TEST 2

DIRECTIONS: Each question or incomplete statement is followed by several suggested answers or completions. Select the one that BEST answers the question or completes the statement. *PRINT THE LETTER OF THE CORRECT ANSWER IN THE SPACE AT THE RIGHT.*

Questions 1-3.

DIRECTIONS: Questions 1 through 3 are to be answered SOLELY on the basis of the following paragraph.

    Every organization needs a systematic method of checking its operation as a means to increase efficiency and promote economy. Many successful private firms have instituted a system of audits or internal inspections to accomplish these ends. Law enforcement organizations, which have an extremely important service to *sell,* should be no less zealous in developing efficiency and economy in their operations. Periodic, organized, and systematic inspections are one means of promoting the achievement of these objectives. The necessity of an organized inspection system is perhaps greatest in those law enforcement groups which have grown to such a size that the principal officer can no longer personally supervise or be cognizant of every action taken. Smooth and effective operation demands that the head of the organization have at hand some tool with which he can study and enforce general policies and procedures and also direct compliance with day-to-day orders, most of which are put into execution outside his sight and hearing. A good inspection system can serve as that tool.

1. The central thought of the above paragraph is that a system of inspections within a police department

   A. is unnecessary for a department in which the principal officer can personally supervise all official actions taken
   B. should be instituted at the first indication that there is any deterioration in job performance by the force
   C. should be decentralized and administered by first-line supervisory officers
   D. is an important aid to the police administrator in the accomplishment of law enforcement objectives

2. The MOST accurate of the following statements concerning the need for an organized inspection system in a law enforcement organization is:
   It is

   A. never needed in an organization of small size where the principal officer can give personal supervision
   B. most needed where the size of the organization prevents direct supervision by the principal officer
   C. more needed in law enforcement organizations than in private firms
   D. especially needed in an organization about to embark upon a needed expansion of services

3. According to the above paragraph, the head of the police organization utilizes the internal inspection system

   A. as a tool which must be constantly re-examined in the light of changing demands for police service
   B. as an administrative technique to increase efficiency and promote economy
   C. by personally visiting those areas of police operation which are outside his sight and hearing
   D. to augment the control of local commanders over detailed field operations

Questions 4-6.

DIRECTIONS: Questions 4 through 6 are to be answered SOLELY on the basis of the following paragraph.

Every officer in a department, from the chief of police to the new recruit, should participate if a human relations program is to be effective. The policies, programs, and examples which the chief initiates become the guide for action by all other officers. Through the command group, lieutenants and above in rank, the chief disseminates throughout the department his policies and ideas for application. It is that group which in essence holds control over a department. Implementation of a human relations program must always be through them, with their full support and understanding obtained. They are the link between the sergeants and the chief; they train and assist the sergeants in all operations and give up some of their authority so the sergeants may have freedom to act. The police sergeant is probably the key to success of any police human relations program, since it is his responsibility to develop a wholesome and loyal attitude in the policemen toward their job, themselves, and toward other officers in the department. Instilling of job satisfaction in the patrolmen becomes his responsibility. If changes are to be made in departmental practices or procedures, it is the sergeant's job to change the policemen's attitudes and to condition them for the change.

4. According to this paragraph, one of the responsibilities of a sergeant is to

   A. inform the command group of any changes in attitude on the part of the policemen
   B. inform the command group of needed changes in practices and procedures and inform the policemen of accomplishments and problems of the command group
   C. insist upon a demonstration of job satisfaction by the policemen
   D. prepare the policemen to accept any impending changes in departmental procedure

5. According to this paragraph, the MOST accurate of the following statements concerning a police human relations program is:

   A. Application of policies and ideas is less the responsibility of the sergeant than of the command group
   B. Newly appointed patrolmen should not participate in a human relations program until the sergeant has had an opportunity to change their attitudes
   C. The key to a successful human relations program is the patrolmen's acceptance of basic departmental procedures
   D. The human relations program can never be successful without being actively supported by the lieutenants

6. According to this paragraph, the command group

   A. assists the sergeant in the accomplishment of police objectives in the area of human relations
   B. delegates responsibility to the sergeant in this critical area of administration so that he has freedom to develop a more wholesome program
   C. initiates the programs and policies which reflect the general views of the chief
   D. should direct but not participate in a human relations program

Questions 7-9.

DIRECTIONS: Questions 7 through 9 are to be answered SOLELY on the basis of the following paragraph.

The sentiment of the community is not always favorable to procedures designed to accomplish the police purpose. Unfavorable public attitudes may make the immediate adoption of a superior procedure impractical. A necessary part of the task of achieving police objectives is the development of public attitudes favorable to their attainment. The police, therefore, must be organized to inform the public regarding the significance and consequences of failures in law enforcement and compliance, and also regarding police requirements and the results of failure to meet them. The police cannot progress ahead of public sentiment since there must be general acceptance by the people of controls that are applied by the police in order to completely accomplish the basic police objectives. The development of favorable public sentiment is a relatively long-range project, whereas organization requirements are immediate. The organizational structure, therefore, must be designed to conform somewhat to public attitudes. As public sentiment changes, modification of the structure may be desirable.

7. According to the above paragraph, modifications of the police organizational structure should

   A. be considered in instances where public sentiment has also changed
   B. be designed to anticipate major changes in public attitudes
   C. be regarded as a relatively long-range project
   D. follow closely any changes in public sentiment

8. According to the above paragraph, the development of favorable public attitudes towards the police is important because

   A. failures in law enforcement activity are thereby more likely to be quickly corrected
   B. the accomplishment of primary police purposes is largely dependent on such favorable attitudes
   C. the improvement of the conditions of work of the police are ultimately determined by the public
   D. no one will comply with police regulations without a favorable public attitude

9. According to the above paragraph, it would be MOST advisable that a decision to adopt a new police procedure

   A. be determined mainly by its crime deterring effect on the community
   B. not be made if any community objection has been expressed towards the procedure

C. be made only after favorable public attitudes have been developed in all community groups
D. be partly based on a consideration of its community acceptance

Questions 10-12.

DIRECTIONS: Questions 10 through 12 are to be answered SOLELY on the basis of the following paragraph.

All members of the police force must recognize that the people, through their representatives, hire and pay the police and that, as in any other employment, there must exist a proper employer-employee relationship. The police officer must understand that the essence of a correct police attitude is a willingness to serve, but at the same time he should distinguish between service and servility, and between courtesy and softness. He must be firm but also courteous, avoiding even an appearance of rudeness. He should develop a position that is friendly and unbiased, pleasant and sympathetic, in his relations with the general public, but firm and impersonal on occasions calling for regulation and control. A police officer should understand that his primary purpose is to prevent violations, not to arrest people. He should recognize the line of demarcation between a police function and passing judgment which is a court function. On the other side, a public that cooperates with the police, that supports them in their efforts and that observes laws and regulations may be said to have a desirable attitude.

10. In accordance with this paragraph, the PROPER attitude for a police officer to take is to

    A. be pleasant and sympathetic at all times
    B. be friendly, firm, and impartial
    C. be stern and severe in meting out justice to all
    D. avoid being rude, except in those cases where the public is uncooperative

11. Assume that an officer is assigned by his superior officer to a busy traffic intersection and is warned to be on the lookout for motorists who skip the light or who are speeding. According to this paragraph, it would be PROPER for the officer in this assignment to

    A. give a summons to every motorist whose car was crossing when the light changed
    B. hide behind a truck and wait for drivers who violate traffic laws
    C. select at random motorists who seem to be impatient and lecture them sternly on traffic safety
    D. stand on post in order to deter violations and give offenders a summons or a warning as required

12. According to this paragraph, a police officer must realize that the PRIMARY purpose of police work is to

    A. provide proper police service in a courteous manner
    B. decide whether those who violate the law should be punished
    C. arrest those who violate laws
    D. establish a proper employer-employee relationship

Questions 13-15.

DIRECTIONS: Questions 13 through 15 are to be answered SOLELY on the basis of the following paragraphs.

In cases of accident, it is most important for an officer to obtain the name, age, residence, occupation, and a full description of the person injured, names and addresses of witnesses. He shall also obtain a statement of the attendant circumstances. He shall carefully note contributory conditions, if any, such as broken pavement, excavation, lights not burning, snow and ice on the roadway, etc. He shall enter all the facts in his memorandum book and on Form 17 or Form 18, and promptly transmit the original of the form to his superior officer and the duplicate to headquarters.

An officer shall render reasonable assistance to sick or injured persons. If the circumstances appear to require the services of a physician, he shall summon a physician by telephoning the superior officer on duty and notifying him of the apparent nature of the illness or accident and the location where the physician will be required. He may summon other officers to assist if circumstances warrant.

In case of an accident or where a person is sick on city property, an officer shall obtain the information necessary to fill out card Form 18 and record this in his memorandum book and promptly telephone the facts to his superior officer. He shall deliver the original card at the expiration of his tour to his superior officer and transmit the duplicate to headquarters.

13. According to this passage, the MOST important consideration in any report on a case of accident or injury is to

    A. obtain all the facts
    B. telephone his superior officer at once
    C. obtain a statement of the attendant circumstances
    D. determine ownership of the property on which the accident occurred

14. According to this passage, in the case of an accident on city property, the officer should ALWAYS

    A. summon a physician before filling out any forms or making any entries in his memorandum book
    B. give his superior officer on duty a prompt report by telephone
    C. immediately bring the original of Form 18 to his superior officer on duty
    D. call at least one other officer to the scene to witness conditions

15. If the procedures stated in this passage were followed for all accidents in the city, an impartial survey of accidents occurring during any period of time in this city may be MOST easily made by

    A. asking a typical officer to show you his memorandum book
    B. having a superior officer investigate whether contributory conditions mentioned by witnesses actually exist
    C. checking all the records of all superior officers
    D. checking the duplicate card files at headquarters

Questions 16-18.

DIRECTIONS: Questions 16 through 18 are to be answered SOLELY on the basis of the following paragraph.

When the frequency of special situations that create extraordinary needs for police service is nearly continuous, as is often the case in a large city, a separate unit for each is desirable even though in some communities these needs are met by the force assigned to deal with the average need. Variations in the manpower needed to deal with special situations further complicate the problem. Special squads created to meet unusual needs are not likely to be adequate to deal with all situations. One unit must be used to supplement the other in some situations. Likewise, the force normally used to meet the average need must be used in some other situations to supplement the efforts of both. For example, the entire force is likely to be pressed into overtime duty when disaster strikes. The existence of special units, however, diminishes the frequency and extent of necessary requisitions of unspecialized manpower from their regular assignments. The special squads should also be used as a manpower reserve to fill vacancies in or absences from regular assignments when the regular services must be maintained exactly as before.

16. The one of the following situations which would MOST justify the creation of a separate unit, according to the above passage, is when

   A. the force assigned to deal with the average need, in small or large cities, is assigned continuously to handle all extraordinary needs for police service
   B. the frequency of the situations that create above average needs is somewhat in proportion to the size of the city
   C. the force assigned to deal with the average need has to give nearly continuous attention to above-average needs
   D. in a large city the separate unit can be used to supplement the force assigned to deal with the average need

16.____

17. When a special squad is unable to meet adequately one of the needs for police service which it was assigned to provide, it would be MOST correct, according to the above passage, to state that

   A. the force normally used to meet the average need should not be used unless some other special squad has first been assigned
   B. the force normally used to meet the average need as well as any other special squad should not both be used at the same time
   C. some other special unit should be used to supplement the special squad while attempting to avoid assigning the force normally used to meet the average need
   D. some other special unit should not be used unless it is likely that its own efforts can be supplemented by the special squad at some future time

17.____

18. The decision as to whether officers assigned to a special unit should be used to replace absent officers in a regular unit depends MAINLY on the

   A. extent to which unspecialized manpower must be requisitioned
   B. effect of the absences on the regular services which should not be even temporarily diminished

18.____

C. extent to which the services provided by the force normally assigned to the regular unit have been diminished by the absences
D. relative importance of maintaining the services of the special squad exactly as before

Questions 19-20.

DIRECTIONS: Questions 19 through 20 are to be answered SOLELY on the basis of the following paragraph.

The traditional characteristics of a police organization, which do not foster group-centered leadership, are being changed daily by progressive police administrators. These characteristics are authoritarian and result in a leader-centered style with all deter- mination of policy and procedure made by the leader. In the group-centered style, policies and procedures are a matter for group discussion and decision. The supposedly modern view is that the group-centered style is the most conducive to improving organizational effectiveness. By contrast, the traditional view regards the group-centered style as an idealistic notion of psychologists. It is questionable, however, that the situation determines the appropriate leadership style. In some circumstances, it will be leader-centered; in others, group-centered. Nevertheless, police supervisors will see more situations calling for a leadership style that, while flexible, is primarily group-centered. Thus, the supervisor in a police department must have a capacity not just to issue orders, but to engage in behavior involving organizational leadership which primarily emphasizes goals and work facilitation.

19. According to the above passage, there is reason to believe that with regard to the effectiveness of different types of leadership, the

    A. leader-centered type is better than the individual-centered type or the group-centered type
    B. leader-centered type is best in some situations and the group-centered type best in other situations
    C. group-centered type is better than the leader-centered type in all situations
    D. authoritarian type is least effective in democratic countries

20. According to the above passage, police administrators today are

    A. more likely than in the past to favor making decisions on the basis of discussions with subordinates
    B. likely in general to favor traditional patterns of leadership in their organizations
    C. more likely to be progressive than conservative
    D. practical and individualistic rather than idealistic in their approach to police problems

KEY (CORRECT ANSWERS)

1.	D	11.	D
2.	B	12.	A
3.	B	13.	A
4.	D	14.	B
5.	D	15.	D
6.	A	16.	C
7.	A	17.	C
8.	B	18.	B
9.	D	19.	B
10.	B	20.	A

READING COMPREHENSION
UNDERSTANDING AND INTERPRETING WRITTEN MATERIAL

EXAMINATION SECTION
TEST 1

DIRECTIONS: Each question or incomplete statement is followed by several suggested answers or completions. Select the one that BEST answers the question or completes the statement. *PRINT THE LETTER OF THE CORRECT ANSWER IN THE SPACE AT THE RIGHT.*

Questions 1-5.

DIRECTIONS: Questions 1 through 5 are to be answered on the basis of the following passage.

The laws with which criminal courts are concerned contain threats of punishment for infraction of specified rules. Consequently, the courts are organized primarily for implementation of the punitive societal reaction of crime. While the informal organization of most courts allows the judge to use discretion as to which guilty persons actually are to be punished, the threat of punishment for all guilty persons always is present. Also, in recent years a number of formal provisions for the use of non-punitive and treatment methods by the criminal courts have been made, but the threat of punishment remains, even for the recipients of the treatment and non-punitive measures. For example, it has become possible for courts to grant probation, which can be non-punitive, to some offenders, but the probationer is constantly under the threat of punishment, for, if he does not maintain the conditions of his probation, he may be imprisoned. As the treatment reaction to crime becomes more popular, the criminal courts may have as their sole function the determination of the guilt or innocence of the accused persons, leaving the problem of correcting criminals entirely to outsiders. Under such conditions, the organization of the court system, the duties and activities of court personnel, and the nature of the trial all would be decidedly different.

1. Which one of the following is the BEST description of the subject matter of the above passage?
   The

   A. value of non-punitive measures for criminals
   B. effect of punishment on guilty individuals
   C. punitive functions of the criminal courts
   D. success of probation as a deterrent of crime

2. It may be INFERRED from the above passage that the present traditional organization of the criminal court system is a result of

   A. the nature of the laws with which these courts are concerned
   B. a shift from non-punitive to punitive measures for correctional purposes
   C. an informal arrangement between court personnel and the government
   D. a formal decision made by court personnel to increase efficiency

3. All persons guilty of breaking certain specified rules, according to the above passage, are subject to the threat of

   A. treatment
   B. punishment
   C. probation
   D. retrial

4. According to the above passage, the decision whether or not to punish a guilty person is a function USUALLY performed by

   A. the jury
   B. the criminal code
   C. the judge
   D. corrections personnel

5. According to the above passage, which one of the following is a possible effect of an increase in the *treatment reactions to crime?*

   A. A decrease in the number of court personnel
   B. An increase in the number of criminal trials
   C. Less reliance on probation as a non-punitive treatment measure
   D. A decrease in the functions of the court following determination of guilt

Questions 6-8.

DIRECTIONS: Questions 6 through 8 are to be answered on the basis of the following passage.

    A glaring exception to the usual practice of the judicial trial as a means of conflict resolution is the utilization of administrative hearings. The growing tendency to create administrative bodies with rule-making and quasi-judicial powers has shattered many standard concepts. A comprehensive examination of the legal process cannot neglect these newer patterns.

    In the administrative process, the legislative, executive, and judicial functions are mixed together, and many functions, such as investigating, advocating, negotiating, testifying, rule making, and adjudicating, are carried out by the same agency. The reason for the breakdown of the separation-of-powers formula is not hard to find. It was felt by Congress, and state and municipal legislatures, that certain regulatory tasks could not be performed efficiently, rapidly, expertly, and with due concern for the public interest by the traditional branches of government. Accordingly, regulatory agencies were delegated powers to consider disputes from the earliest stage of investigation to the final stages of adjudication entirely within each agency itself, subject only to limited review in the regular courts.

6. The above passage states that the usual means for conflict resolution is through the use of

   A. judicial trial
   B. administrative hearing
   C. legislation
   D. regulatory agencies

7. The above passage IMPLIES that the use of administrative hearing in resolving conflict is a(n) _____ approach.

   A. traditional
   B. new
   C. dangerous
   D. experimental

8. The above passage states that the reason for the breakdown of the separation-of-powers formula in the administrative process is that

A. Congress believed that certain regulatory tasks could be better performed by separate agencies
B. legislative and executive functions are incompatible in the same agency
C. investigative and regulatory functions are not normally reviewed by the courts
D. state and municipal legislatures are more concerned with efficiency than with legality

Questions 9-10.

DIRECTIONS: Questions 9 and 10 are to be answered SOLELY on the basis of the information given in the following paragraph.

An assumption commonly made in regard to the reliability of testimony is that when a number of persons report upon the same matter, those details upon which there is an agreement may, in general, be considered as substantiated. Experiments have shown, however, that there is a tendency for the same errors to appear in the testimony of different individuals, and that, quite apart from any collusion, agreement of testimony is no proof of dependability.

9. According to the above paragraph, it is commonly assumed that details of an event are substantiated when

A. a number of persons report upon them
B. a reliable person testifies to them
C. no errors are apparent in the testimony of different individuals
D. several witnesses are in agreement about them

9.____

10. According to the above paragraph, agreement in the testimony of different witnesses to the same event is

A. evaluated more reliably when considered apart from collusion
B. not the result of chance
C. not a guarantee of the accuracy of the facts
D. the result of a mass reaction of the witnesses

10.____

Questions 11-12.

DIRECTIONS: Questions 11 and 12 are to be answered SOLELY on the basis of the information given in the following paragraph.

The accuracy of the information about past occurrence obtainable in an interview is so low that one must take the stand that the best use to be made of the interview in this connection is a means of finding clues and avenues of access to more reliable sources of information. On the other hand, feelings and attitudes have been found to be clearly and correctly revealed in a properly conducted personal interview.

11. According to the above paragraph, information obtained in a personal interview

A. can be corroborated by other clues and more reliable sources of information revealed at the interview
B. can be used to develop leads to other sources of information about past events
C. is not reliable
D. is reliable if it relates to recent occurrences

11.____

12. According to the above paragraph, the personal interview is suitable for obtaining

    A. emotional reactions to a given situation
    B. fresh information on factors which may be forgotten
    C. revived recollection of previous events for later use as testimony
    D. specific information on material already reduced to writing

Questions 13-15.

DIRECTIONS: Questions 13 through 15 are to be answered on the basis of the following paragraph.

Admissibility of handwriting standards (samples of handwriting for the purpose of comparison) as a basis for expert testimony is frequently necessary when the authenticity of disputed documents may be at issue. Under the older rules of common law, only that writing relating to the issues in the case could be used as a basis for handwriting testimony by an expert. Today, most jurisdictions admit irrelevant writings as standards for comparison. However, their genuineness, in all instances, must be established to the satisfaction of the court. There are a number of types of documents, however, not ordinarily relevant to the issues which are seldom acceptable to the court as handwriting standards, such as bail bonds, signatures on affidavits, depositions, etc. These are usually already before the court as part of the record in a case. Exhibits written in the presence of a witness or prepared voluntarily for a law enforcement officer are readily admissible in most jurisdictions. Testimony of a witness who is considered familiar with the writing is admissible in some jurisdictions. In criminal cases, it is possible that the signature on the fingerprint card obtained in connection with the arrest of the defendant for the crime currently charged may be admitted as a handwriting standard. In order to give the defendant the fairest possible treatment, most jurisdictions do not admit the signatures on fingerprint cards pertaining to prior arrests. However, they are admitted sometimes. In such instances, the court usually requires that the signature be photographed or removed from the card and no reference be made to the origin of the signature.

13. Of the following, the types of handwriting standards MOST likely to be admitted in evidence by most jurisdictions are those

    A. appearing on depositions and bail bonds
    B. which were written in the presence of a witness or voluntarily given to a law enforcement officer
    C. identified by witnesses who claim to be familiar with the handwriting
    D. which are in conformity with the rules of common law only

14. The PRINCIPAL factor which generally determines the acceptance of handwriting standards by the courts is

    A. the relevance of the submitted documents to the issues of the case
    B. the number of witnesses who have knowledge of the submitted documents
    C. testimony that the writing has been examined by a handwriting expert
    D. acknowledgment by the court of the authenticity of the submitted documents

15. The MOST logical reason for requiring the removal of the signature of a defendant from fingerprint cards pertaining to prior arrests, before admitting the signature in court as a handwriting standard, is that

A. it simplifies the process of identification of the signature as a standard for comparison
B. the need for identifying the fingerprints is eliminated
C. mention of prior arrests may be prejudicial to the defendant
D. a handwriting expert does not need information pertaining to prior arrests in order to make his identification

Questions 16-20.

DIRECTIONS: Questions 16 through 20 are to be answered SOLELY on the basis of the information contained in the following paragraph.

A statement which is offered in an attempt to prove the truth of the matters therein stated, but which is not made by the author as a witness before the court at the particular trial in which it is so offered, is hearsay. This is so whether the statement consists of words (oral or written), of symbols used as a substitute for words, or of signs or other conduct offered as the equivalent of a statement. Subject to some well-established exceptions, hearsay is not generally acceptable as evidence, and it does not become competent evidence just because it is received by the court without objection. One basis for this rule is simply that a fact cannot be proved by showing that somebody stated it was a fact. Another basis for the rule is the fundamental principle that in a criminal prosecution the testimony of the witness shall be taken before the court, so that at the time he gives the testimony offered in evidence he will be sworn and subject to cross-examination, the scrutiny of the court, and confrontation by the accused.

16. Which of the following is hearsay? 16.____
    A(n)

    A. written statement by a person not present at the court hearing where the statement is submitted as proof of an occurrence
    B. oral statement in court by a witness of what he saw
    C. written statement of what he saw by a witness present in court
    D. re-enactment by a witness in court of what he saw

17. In a criminal case, a statement by a person not present in court is 17.____

    A. *acceptable* evidence if not objected to by the prosecutor
    B. *acceptable* evidence if not objected to by the defense lawyer
    C. *not acceptable* evidence except in certain well-settled circumstances
    D. *not acceptable* evidence under any circumstances

18. The rule on hearsay is founded on the belief that 18.____

    A. proving someone said an act occurred is not proof that the act did occur
    B. a person who has knowledge about a case should be willing to appear in court
    C. persons not present in court are likely to be unreliable witnesses
    D. permitting persons to testify without appearing in court will lead to a disrespect for law

19. One reason for the general rule that a witness in a criminal case must give his testimony in court is that

    A. a witness may be influenced by threats to make untrue statements
    B. the opposite side is then permitted to question him
    C. the court provides protection for a witness against unfair questioning
    D. the adversary system is designed to prevent a miscarriage of justice

20. Of the following, the MOST appropriate title for the above passage would be

    A. WHAT IS HEARSAY?
    B. RIGHTS OF DEFENDANTS
    C. TRIAL PROCEDURES
    D. TESTIMONY OF WITNESSES

21. A person's statements are independent of who he is or what he is. Statements made by a person are not proved true or false by questioning his character or his position. A statement should stand or fall on its merits, regardless of who makes the statement. Truth is determined by evidence only. A person's character or personality should not be the determining factor in logic. Discussions should not become incidents of name calling.
    According to the above, whether or not a statement is true depends on the

    A. recipient's conception of validity
    B. maker's reliability
    C. extent of support by facts
    D. degree of merit the discussion has

Question 22-25.

DIRECTIONS: Questions 22 through 25 are to be answered on the basis of the following passage.

The question, whether an act, repugnant to the Constitution, can become the law of the land, is a question deeply interesting to the United States; but, happily, not of an intricacy proportioned to its interest. It seems only necessary to recognize certain principles, supposed to have been long and well-established, to decide it. That the people have an original right to establish, for their future government, such principles as, in their opinion, shall most conduce to their own happiness, is the basis on which the whole American fabric has been erected. The exercise of this original right is a very great exertion; nor can it, nor ought it, to be frequently repeated. The principles, therefore, so established are deemed fundamental; and as the authority from which they proceed is supreme, and can seldom act, they are designed to be permanent.

22. The BEST title for the above passage would be

    A. PRINCIPLES OF THE CONSTITUTION
    B. THE ROOT OF CONSTITUTIONAL CHANGE
    C. ONLY PEOPLE CAN CHANGE THE CONSTITUTION
    D. METHODS OF CONSTITUTIONAL CHANGE

23. According to the above passage, original right is

    A. fundamental to the principle that the people may choose their own form of government
    B. established by the Constitution

C. the result of a very great exertion and should not often be repeated
D. supreme, can seldom act, and is designed to be permanent

24. Whether an act not in keeping with Constitutional principles can become law is, according to the above passage,

    A. an intricate problem requiring great thought and concentration
    B. determined by the proportionate interests of legislators
    C. determined by certain long established principles, fundamental to Constitutional Law
    D. an intricate problem, but less intricate than it would seem from the interest shown in it

24._____

25. According to the above passage, the phrase *and can seldom act* refers to the

    A. principle enacted early into law by Americans when they chose their future form of government
    B. original rights of the people as vested in the Constitution
    C. original framers of the Constitution
    D. established, fundamental principles of government

25._____

KEY (CORRECT ANSWERS)

1. C	11. B
2. A	12. A
3. B	13. B
4. C	14. D
5. D	15. C
6. A	16. A
7. B	17. C
8. A	18. A
9. D	19. B
10. C	20. A

21. C
22. B
23. A
24. D
25. A

TEST 2

DIRECTIONS: Each question or incomplete statement is followed by several suggested answers or completions. Select the one that BEST answers the question or completes the statement. *PRINT THE LETTER OF THE CORRECT ANSWER IN THE SPACE AT THE RIGHT.*

Questions 1-3.

DIRECTIONS: Questions 1 through 3 are to be answered SOLELY on the basis of the following paragraph.

    The police laboratory performs a valuable service in crime investigation by assisting in the reconstruction of criminal action and by aiding in the identification of persons and things. When studied by a technician, physical things found at crime scenes often reveal facts useful in identifying the criminal and in determining what has occurred. The nature of substances to be examined and the character of the examination to be made vary so widely that the services of a large variety of skilled scientific persons are needed in crime investigations. To employ such a complete staff and to provide them with equipment and standards needed for all possible analysis and comparisons is beyond the means and the needs of any but the largest police departments. The search of crime scenes for physical evidence also calls for the services of specialists supplied with essential equipment and assigned to each tour of duty so as to provide service at any hour.

1. If a police department employs a large staff of technicians of various types in its laboratory, it will affect crime investigations to the extent that 1.____

    A. most crimes will be speedily solved
    B. identification of criminals will be aided
    C. search of crime scenes for physical evidence will become of less importance
    D. investigation by police officers will not usually be required

2. According to the above paragraph, the MOST complete study of objects found at the scenes of crimes is 2.____

    A. always done in all large police departments
    B. based on assigning one technician to each tour of duty
    C. probably done only in large police departments
    D. probably done in police departments of communities with low crime rates

3. According to the above paragraph, a large variety of skilled technicians is useful in criminal investigations because 3.____

    A. crimes cannot be solved without their assistance as part of the police team
    B. large police departments need large staffs
    C. many different kinds of tests on various substances can be made
    D. the police cannot predict what methods may be tried by wily criminals

Questions 4-6.

DIRECTIONS: Questions 4 through 6 are to be answered SOLELY on the basis of the following passage.

Probably the most important single mechanism for bringing the resources of science and technology to bear on the problems of crime would be the establishment of a major prestigious science and technology research program within a research institute. The program would create interdisciplinary teams of mathematicians, computer scientists, electronics engineers, physicists, biologists, and other natural scientists, psychologists, sociologists, economists, and lawyers. The institute and the program must be significant enough to attract the best scientists available, and, to this end, the director of this institute must himself have a background in science and technology and have the respect of scientists. Because it would be difficult to attract such a staff into the Federal government, the institute should be established by a university, a group of universities, or an independent nonprofit organization, and should be within a major metropolitan area. The institute would have to establish close ties with neighboring criminal justice agencies that would receive the benefit of serving as experimental laboratories for such an institute. In fact, the proposal for the institute might be jointly submitted with the criminal justice agencies. The research program would require, in order to bring together the necessary *critical mass* of competent staff, an annual budget which might reach 5 million dollars, funded with at least three years of lead time to assure continuity. Such a major scientific and technological research institute should be supported by the Federal government.

4. Of the following, the MOST appropriate title for the foregoing passage is

   A. RESEARCH - AN INTERDISCIPLINARY APPROACH TO FIGHTING CRIME
   B. A CURRICULUM FOR FIGHTING CRIME
   C. THE ROLE OF THE UNIVERSITY IN THE FIGHT AGAINST CRIME
   D. GOVERNMENTAL SUPPORT OF CRIMINAL RESEARCH PROGRAMS

5. According to the above passage, in order to attract the best scientists available, the research institute should

   A. provide psychologists and sociologists to counsel individual members of interdisciplinary teams
   B. encourage close ties with neighboring criminal justice agencies
   C. be led by a person who is respected in the scientific community
   D. be directly operated and funded by the Federal government

6. The term *critical mass,* as used in the above passage, refers MAINLY to

   A. a staff which would remain for three years of continuous service to the institute
   B. staff members necessary to carry out the research program of the institute successfully
   C. the staff necessary to establish relations with criminal justice agencies which will serve as experimental laboratories for the institute
   D. a staff which would be able to assist the institute in raising adequate funds

Questions 7-9.

DIRECTIONS: Questions 7 through 9 are to be answered SOLELY on the basis of the following paragraph.

The use of modern scientific methods in the examination of physical evidence often provides information to the investigator which he could not otherwise obtain. This applies particularly to small objects and materials present in minute quantities or trace evidence because the quantities here are such that they may be overlooked without methodical searching, and often special means of detection are needed. Whenever two objects come in contact with one another, there is a transfer of material, however slight. Usually, the softer object will transfer to the harder, but the transfer may be mutual. The quantity of material transferred differs with the type of material involved and the more violent the contact the greater the degree of transference. Through scientific methods of determining physical properties and chemical composition, we can add to the facts observable by the investigator's unaided senses, and thereby increase the chances of identification.

7. According to the above paragraph, the amount of material transferred whenever two objects come in contact with one another

   A. varies directly with the softness of the objects involved
   B. varies directly with the violence of the contact of the objects
   C. is greater when two soft, rather than hard, objects come into violent contact with each other
   D. is greater when coarse-grained, rather than smooth-grained, materials are involved

8. According to the above paragraph, the PRINCIPAL reason for employing scientific methods in obtaining trace evidence is that

   A. other methods do not involve a methodical search of the crime scene
   B. scientific methods of examination frequently reveal physical evidence which did not previously exist
   C. the amount of trace evidence may be so sparse that other methods are useless
   D. trace evidence cannot be properly identified unless special means of detection are employed

9. According to the above paragraph, the one of the following statements which BEST describes the manner in which scientific methods of analyzing physical evidence assists the investigator is that such methods

   A. add additional valuable information to the investigator's own knowledge of complex and rarely occurring materials found as evidence
   B. compensate for the lack of important evidential material through the use of physical and chemical analyses
   C. make possible an analysis of evidence which goes beyond the ordinary capacity of the investigator's senses
   D. identify precisely those physical characteristics of the individual which the untrained senses of the investigator are unable to discern

Questions 10-13.

DIRECTIONS: Questions 10 through 13 are to be answered SOLELY on the basis of the information contained in the following paragraph.

Under the provisions of the Bank Protection Act of 1968, enacted July 8, 1968, each Federal banking supervisory agency, as of January 7, 1969, had to issue rules establishing minimum standards with which financial institutions under their control must comply with respect to the installation, maintenance, and operation of security devices and procedures, reasonable in cost, to discourage robberies, burglaries, and larcenies, and to assist in the identification and apprehension of persons who commit such acts. The rules set the time limits within which the affected banks and savings and loan associations must comply with the standards, and the rules require the submission of periodic reports on the steps taken. A violator of a rule under this Act is subject to a civil penalty not to exceed $100 for each day of the violation. The enforcement of these regulations rests with the responsible banking supervisory agencies.

10. The Bank Protection Act of 1968 was designed to

    A. provide Federal police protection for banks covered by the Act
    B. have organizations covered by the Act take precautions against criminals
    C. set up a system for reporting all bank robberies to the FBI
    D. insure institutions covered by the Act from financial loss due to robberies, burglaries, and larcenies

11. Under the provisions of the Bank Protection Act of 1968, each Federal banking supervisory agency was required to set up rules for financial institutions covered by the Act governing the

    A. hiring of personnel
    B. punishment of burglars
    C. taking of protective measures
    D. penalties for violations

12. Financial institutions covered by the Bank Protection Act of 1968 were required to

    A. file reports at regular intervals on what they had done to prevent theft
    B. identify and apprehend persons who commit robberies, burglaries, and larcenies
    C. draw up a code of ethics for their employees
    D. have fingerprints of their employees filed with the FBI

13. Under the provisions of the Bank Protection Act of 1968, a bank which is subject to the rules established under the Act and which violates a rule is liable to a penalty of NOT _____ than $100 for each _____.

    A. more; violation
    B. less; day of violation
    C. less; violation
    D. more; day of violation

Questions 14-17.

DIRECTIONS: Questions 14 through 17 are to be answered SOLELY on the basis of the following passage.

Specific measures for prevention of pilferage will be based on careful analysis of the conditions at each agency. The most practical and effective method to control casual pilferage is the establishment of psychological deterrents.

One of the most common means of discouraging casual pilferage is to search individuals leaving the agency at unannounced times and places. These spot searches may occasionally detect attempts at theft, but greater value is realized by bringing to the attention of individuals the fact that they may be apprehended if they do attempt the illegal removal of property.

An aggressive security education program is an effective means of convincing employees that they have much more to lose than they do to gain by engaging in acts of theft. It is important for all employees to realize that pilferage is morally wrong no matter how insignificant the value of the item which is taken. In establishing any deterrent to casual pilferage, security officers must not lose sight of the fact that most employees are honest and disapprove of thievery. Mutual respect between security personnel and other employees of the agency must be maintained if the facility is to be protected from other more dangerous forms of human hazards. Any security measure which infringes on the human rights or dignity of others will jeopardize, rather than enhance, the overall protection of the agency.

14. The $100,000 yearly inventory of an agency revealed that $50 worth of goods had been stolen; the only individuals with access to the stolen materials were the employees. Of the following measures, which would the author of the above passage MOST likely recommend to a security officer?

    A. Conduct an intensive investigation of all employees to find the culprit.
    B. Make a record of the theft, but take no investigative or disciplinary action against any employee.
    C. Place a tight security check on all future movements of personnel.
    D. Remove the remainder of the material to an area with much greater security.

15. What does the passage imply is the percentage of employees whom a security officer should expect to be honest?

    A. No employee can be expected to be honest all of the time
    B. Just 50%
    C. Less than 50%
    D. More than 50%

16. According to the above passage, the security officer would use which of the following methods to minimize theft in buildings with many exits when his staff is very small?

    A. Conduct an inventory of all material and place a guard near that which is most likely to be pilfered
    B. Inform employees of the consequences of legal prosecution for pilfering
    C. Close off the unimportant exits and have all his men concentrate on a few exits
    D. Place a guard at each exit and conduct a casual search of individuals leaving the premises

17. Of the following, the title BEST suited for this passage is

    A. CONTROL MEASURES FOR CASUAL PILFERING
    B. DETECTING THE POTENTIAL PILFERER
    C. FINANCIAL LOSSES RESULTING FROM PILFERING
    D. THE USE OF MORAL PERSUASION IN PHYSICAL SECURITY

Questions 18-24.

DIRECTIONS: Questions 18 through 24 are to be answered SOLELY on the basis of the following passage.

Burglar alarms are designed to detect intrusion automatically. Robbery alarms enable a victim of a robbery or an attack to signal for help. Such devices can be located in elevators, hallways, homes and apartments, businesses and factories, and subways, as well as on the street in high-crime areas. Alarms could deter some potential criminals from attacking targets so protected. If alarms were prevalent and not visible, then they might serve to suppress crime generally. In addition, of course, the alarms can summon the police when they are needed.

All alarms must perform three functions: sensing or initiation of the signal, transmission of the signal and annunciation of the alarm. A burglar alarm needs a sensor to detect human presence or activity in an unoccupied enclosed area like a building or a room. A robbery victim would initiate the alarm by closing a foot or wall switch, or by triggering a portable transmitter which would send the alarm signal to a remote receiver. The signal can sound locally as a loud noise to frighten away a criminal, or it can be sent silently by wire to a central agency. A centralized annunciator requires either private lines from each alarmed point, or the transmission of some information on the location of the signal.

18. A conclusion which follows LOGICALLY from the above passage is that

    A. burglar alarms employ sensor devices; robbery alarms make use of initiation devices
    B. robbery alarms signal intrusion without the help of the victim; burglar alarms require the victim to trigger a switch
    C. robbery alarms sound locally; burglar alarms are transmitted to a central agency
    D. the mechanisms for a burglar alarm and a robbery alarm are alike

19. According to the above passage, alarms can be located

    A. in a wide variety of settings
    B. only in enclosed areas
    C. at low cost in high-crime areas
    D. only in places where potential criminals will be deterred

20. According to the above passage, which of the following is ESSENTIAL if a signal is to be received in a central office?

    A. A foot or wall switch
    B. A noise-producing mechanism
    C. A portable reception device
    D. Information regarding the location of the source

21. According to the above passage, an alarm system can function WITHOUT a

    A. centralized annunciating device
    B. device to stop the alarm
    C. sensing or initiating device
    D. transmission device

22. According to the above passage, the purpose of robbery alarms is to

    A. find out automatically whether a robbery has taken place
    B. lower the crime rate in high-crime areas
    C. make a loud noise to frighten away the criminal
    D. provide a victim with the means to signal for help

23. According to the above passage, alarms might aid in lessening crime if they were   23._____

    A. answered promptly by police
    B. completely automatic
    C. easily accessible to victims
    D. hidden and widespread

24. Of the following, the BEST title for the above passage is   24._____

    A. DETECTION OF CRIME BY ALARMS
    B. LOWERING THE CRIME RATE
    C. SUPPRESSION OF CRIME
    D. THE PREVENTION OF ROBBERY

25. Although the rural crime reporting area is much less developed than that for cities and   25._____
    towns, current data are collected in sufficient volume to justify the generalization that
    rural crime rates are lower than those or urban communities.
    According to this statement,

    A. better reporting of crime occurs in rural areas than in cities
    B. there appears to be a lower proportion of crime in rural areas than in cities
    C. cities have more crime than towns
    D. crime depends on the amount of reporting

KEY (CORRECT ANSWERS)

1.	B	11.	C
2.	C	12.	A
3.	C	13.	D
4.	A	14.	B
5.	C	15.	D
6.	B	16.	B
7.	B	17.	A
8.	C	18.	A
9.	C	19.	A
10.	B	20.	D

21. A
22. D
23. D
24. A
25. B

FILLING OUT STANDARD FORMS

Police Officers must be able to remember how to record information properly on standard forms. The exam will test your knowledge of how well you remember the correct way to fill out the following five forms: the Incident Report Form, the Medical History Form, the Arrest Record Form, the Firearms Record Form, and the Stolen Car Report Form. The directions for filling out each form should be memorized.

Below is a sample Incident Report Form.

INCIDENT REPORT (12-7)			
1. Date	2. District Occurrence	3. Case Number	4. Car Number
5. Offense/Incident	6. Address of Occurrence		
7. Name of Complainant	8. Sex	9. Race	10. Birthdate
11. Address	12. Occupation		
13. Phone:　Business　Home	14. Employer	15. Hours Per Week:	
16. Details:			
17. Report to follow: _____ Yes _____ No			
18. Time out: ___ A.M. ___ P.M.	19. Time In ___ A.M. ___ P.M.		
20. Police Officer	21. District		
22. Signature of Officer			

Below is a listing of the block numbers and a description of the precise information that is to be entered in each block. You will not have these instructions in front of you when you take the test. It is important that you learn the instructions or you will not be able to do your best.

173

Directions for Incident Report Form (12-7)

Block 1. The date block will have the current date listed numerically with month first, day, and then year separated by slashes. The name of the day of the week will be abbreviated after the date. Wednesday, March 24, 2012 would appear as 3/24/12 Wed. If the date of the incident is different from the current date, enter the date of the incident as a detail in Block 16.

Block 2. List the district where the incident occurred.

Block 3. Case numbers will be assigned by the dispatcher and the same numbers will be used on all follow-up reports.

Block 4. List patrol car number.

Block 5. Offense/Incident will use titles for crimes from the City Police Code and will be followed by code numbers.

Block 6. List address of incident occurrence.

Block 7. Complainant's name will list last name first, followed by first name and middle name. If the complainant and victim are two different persons, enter pertinent information about the victim, such as the victim's name, in the detail section in Block 16.

Block 8. Use M or F for male or female.

Block 9. Use W for white, B for black, H for hispanic, or O for other.

Block 10. The birthdate will be written in the same way as the date in Block 1.

Block 11. List address of complainant.

Block 12. Under occupation, list the complainant's job title. If the complainant is unemployed, a student, or a homemaker, list this. For students, list grade.

Block 13. List business and home telephone numbers of the complainant.

Block 14. List name and address of complainant's employer or school. If none, write "none."

Block 15. Write the hours per week that the complainant spends working at place of employment or in school attendance. If complainant works shifts, write "shift." If hours of school or work are irregular, write "irreg."

Block 16. Include a description of the incident. If the victim and complainant are two different people, then describe the victim by using the same kind of information used to describe the complainant in Blocks 7-15 above.

Block 17. Indicate whether or not a report of the incident will be written.

Block 18.	For time out, write the time the officer arrived on scene.

Block 19.	For time in, write the time the officer left scene.

Block 20.	Under police officer, officer will print name and badge number. The police officer's name will be written in the following order: first name, middle initial (if used), last name.

Block 21.	District means the district of officer's assignment.

Block 22.	Officer will sign the Incident Report. Complainant will be given pink copy of report.

Below is a sample Medical History Form.

MEDICAL HISTORY FORM			
1. Name Johnson, Freida C.		2. Precinct and Rank 3rd, Police Officer	
3. Height 5' 9"	4. Weight 160 Lbs.	5. Age 35	6. Date of last physical examination February 15, 2012
7. Performed By: Dr. Myers, 1620 Turner Ave., Washington, D.C			
8. Do you or have you ever had any of the following? _x_ Yes ___ No If yes, indicate the year the illness was first diagnosed in the space provided. _____ Pneumonia _____ Measles _____ Scarlet Fever _____ Tuberculosis _____ Mumps _____ Asthma _____ Diabetes _____ Chicken Pox 2009 Hay Fever			

Below is a listing of the block numbers and a description of the precise information that is to be entered in each block. You will NOT have these instructions in front of you when you take the test. It is important that you learn the instructions or you will not be able to do your best.

Directions for Medical History Form

Block 1:	Officer's last name, first name, and middle initial

Block 2:	Precinct to which officer is currently assigned and present rank

Block 3:	Height without shoes

Block 4:   Current weight

Block 5:   Age

Block 6:   Date of last physical examination

Block 7:   Name and address of doctor seen at time of last physical

Block 8:   Indicate whether or not the officer has had any of the illnesses listed. If the officer has had illnesses, indicate the year the illness was first diagnosed in the space to the left of the illness.

Below is a sample Arrest Record Form.

ARREST RECORD FORM	
1. Name Thames, Earl M.	2. Age 28
3. Address 2722 Alton Place, Hammond, Iowa	
4. Date September 20, 2012	5. Time 8:45 P.M.
6. Location 916 13th Street, Hammond, Iowa	
7. Offence Attempted robbery	
8. Witnesses Martin Vantreuren	
9. Previous Arrests None	
10. Arresting Officer Joseph Novello, #1234	

Below is a listing of the block numbers and a description of the precise information that is to be entered in each block. You will NOT have these instructions in front of you when you take the test. It is important that you learn the instructions or you will not be able to do your best.

Directions for Arrest Record Form

Block 1:   Last name, first name, and middle initial of suspect arrested

Block 2:   Age of suspect

Block 3:   Home address of suspect

Block 4:   Date of arrest

Block 5:   Time of arrest; indicate a.m. or p.m.

Block 6: Location of the arrest

Block 7: Offense for which the suspect has been arrested

Block 8: Witnesses to the offense and where they can be reached. Anyone directly involved with the crime, other than the criminal, is a witness including the victim.

Block 9: Previous arrests, if records are available (if not, write "none")

Block 10: Name and badge number of arresting officer

Below is a sample Firearms Record Form.

FIREARMS RECORD FORM
1. Type of Firearm   Pistol
2. Number   9860023
3. Caliber or Gauge   .38 caliber
4. Issued to   Janice Fleming, #6423
5. Precinct   6th
6. Instruction   August 14, 2010
7. Authorization   Anderson
8. Issuing Officer   Minich

Directions for Firearms Record Form

Block 1: Type of firearm (e.g., revolver, automatic pistol, rifle)

Block 2: Serial number of firearm

Block 3: Caliber or gauge of ammunition used in the firearm

Block 4: First and last names and badge number of individual receiving the firearm

Block 5: Precinct to which the individual receiving the firearm is assigned

Block 6: Date on which the individual receiving the firearm was trained in the use of the particular firearm

Block 7: Last name of the officer authorizing the use of the firearm

Block 8: Last name of the supply officer issuing the firearm

Below is a sample Stolen Car Report Form.

STOLEN CAR REPORT	
1. Name Lana Berghoff	
2. Address 1812 Tulip Lane, Sacramento, California	

3. Description
    3a. Make   Volvo   3b. Model   Station Wagon
    3c. Year 2012 3d. Color Blue	

4. License No.
    YMD-124 CA
	5. Time Theft Discovered
	    5:15 P.M. 1-11-07

6. Last Seen: Tower Parking Lot, Sacramento, California	
7. Reporting Officer Terra, 3rd Precinct	

Below is a listing of the block numbers and a description of the precise information that is to be entered in each block. You will NOT have these instructions in front of you when you take the test. It is important that you learn the instructions or you will not be able to do your best.

Directions for Stolen Car Report Form

Block 1:   Name of owner of car

Block 2:   Address of owner of car

Block 3a,b,c,d: Information on make, model, year, and color of vehicle

Block 4:   License number of vehicle and state of issue

Block 5:   Time and date theft was discovered

Block 6:   Location of car when it was last seen

Block 7:   Last name and precinct number of officer filling out report

In the exam, you will be given questions like the sample questions below.

Sample Questions

1. On Monday, July 19, 2012, George Mason of 1620 Rockman Street, Tripton, new Mexico, called the police and reported that his next door neighbor had slashed the tires of all the cars parked on Rockman Street. Police Officer Antonia Randall of the 9th precinct answered the call.

INCIDENT REPORT(12-7)			
1. Date	2. District Occurrence	3. Case Number	4. Car Number
5. Offence/Incident	6. Address of Occurrence		
7. Name of Complainant	8. Sex	9. Race	10. Birthdate
11. Address	12. Occupation		
13. Phone: Business Home	14. Employer		15. Hours Per Week:
16. Details:			
17. Report to follow:	_____ Yes	_____ No	
18. Time out: ___ A.M. ___ P.M.		19. Time In: ___ A.M. ___ P.M.	
20. Police Officer		21. District	
22. Signature of Officer			

Which of the following should be in Block 1?

A. Monday July 19, 2012.
B. July 19, 2012
C. 19 July 2012
D. 7/19/12 Mon.

2. Police Officer Randolph Curtis (badge #142) arrested Marilyn O. Exner in her home at 103 Orange St., Merville, Nevada for the attempted robbery of a convenience store owned by Patti Scuderi. Officer Curtis made the arrest at 6:32 P.M. on March 3, 2007.

ARREST RECORD FORM		
1. Name Exner, Marilyn O	2. Age	42
3. Address 103 Orange St.		
Merville, Nevada		
4. Date March 3, 2012	5. Time	6 : 32 P.M.
6. Location 103 Orange St., Merville, Nevada		
7. Offense arson		
8. Witnesses Patti Scuderi		
9. Previous Arrests none		
10. Arresting Officer Randolph Curtis, #142		

Of the following, which Block was incorrectly filled out?
Block

A. 1   B. 3   C. 7   D. 10

KEY (CORRECT ANSWERS)

1. D
2. C

REPORT WRITING

EXAMINATION SECTION
TEST 1

DIRECTIONS: Each question or incomplete statement is followed by several suggested answers or completions. Select the one that BEST answers the question or completes the statement. *PRINT THE LETTER OF THE CORRECT ANSWER IN THE SPACE AT THE RIGHT.*

1. Police Officer Johnson responds to the scene of an assault and obtains the following information:
   Time of Occurrence: 8:30 P.M.
   Place of Occurrence: 120-18 119th Avenue, Apt. 2A
   Suspects: John Andrews, victim's ex-husband and unknown white male
   Victim: Susan Andrews
   Injury: Broken right arm
   Officer Johnson is preparing a complaint report on the incident.
   Which one of the following expresses the above information MOST clearly and accurately?

   A. Susan Andrews was assaulted at 120-18 119th Avenue, Apt. 2A. At 8:30 P.M., her ex-husband, John Andrews, and an unknown white male broke her arm.
   B. At 8:30 P.M., Susan Andrews was assaulted at 120-18 119th Avenue, Apt. 2A, by her ex-husband, John Andrews, and an unknown white male. Her right arm was broken.
   C. John Andrews, an unknown white male, and Susan Andrews' ex-husband, assaulted and broke her right arm at 8:30 P.M., at 120-18 119th Avenue, Apt. 2A.
   D. John Andrews, ex-husband of Susan Andrews, broke her right arm with an unknown white male at 120-18 119th Avenue, at 8:30 P.M. in Apt. 2A.

2. While on patrol, Officers Banks and Thompson see a man lying on the ground bleeding. Officer Banks records the following details about the incident:
   Time of Incident: 3:15 P.M.
   Place of Incident: Sidewalk in front of 517 Rock Avenue
   Incident: Tripped and fell
   Name of Injured: John Blake
   Injury: Head wound
   Action Taken: Transported to Merry Hospital
   Officer Banks is completing a report on the incident.
   Which one of the following expresses the above information MOST clearly and accurately?

   A. At 3:15 P.M., Mr. John Blake was transported to Merry Hospital. He tripped and fell, injuring his head on sidewalk in front of 517 Rock Avenue.
   B. Mr. John Blake tripped and fell on the sidewalk at 3:15 P.M. in front of 517 Rock Avenue. He was transported to Merry Hospital while he sustained a head wound.
   C. Mr. John Blake injured his head when he tripped and fell on the sidewalk in front of 517 Rock Avenue at 3:15 P.M. He was transported to Merry Hospital.
   D. A head was wounded on the sidewalk in front of 517 Rock Avenue at 3:15 P.M. Mr. John Blake tripped and fell and was transported to Merry Hospital.

3. When assigned to investigate a complaint, a police officer should
   I. Interview witnesses and obtain facts
   II. Conduct a thorough investigation of circumstances concerning the complaint
   III. Prepare a complaint report
   IV. Determine if the complaint report should be closed or referred for further investigation
   V. Enter complaint report on the Complaint Report Index and obtain a complaint report number at the station house

   While on patrol, Police Officer John is instructed by his supervisor to investigate a complaint by Mr. Stanley Burns, who was assaulted by his brother-in-law, Henry Traub. After interviewing Mr. Burns, Officer John learns that Mr. Traub has been living with Mr. Burns for the past two years. Officer John accompanies Mr. Burns to his apartment but Mr. Traub is not there. Officer John fills out the complaint report and takes the report back to the station house where it is entered on the Complaint Report Index and assigned a complaint report number. Officer John's actions were

   A. *improper,* primarily because he should have stayed at Mr. Burns' apartment and waited for Mr. Traub to return in order to arrest him
   B. *proper,* primarily because after obtaining all the facts, he took the report back to the station house and was assigned a complaint report number
   C. *improper,* primarily because he should have decided whether to close the report or refer it for further investigation
   D. *proper,* primarily because he was instructed by his supervisor to take the report from Mr. Burns even though it involved his brother-in-law

4. Police Officer Waters was the first person at the scene of a fire which may have been the result of arson. He obtained the following information:
   Place of Occurrence: 35 John Street, Apt. 27
   Time of Occurrence: 4:00 P.M.
   Witness: Daisy Logan
   Incident: Fire (possible arson)
   Suspect: Male, white, approximately 18 years old, wearing blue jeans and a plaid shirt, running away from the incident Officer Waters is completing a report on the incident.

   Which one of the following expresses the above information MOST clearly and accurately?

   A. At 4:00 P.M., Daisy Logan saw a white male, approximately 18 years old who was wearing blue jeans and a plaid shirt, running from the scene of a fire at 35 John Street, Apt. 27.
   B. Seeing a fire at 35 John Street, a white male approximately 18 years old, wearing blue jeans and a plaid shirt, was seen running from Apt. 27 at 4:00 P.M. reported Daisy Logan.
   C. Approximately 18 years old and wearing blue jeans and a plaid shirt, Daisy Logan saw a fire and a white male running from 35 John Street, Apt. 27 at 4:00 P.M.
   D. Running from 35 John Street, Apt. 27, the scene of the fire, reported Daisy Logan at 4:00 P.M., was a white male approximately 18 years old and wearing blue jeans and a plaid shirt.

5. Police Officer Sullivan obtained the following information at the scene of a two-car accident:

   Place of Occurrence: 2971 William Street
   Drivers and Vehicles Involved: Mrs. Wilson, driver of blue 2004 Toyota Camry; Mr. Bailey, driver of white 2001 Dodge
   Injuries Sustained: Mr. Bailey had a swollen right eye; Mrs. Wilson had a broken left hand

   Which one of the following expresses the above information MOST clearly and accurately?

   A. Mr. Bailey, owner of a white 2001 Dodge, at 2971 William Street, had a swollen right eye. Mrs. Wilson, with a broken left hand, is the owner of the blue 2004 Toyota Camry. They were in a car accident.
   B. Mrs. Wilson got a broken left hand and Mr. Bailey a swollen right eye at 2971 William Street. The vehicles involved in the car accident were a 2001 Dodge, white, owned by Mr. Bailey, and Mrs. Wilson's blue 2004 Toyota Camry.
   C. Mrs. Wilson, the driver of the blue 2004 Toyota Camry, and Mr. Bailey, the driver of the white 2001 Dodge, were involved in a car accident at 2971 William Street. Mr. Bailey sustained a swollen right eye, and Mrs. Wilson broke her left hand.
   D. Mr. Bailey sustained a swollen right eye and Mrs. Wilson broke her left hand in a car accident at 2971 William Street. They owned a 2001 white Dodge and a 2004 blue Toyota Camry.

6. Officer Johnson has issued a summons to a driver and has obtained the following information:

   Place of Occurrence: Corner of Foster Road and Woodrow Avenue
   Time of Occurrence: 7:10 P.M.
   Driver: William Grant
   Offense: Driving through a red light
   Age of Driver: 42
   Address of Driver: 23 Richmond Avenue

   Officer Johnson is making an entry in his Memo Book regarding the incident.
   Which one of the following expresses the above information MOST clearly and accurately?

   A. William Grant, lives at 23 Richmond Avenue at 7:10 P.M., went through a red light. He was issued a summons at the corner of Foster Road and Woodrow Avenue. The driver is 42 years old.
   B. William Grant, age 42, who lives at 23 Richmond Avenue, was issued a summons for going through a red light at 7:10 P.M. at the corner of Foster Road and Woodrow Avenue.
   C. William Grant, age 42, was issued a summons on the corner of Foster Road and Woodrow Avenue for going through a red light. He lives at 23 Richmond Avenue at 7:10 P.M.
   D. A 42-year-old man who lives at 23 Richmond Avenue was issued a summons at 7:10 P.M. William Grant went through a red light at the corner of Foster Road and Woodrow Avenue.

7. Police Officer Frome has completed investigating a report of a stolen auto and obtained the following information:

Date of Occurrence: October 26, 2004
Place of Occurrence: 51st Street and 8th Avenue
Time of Occurrence: 3:30 P.M.
Crime: Auto theft
Suspect: Michael Wadsworth
Action Taken: Suspect arrested

Which one of the following expresses the above information MOST clearly and accurately?

A. Arrested on October 26, 2004 was a stolen auto at 51st Street and 8th Avenue at 3:30 P.M. driven by Michael Wadsworth.
B. For driving a stolen auto at 3:30 P.M., Michael Wadsworth was arrested at 51st Street and 8th Avenue on October 26, 2004.
C. On October 26, 2004 at 3:30 P.M., Michael Wadsworth was arrested at 51st Street and 8th Avenue for driving a stolen auto.
D. Michael Wadsworth was arrested on October 26, 2004 at 3:30 P.M. for driving at 51st Street and 8th Avenue. The auto was stolen.

8. Police Officer Wright has finished investigating a report of Grand Larceny and has obtained the following information:

Time of Occurrence: Between 1:00 P.M. and 2:00 P.M.
Place of Occurrence: In front of victim's home, 85 Montgomery Avenue
Victim: Mr. Williams, owner of the vehicle
Crime: Automobile broken into
Property Taken: Stereo valued at $1,200

Officer Wright is preparing a report on the incident. Which one of the following expresses the above information MOST clearly and accurately?

A. While parked in front of his home Mr. Williams states that between 1:00 P.M. and 2:00 P.M. an unknown person broke into his vehicle. Mr. Williams, who lives at 85 Montgomery Avenue, lost his $1,200 stereo.
B. Mr. Williams, who lives at 85 Montgomery Avenue, states that between 1:00 P.M. and 2:00 P.M. his vehicle was parked in front of his home when an unknown person broke into his car and took his stereo worth $1,200.
C. Mr. Williams was parked in front of 85 Montgomery Avenue, which is his home, when it was robbed of a $1,200 stereo. When he came out, he observed between 1:00 P.M. and 2:00 P.M. that his car had been broken into by an unknown person.
D. Mr. Williams states between 1:00 P.M. and 2:00 P.M. that an unknown person broke into his car in front of his home. Mr. Williams further states that he was robbed of a $1,200 stereo at 85 Montgomery Avenue.

9. Police Officer Fontaine obtained the following details relating to a suspicious package:

   Place of Occurrence: Case Bank, 2 Wall Street
   Time of Occurrence: 10:30 A.M.
   Date of Occurrence: October 10, 2004
   Complaint: Suspicious package in doorway
   Found By: Emergency Service Unit

   Officer Fontaine is preparing a report for department records.
   Which one of the following expresses the above information MOST clearly and accurately?

   A. At 10:30 A.M., the Emergency Service Unit reported they found a package on October 10, 2004 which appeared suspicious. This occurred in a doorway at 2 Wall Street, Case Bank.
   B. A package which appeared suspicious was in the doorway of Case Bank. The Emergency Service Unit reported this at 2 Wall Street at 10:30 A.M. on October 10, 2004 when found.
   C. On October 10, 2004 at 10:30 A.M., a suspicious package was found by the Emergency Service Unit in the doorway of Case Bank at 2 Wall Street.
   D. The Emergency Service Unit found a package at the Case Bank. It appeared suspicious at 10:30 A.M. in the doorway of 2 Wall Street on October 10, 2004.

10. Police Officer Reardon receives the following information regarding a case of child abuse:

    Victim: Joseph Mays
    Victim's Age: 10 years old
    Victim's Address: Resides with his family at 42 Columbia Street, Apt. 1B
    Complainant: Victim's uncle, Kevin Mays
    Suspects: Victim's parents

    Police Officer Reardon is preparing a report to send to the Department of Social Services.
    Which one of the following expresses the above information MOST clearly and accurately?

    A. Kevin Mays reported a case of child abuse to his ten-year-old nephew, Joseph Mays, by his parents. He resides with his family at 42 Columbia Street, Apt. 1B.
    B. Kevin Mays reported that his ten-year-old nephew, Joseph Mays, has been abused by the child's parents. Joseph Mays resides with his family at 42 Columbia Street, Apt. 1B.
    C. Joseph Mays has been abused by his parents. Kevin Mays reported that his nephew resides with his family at 42 Columbia Street, Apt. 1B. He is ten years old.
    D. Kevin Mays reported that his nephew is ten years old. Joseph Mays has been abused by his parents. He resides with his family at 42 Columbia Street, Apt. 1B.

11. While on patrol, Police Officer Hawkins was approached by Harry Roland, a store owner, who found a leather bag valued at $200.00 outside his store. Officer Hawkins took the property into custody and removed the following items:

2 Solex watches, each valued at	$500.00
4 14-kt. gold necklaces, each valued at	$315.00
Cash	$519.00
1 diamond ring, valued at	$400.00

Officer Hawkins is preparing a report on the found property.
Which one of the following is the TOTAL value of the property and cash found?

   A. $1,734   B. $3,171   C. $3,179   D. $3,379

12. While on patrol, Police Officer Blake observes a man running from a burning abandoned building. Officer Blake radios the following information:

Place of Occurrence:	310 Hall Avenue
Time of Occurrence:	8:30 P.M.
Type of Building:	Abandoned
Suspect:	Male, white, about 35 years old
Crime:	Arson

Officer Blake is completing a report on the incident.
Which one of the following expresses the above information MOST clearly and accurately?

   A. An abandoned building located at 310 Hall Avenue was on fire at 8:30 P.M. A white male, approximately 35 years old, was observed fleeing the scene.
   B. A white male, approximately 35 years old, at 8:30 P.M. was observed fleeing 310 Hall Avenue. The fire was set at an abandoned building.
   C. An abandoned building was set on fire. A white male, approximately 35 years old, was observed fleeing the scene at 8:30 P.M. at 310 Hall Avenue.
   D. Observed fleeing a building at 8:30 P.M. was a white male, approximately 35 years old. An abandoned building, located at 310 Hall Avenue, was set on fire.

13. Police Officer Winters responds to a call regarding a report of a missing person. The following information was obtained by the Officer:

Time of Occurrence:	3:30 P.M.
Place of Occurrence:	Harrison Park
Reported By:	Louise Dee - daughter
Description of Missing Person:	Sharon Dee, 70 years old, 5'5", brown eyes, black hair - mother

Officer Winters is completing a report on the incident. Which one of the following expresses the above information MOST clearly and accurately?

   A. Mrs. Sharon Dee, reported missing by her daughter, Louise, was seen in Harrison Park. The last time she saw her was at 3:30 P.M. She is 70 years old with black hair, brown eyes, and 5'5".
   B. Louise Dee reported that her mother, Sharon Dee, is missing. Sharon Dee is 70 years old, has black hair, brown eyes, and is 5'5". She was last seen at 3:30 P.M. in Harrison Park.
   C. Louise Dee reported Sharon, her 70-year-old mother at 3:30 P.M., to be missing after being seen last at Harrison Park. Described as being 5'5", she has black hair and brown eyes.

D. At 3:30 P.M. Louise Dee's mother was last seen by her daughter in Harrison Park. She has black hair and brown eyes. Louise reported Sharon is 5'5" and 70 years old.

14. While on patrol, Police Officers Mertz and Gallo receive a call from the dispatcher regarding a crime in progress.
When the Officers arrive, they obtain the following information:
Time of Occurrence: 2:00 P.M.
Place of Occurrence: In front of 2124 Bristol Avenue
Crime: Purse snatch
Victim: Maria Nieves
Suspect: Carlos Ortiz
Witness: Jose Perez, who apprehended the subject
The Officers are completing a report on the incident.
Which one of the following expresses the above information MOST clearly and accurately?

14.____

 A. At 2:00 P.M., Jose Perez witnessed Maria Nieves. Her purse was snatched. The suspect, Carlos Ortiz, was apprehended in front of 2124 Bristol Avenue.
 B. In front of 2124 Bristol Avenue, Carlos Ortiz snatched the purse belonging to Maria Nieves. Carlos Ortiz was apprehended by a witness to the crime after Jose Perez saw the purse snatch at 2:00 P.M.
 C. At 2:00 P.M., Carlos Ortiz snatched a purse from Maria Nieves in front of 2124 Bristol Avenue. Carlos Ortiz was apprehended by Jose Perez, a witness to the crime.
 D. At 2:00 P.M., Carlos Ortiz was seen snatching the purse of Maria Nieves as seen and apprehended by Jose Perez in front of 2124 Bristol Avenue.

15. Police Officers Willis and James respond to a crime in progress and obtain the following information:
Time of Occurrence: 8:30 A.M.
Place of Occurrence: Corner of Hopkin Avenue and Amboy Place
Crime: Chain snatch
Victim: Mrs. Paula Evans
Witness: Mr. Robert Peters
Suspect: White male
Officers Willis and James are completing a report on the incident.
Which one of the following expresses the above information MOST clearly and accurately?

15.____

 A. Mrs. Paula Evans was standing on the corner of Hopkin Avenue and Amboy Place at 8:30 A.M. when a white male snatched her chain. Mr. Robert Peters witnessed the crime.
 B. At 8:30 A.M., Mr, Robert Peters witnessed Mrs. Paula Evans and a white male standing on the corner of Hopkin Avenue and Amboy Place. Her chain was snatched.
 C. At 8:30 A.M., a white male was standing on the corner of Hopkin Avenue and Amboy Place. Mrs. Paula Evans' chain was snatched, and Mr. Robert Peters witnessed the crime.

D. At 8:30 A.M., Mr. Robert Peters reported he witnessed a white male snatching Mrs. Paula Evans' chain while standing on the corner of Hopkin Avenue and Amboy Place.

16. Police Officers Cleveland and Logan responded to an assault that had recently occurred. The following information was obtained at the scene:

    Place of Occurrence: Broadway and Roosevelt Avenue
    Time of Occurrence: 1:00 A.M.
    Crime: Attempted robbery, assault
    Victim: Chuck Brown, suffered a broken tooth
    Suspect: Lewis Brown, victim's brother

    Officer Logan is completing a report on the incident.
    Which one of the following expresses the above information MOST clearly and accurately?

    A. Lewis Brown assaulted his brother Chuck on the corner of Broadway and Roosevelt Avenue. Chuck Brown reported his broken tooth during the attempted robbery at 1:00 A.M.
    B. Chuck Brown had his tooth broken when he was assaulted at 1:00 A.M. on the corner of Broadway and Roosevelt Avenue by his brother, Lewis Brown, while Lewis was attempting to rob him.
    C. An attempt at 1:00 A.M. to rob Chuck Brown turned into an assault at the corner of Broadway and Roosevelt Avenue when his brother Lewis broke his tooth.
    D. At 1:00 A.M., Chuck Brown reported that he was assaulted during his brother's attempt to rob him. Lewis Brown broke his tooth. The incident occurred on the corner of Broadway and Roosevelt Avenue.

17. Police Officer Mannix has just completed an investigation regarding a hit-and-run accident which resulted in a pedestrian being injured. Officer Mannix has obtained the following information:

    Make and Model of Car: Pontiac, Trans Am
    Year and Color of Car: 2006, white
    Driver of Car: Male, black
    Place of Occurrence: Corner of E. 15th Street and 8th Avenue
    Time of Occurrence: 1:00 P.M.

    Officer Mannix is completing a report on the accident.
    Which one of the following expresses the above information MOST clearly and accurately?

    A. At 1:00 P.M., at the corner of E. 15th Street and 8th Avenue, a black male driving a white 2006 Pontiac Trans Am was observed leaving the scene of an accident after injuring a pedestrian with the vehicle.
    B. On the corner of E. 15th Street and 8th Avenue, a white Pontiac, driven by a black male, a 2006 Trans Am injured a pedestrian and left the scene of the accident at 1:00 P.M.
    C. A black male driving a white 2006 Pontiac Trans Am injured a pedestrian and left with the car while driving on the corner of E. 15th Street and 8th Avenue at 1:00 P.M.
    D. At the corner of E. 15th Street and 8th Avenue, a pedestrian was injured by a black male. He fled in his white 2006 Pontiac Trans Am at 1:00 P.M.

18. The following details were obtained by Police Officer Dwight at the scene of a family dispute:

    Place of Occurrence: 77 Baruch Drive
    Victim: Andrea Valdez, wife of Walker
    Violator: Edward Walker
    Witness: George Valdez, victim's brother
    Crime: Violation of Order of Protection
    Action Taken: Violator arrested

    Police Officer Dwight is preparing a report on the incident.
    Which one of the following expresses the above information MOST clearly and accurately?

    A. George Valdez saw Edward Walker violate his sister's Order of Protection at 77 Baruch Drive. Andrea Valdez's husband was arrested for this violation.
    B. Andrea Valdez's Order of Protection was violated at 77 Baruch Drive. George Valdez saw his brother-in-law violate his sister's Order. Edward Walker was arrested.
    C. Edward Walker was arrested for violating an Order of Protection held by his wife, Andrea Valdez. Andrea's brother, George Valdez, witnessed the violation at 77 Baruch Drive.
    D. An arrest was made at 77 Baruch Drive when an Order of Protection held by Andrea Valdez was violated by her husband. George Valdez, her brother, witnessed Edward Walker.

19. The following details were obtained by Police Officer Jackson at the scene of a robbery:

    Place of Occurrence: Chambers Street, northbound A platform
    Victim: Mr. John Wells
    Suspect: Joseph Miller
    Crime: Robbery, armed with knife, wallet taken
    Action Taken: Suspect arrested

    Officer Jackson is completing a report on the incident.
    Which one of the following expresses the above information MOST clearly and accurately?

    A. At Chambers Street northbound A platform, Joseph Miller used a knife to remove the wallet of John Wells while waiting for the train. Police arrested him.
    B. Mr. John Wells, while waiting for the northbound A train at Chambers Street, had his wallet forcibly removed at knifepoint by Joseph Miller. Joseph Miller was later arrested.
    C. Joseph Miller was arrested for robbery. At Chambers Street, John Wells stated that his wallet was taken. The incident occurred at knifepoint while waiting on a northbound A platform.
    D. At the northbound Chambers Street platform, John Wells was waiting for the A train. Joseph Miller produced a knife and removed his wallet. He was arrested.

20. Police Officer Bellows responds to a report of drugs being sold in the lobby of an apartment building. He obtains the following information at the scene:

Time of Occurrence: 11:30 P.M.
Place of Occurrence: 1010 Bath Avenue
Witnesses: Mary Markham, John Silver
Suspect: Harry Stoner
Crime: Drug sales
Action Taken: Suspect was gone when police arrived

Officer Bellows is completing a report of the incident. Which one of the following expresses the above information MOST clearly and accurately?

- A. Mary Markham and John Silver witnessed drugs being sold and the suspect flee at 1010 Bath Avenue. Harry Stoner was conducting his business at 11:30 P.M. before police arrival in the lobby.
- B. In the lobby, Mary Markham reported at 11:30 P.M. she saw Harry Stoner, along with John Silver, selling drugs. He ran from the lobby at 1010 Bath Avenue before police arrived.
- C. John Silver and Mary Markham reported that they observed Harry Stoner selling drugs in the lobby of 1010 Bath Avenue at 11:30 P.M. The witnesses stated that Stoner fled before police arrived.
- D. Before police arrived, witnesses stated that Harry Stoner was selling drugs. At 1010 Bath Avenue, in the lobby, John Silver and Mary Markham said they observed his actions at 11:30 P.M.

21. While on patrol, Police Officer Fox receives a call to respond to a robbery. Upon arriving at the scene, he obtains the following information:

Time of Occurrence: 6:00 P.M.
Place of Occurrence: Sal's Liquor Store at 30 Fordham Road
Victim: Sal Jones
Suspect: White male wearing a beige parka
Description of Crime: Victim was robbed in his store at gunpoint

Officer Fox is completing a report on the incident. Which one of the following expresses the above information MOST clearly and accurately?

- A. I was informed at 6:00 P.M. by Sal Jones that an unidentified white male robbed him at gunpoint at 30 Fordham Road while wearing a beige parka at Sal's Liquor Store.
- B. At 6:00 P.M., Sal Jones was robbed at gunpoint in his store. An unidentified white male wearing a beige parka came into Sal's Liquor Store at 30 Fordham Road, he told me.
- C. I was informed at 6:00 P.M. while wearing a beige parka an unidentified white male robbed Sal Jones at gunpoint at Sal's Liquor Store at 30 Fordham Road.
- D. Sal Jones informed me that at 6:00 P.M. he was robbed at gunpoint in his store, Sal's Liquor Store, located at 30 Fordham Road, by an unidentified white male wearing a beige parka.

22. The following details were obtained by Police Officer Connors at the scene of a bank robbery: 22.____

Time of Occurrence:	10:21 A.M.
Place of Occurrence:	Westbury Savings and Loan
Crime:	Bank Robbery
Suspect:	Male, dressed in black, wearing a black woolen face mask
Witness:	Mary Henderson of 217 Westbury Ave.
Amount Stolen:	$6141 U.S. currency

Officer Connors is completing a report on the incident. Which one of the following expresses the above information MOST clearly and accurately?

- A. At 10:21 A.M., the Westbury Savings and Loan was witnessed being robbed by Mary Henderson of 217 Westbury Avenue. The suspect fled dressed in black with a black woolen face mask. He left the bank with $6141 in U.S. currency.
- B. Dressed in black wearing a black woolen face mask, Mary Henderson of 217 Westbury Avenue saw a suspect flee with $6141 in U.S. currency after robbing the Westbury Savings and Loan. The robber was seen at 10:21 A.M.
- C. At 10:21 A.M., Mary Henderson of 217 Westbury Avenue, witness to the robbery of the Westbury Savings and Loan, reports that a male, dressed in black, wearing a black face mask, did rob said bank and fled with $6141 in U.S. currency.
- D. Mary Henderson, of 217 Westbury Avenue, witnessed the robbery of the Westbury Savings and Loan at 10:21 A.M. The suspect, a male, was dressed in black and was wearing a black woolen face mask. He fled with $6141 in U.S. currency.

23. At the scene of a dispute, Police Officer Johnson made an arrest after obtaining the following information: 23.____

Place of Occurrence:	940 Baxter Avenue
Time of Occurrence:	3:40 P.M.
Victim:	John Mitchell
Suspect:	Robert Holden, arrested at scene
Crime:	Menacing
Weapon:	Knife
Time of Arrest:	4:00 P.M.

Officer Johnson is completing a report of the incident.
Which one of the following expresses the above information MOST clearly and accurately?

- A. John Mitchell was menaced by a knife at 940 Baxter Avenue. Robert Holden, owner of the weapon, was arrested at 4:00 P.M., twenty minutes later, at the scene.
- B. John Mitchell reports at 3:40 P.M. he was menaced at 940 Baxter Avenue by Robert Holden. He threatened him with his knife and was arrested at 4:00 P.M. at the scene.
- C. John Mitchell stated that at 3:40 P.M. at 940 Baxter Avenue he was menaced by Robert Holden, who was carrying a knife. Mr. Holden was arrested at the scene at 4:00 P.M.
- D. With a knife, Robert Holden menaced John Mitchell at 3:40 P.M. The knife belonged to him, and he was arrested at the scene of 940 Baxter Avenue at 4:00 P.M.

24. Officer Nieves obtained the following information after he was called to the scene of a large gathering:
    Time of Occurrence: 2:45 A.M.
    Place of Occurrence: Mulberry Park
    Complaint: Loud music
    Complainant: Mrs. Simpkins, 42 Mulberry Street, Apt. 25
    Action Taken: Police officer dispersed the crowd
    Officer Nieves is completing a report on the incident. Which one of the following expresses the above information MOST clearly and accurately?

    A. Mrs. Simpkins, who lives at 42 Mulberry Street, Apt. 25, called the police to make a complaint. A large crowd of people were playing loud music in Mulberry Park at 2:45 A.M. Officer Nieves responded and dispersed the crowd.
    B. Officer Nieves responded to Mulberry Park because Mrs. Simpkins, the complainant, lives at 42 Mulberry Street, Apt. 25. Due to a large crowd of people who were playing loud music at 2:45 A.M., he immediately dispersed the crowd.
    C. Due to a large crowd of people who were playing loud music in Mulberry Park at 2:45 A.M., Officer Nieves responded and dispersed the crowd. Mrs. Simpkins called the police and complained. She lives at 42 Mulberry Street, Apt. 25.
    D. Responding to a complaint by Mrs. Simpkins, who resides at 42 Mulberry Street, Apt. 25, Officer Nieves dispersed a large crowd in Mulberry Park. They were playing loud music. It was 2:45 A.M.

25. While patroling the subway, Police Officer Clark responds to the scene of a past robbery where he obtains the following information:
    Place of Occurrence: Northbound E train
    Time of Occurrence: 6:30 P.M.
    Victim: Robert Brey
    Crime: Wallet and jewelry taken
    Suspects: 2 male whites armed with knives
    Officer Clark is completing a report on the incident.
    Which one of the following expresses the above information MOST clearly and accurately?

    A. At 6:30 P.M., Robert Brey reported he was robbed of his wallet and jewelry. On the northbound E train, two white males approached Mr. Brey. They threatened him before taking his property with knives.
    B. While riding the E train northbound, two white men approached Robert Brey at 6:30 P.M. They threatened him with knives and took his wallet and jewelry.
    C. Robert Brey was riding the E train at 6:30 P.M. when he was threatened by two whites. The men took his wallet and jewelry as he was traveling northbound.
    D. Robert Brey reports at 6:30 P.M. he lost his wallet to two white men as well as his jewelry. They were carrying knives and threatened him aboard the northbound E train.

KEY (CORRECT ANSWERS)

1.	B	11.	D
2.	C	12.	A
3.	C	13.	B
4.	A	14.	C
5.	C	15.	A
6.	B	16.	B
7.	C	17.	A
8.	B	18.	C
9.	C	19.	B
10.	B	20.	C

21. D
22. D
23. C
24. A
25. B

TEST 2

DIRECTIONS: Each question or incomplete statement is followed by several suggested answers or completions. Select the one that BEST answers the question or completes the statement. *PRINT THE LETTER OF THE CORRECT ANSWER IN THE SPACE AT THE RIGHT.*

1. Police Officer Johnson has just finished investigating a report of a burglary and has obtained the following information:
   Place of Occurrence: Victim's residence
   Time of Occurrence: Between 8:13 P.M. and 4:15 A.M.
   Victim: Paul Mason of 1264 Twentieth Street, Apt. 3D
   Crime: Burglary
   Damage: Filed front door lock
   Officer Johnson is preparing a report of the incident. Which one of the following expresses the above information MOST clearly and accurately?

   A. Paul Mason's residence was burglarized at 1264 Twentieth Street, Apt. 3D, between 8:13 P.M. and 4:15 A.M. by filing the front door lock.
   B. Paul Mason was burglarized by filing the front door lock and he lives at 1264 Twentieth Street, Apt. 3D, between 8:13 P.M. and 4:15 A.M.
   C. Between 8:13 P.M. and 4:15 A.M., the residence of Paul Mason, located at 1264 Twentieth Street, Apt. 3D, was burglarized after the front door lock was filed.
   D. Between 8:13 P.M. and 4:15 A.M., at 1264 Twentieth Street, Apt. 3D, after the front door lock was filed, the residence of Paul Mason was burglarized.

2. Police Officer Lowell has just finished investigating a burglary and has received the following information:
   Place of Occurrence: 117-12 Sutphin Boulevard
   Time of Occurrence: Between 9:00 A.M. and 5:00 P.M.
   Victim: Mandee Cotton
   Suspects: Unknown
   Officer Lowell is completing a report on this incident.
   Which one of the following expresses the above information MOST clearly and accurately?

   A. Mandee Cotton reported that her home was burglarized between 9:00 A.M. and 5:00 P.M. Ms. Cotton resides at 117-12 Sutphin Boulevard. Suspects are unknown.
   B. A burglary was committed at 117-12 Sutphin Boulevard reported Mandee Cotton between 9:00 A.M. and 5:00 P.M. Ms. Cotton said unknown suspects burglarized her home.
   C. Unknown suspects burglarized a home at 117-12 Sutphin Boulevard between 9:00 A.M. and 5:00 P.M. Mandee Cotton, homeowner, reported.
   D. Between the hours of 9:00 A.M. and 5:00 P.M., it was reported that 117-12 Sutphin Boulevard was burglarized. Mandee Cotton reported that unknown suspects are responsible.

3. Police Officer Dale has just finished investigating a report of attempted theft and has obtained the following information:

   Place of Occurrence: In front of 103 W. 105th Street
   Time of Occurrence: 11:30 A.M.
   Victim: Mary Davis
   Crime: Attempted theft
   Suspect: Male, black, scar on right side of face
   Action Taken: Drove victim around area to locate suspect

   Officer Dale is preparing a report on the incident. Which one of the following expresses the above information MOST clearly and accurately?

   A. Mary Davis was standing in front of 103 W. 105th Street when Officer Dale arrived after an attempt to steal her pocketbook failed at 11:30 A.M. Officer Dale canvassed the area looking for a black male with a scar on the right side of his face with Ms. Davis in the patrol car.
   B. Mary Davis stated that, at 11:30 A.M., she was standing in front of 103 W. 105th Street when a black male with a scar on the right side of his face attempted to steal her pocketbook. Officer Dale canvassed the area with Ms. Davis in the patrol car.
   C. Officer Dale canvassed the area by putting Mary Davis in a patrol car looking for a black male with a scar on the right side of his face. At 11:30 A.M. in front of 103 W. 105th Street, she said he attempted to steal her pocketbook.
   D. At 11:30 A.M., in front of 103 W. 105th Street, Officer Dale canvassed the area with Mary Davis in a patrol car who said that a black male with a scar on the right side of his face attempted to steal her pocketbook.

4. While on patrol, Police Officer Santoro received a call to respond to the scene of a shooting. The following details were obtained at the scene:

   Time of Occurrence: 4:00 A.M.
   Place of Occurrence: 232 Senator Street
   Victim: Mike Nisman
   Suspect: Howard Conran
   Crime: Shooting
   Witness: Sheila Norris

   Officer Santoro is completing a report on the incident.
   Which one of the following expresses the above information MOST clearly and accurately?

   A. Sheila Norris stated at 4:00 A.M. she witnessed a shooting of her neighbor in front of her building. Howard Conran shot Mike Nisman and ran from 232 Senator Street.
   B. Mike Nisman was the victim of a shooting incident seen by his neighbor. At 4:00 A.M., Sheila Norris saw Howard Conran shoot him and run in front of their building. Norris and Nisman reside at 232 Senator Street.
   C. Sheila Norris states that at 4:00 A.M. she witnessed Howard Conran shoot Mike Nisman, her neighbor, in front of their building at 232 Senator Street. She further states she saw the suspect running from the scene.
   D. Mike Nisman was shot by Howard Conran at 4:00 A.M. His neighbor, Sheila Norris, witnessed him run from the scene in front of their building at 232 Senator Street.

5. Police Officer Taylor responds to the scene of a serious traffic accident in which a car struck a telephone pole, and obtains the following information:

Place of Occurrence: Intersection of Rock Street and Amboy Place
Time of Occurrence: 3:27 A.M.
Name of Injured: Carlos Black
Driver of Car: Carlos Black
Action Taken: Injured taken to Beth-El Hospital

Officer Taylor is preparing a report on the accident. Which one of the following expresses the above information MOST clearly and accurately?

A. At approximately 3:27 A.M., Carlos Black drove his car into a telephone pole located at the intersection of Rock Street and Amboy Place. Mr. Black, who was the only person injured, was taken to Beth-El Hospital.
B. Carlos Black, injured at the intersection of Rock Street and Amboy Place, hit a telephone pole. He was taken to Beth-El Hospital after the car accident which occurred at 3:27 A.M.
C. At the intersection of Rock Street and Amboy Place, Carlos Black injured himself and was taken to Beth-El Hospital. His car hit a telephone pole at 3:27 A.M.
D. At the intersection of Rock Street and Amboy Place at 3:27 A.M., Carlos Black was taken to Beth-El Hospital after injuring himself by driving into a telephone pole.

6. While on patrol in the Jefferson Housing Projects, Police Officer Johnson responds to the scene of a Grand Larceny.

The following information was obtained by Officer Johnson:

Time of Occurrence: 6:00 P.M.
Place of Occurrence: Rear of Building 12A
Victim: Maria Lopez
Crime: Purse snatched
Suspect: Unknown

Officer Johnson is preparing a report on the incident.
Which one of the following expresses the above information MOST clearly and accurately?

A. At the rear of Building 12A, at 6:00 P.M., by an unknown suspect, Maria Lopez reported her purse snatched in the Jefferson Housing Projects.
B. Maria Lopez reported that at 6:00 P.M. her purse was snatched by an unknown suspect at the rear of Building 12A in the Jefferson Housing Projects.
C. At the rear of Building 12A, Maria Lopez reported at 6:00 P.M. that her purse had been snatched by an unknown suspect in the Jefferson Housing Projects.
D. In the Jefferson Housing Projects, Maria Lopez reported at the rear of Building 12A that her purse had been snatched by an unknown suspect at 6:00 P.M.

7. Criminal Possession of Stolen Property 2nd Degree occurs when a person knowingly possesses stolen property with intent to benefit himself or a person other than the owner, or to prevent its recovery by the owner, and when the
    I. value of the property exceeds two hundred fifty dollars; or
    II. property consists of a credit card; or
    III. person is a pawnbroker or is in the business of buying, selling, or otherwise dealing in property; or
    IV. property consists of one or more firearms, rifles, or shotguns.

    Which one of the following is the BEST example of Criminal Possession of Stolen Property in the Second Degree?

    A. Mary knowingly buys a stolen camera valued at $225 for her mother's birthday.
    B. John finds a wallet containing $100 and various credit cards. John keeps the money and turns the credit cards in at his local precinct.
    C. Mr. Varrone, a pawnbroker, refuses to buy Mr. Cutter's stolen VCR valued at $230.
    D. Mr. Aquista, the owner of a toy store, knowingly buys a crate of stolen water pistols valued at $260.

8. Police Officer Dale has just finished investigating a report of menacing and obtained the following information:
    Time of Occurrence: 10:30 P.M.
    Place of Occurrence: (Hallway) 77 Hill Street
    Victim: Grace Jackson
    Suspect: Susan, white female, 30 years of age
    Crime: Menacing with a knife

    Officer Dale is preparing a report on the incident.
    Which one of the following expresses the above information MOST clearly and accurately?

    A. At 10:30 P.M., Grace Jackson was stopped in the hallway of 77 Hill Street by a 30-year-old white female known to Grace as Susan. Susan put a knife to Grace's throat and demanded that Grace stay out of the building or Susan would hurt her.
    B. Grace Jackson was stopped in the hallway at knifepoint and threatened to stay away from the building located at 77 Hill Street. The female who is 30 years of age known as Susan by Jackson stopped her at 10:30 P.M.
    C. At 10:30 P.M. in the hallway of 77 Hill Street, Grace Jackson reported a white female 30 years of age put a knife to her throat. She knew her as Susan and demanded she stay away from the building or she would get hurt.
    D. A white female 30 years of age known to Grace Jackson as Susan stopped her in the hallway of 77 Hill Street. She put a knife to her throat and at 10:30 P.M. demanded she stay away from the building or she would get hurt.

9. Police Officer Bennett responds to the scene of a car accident and obtains the following information from the witness:
    Time of Occurrence: 3:00 A.M.
    Victim: Joe Morris, removed to Methodist Hospital
    Crime: Struck pedestrian and left the scene of accident
    Description of Auto: Blue 2008 Pontiac, license plate EOT-3745

    Officer Bennett is preparing an accident report. Which one of the following expresses the above information MOST clearly and accurately?

- A. Joe Morris, a pedestrian, was hit at 3:00 A.M. and removed to Methodist Hospital. Also a blue Pontiac, 2008 model left the scene, license plate BOT-3745.
- B. A pedestrian was taken to Methodist Hospital after being struck at 3:00 A.M. A blue automobile was seen leaving the scene with license plate BOT-3745. Joe Morris was knocked down by a 2008 Pontiac.
- C. At 3:00 A.M., Joe Morris, a pedestrian, was struck by a blue 2008 Pontiac. The automobile, license plate BOT-3745, left the scene. Mr. Morris was taken to Methodist Hospital.
- D. Joe Morris, a pedestrian at 3:00 A.M. was struck by a Pontiac. A 2008 model, license plate BOT-3745, blue in color, left the scene and the victim was taken to Methodist Hospital.

10. At 11:30 A.M., Police Officers Newman and Johnson receive a radio call to respond to a reported robbery. The Officers obtained the following information:

    Time of Occurrence: 11:20 A.M.
    Place of Occurrence: Twenty-four hour newsstand at 2024 86th Street
    Victim: Sam Norris, owner
    Amount Stolen: $450.00
    Suspects: Two male whites

    Officer Newman is completing a complaint report on the incident.
    Which one of the following expresses the above information MOST clearly and accurately?

    - A. At 11:20 A.M., it was reported by the newsstand owner that two male whites robbed $450.00 from Sam Norris. The Twenty-four hour newsstand is located at 2024 86th Street.
    - B. At 11:20 A.M., Sam Norris, the newsstand owner, reported that the Twenty-four hour newsstand located at 2024 86th Street was robbed by two male whites who took $450.00.
    - C. Sam Norris, the owner of the Twenty-four hour newsstand located at 2024 86th Street, reported that at 11:20 A.M. two white males robbed his newsstand of $450.00.
    - D. Sam Norris reported at 11:20 A.M. that $450.00 had been taken from the owner of the Twenty-four hour newsstand located at 2024 86th Street by two male whites.

11. While on patrol, Police Officers Carter and Popps receive a call to respond to an assault in progress. Upon arrival, they receive the following information:

    Place of Occurrence: 27 Park Avenue
    Victim: John Dee
    Suspect: Michael Jones
    Crime: Stabbing during a fight
    Action Taken: Suspect arrested

    The Officers are completing a report on the incident.
    Which one of the following expresses the above information MOST clearly and accurately?

    - A. In front of 27 Park Avenue, Michael Jones was arrested for stabbing John Dee during a fight.
    - B. Michael Jones was arrested for stabbing John Dee during a fight in front of 27 Park Avenue.

C. During a fight, Michael Jones was arrested for stabbing John Dee in front of 27 Park Avenue.
D. John Dee was stabbed by Michael Jones, who was arrested for fighting in front of 27 Park Avenue.

12. Police Officer Gattuso responded to a report of a robbery and obtained the following information regarding the incident:

    Place of Occurrence: Princess Grocery, 6 Button Place
    Time of Occurrence: 6:00 P.M.
    Crime: Robbery of $200
    Victim: Sara Davidson, owner of Princess Grocery
    Description of Suspect: White, female, red hair, blue jeans, and white T-shirt
    Weapon: Knife

    Officer Gattuso is preparing a report on the incident.
    Which one of the following expresses the above information MOST clearly and accurately?

    A. Sara Davidson reported at 6:00 P.M. her store Princess Grocery was robbed at knifepoint at 6 Button Place. A white woman with red hair took $200 from her wearing blue jeans and a white T-shirt.
    B. At 6:00 P.M., a red-haired woman took $200 from 6 Button Place at Princess Grocery owned by Sara Davidson, who was robbed by the white woman. She was wearing blue jeans and a white T-shirt and used a knife.
    C. In a robbery that occurred at knifepoint, a red-haired white woman robbed the owner of Princess Grocery. Sara Davidson, the owner of the 6 Button Place store which was robbed of $200, said she was wearing blue jeans and a white T-shirt at 6:00 P.M.
    D. At 6:00 P.M., Sara Davidson, owner of Princess Grocery, located at 6 Button Place, was robbed of $200 at knifepoint. The suspect is a white female with red hair wearing blue jeans and a white T-shirt.

13. Police Officer Martinez responds to a report of an assault and obtains the following information regarding the incident:

    Place of Occurrence: Corner of Frank and Lincoln Avenues
    Time of Occurrence: 9:40 A.M.
    Crime: Assault
    Victim: Mr. John Adams of 31 20th Street
    Suspect: Male, white, 5'11", 170 lbs., dressed in gray
    Injury: Victim suffered a split lip
    Action Taken: Victim transported to St. Mary's Hospital

    Officer Martinez is completing a report on the incident. Which one of the following expresses the above information MOST clearly and accurately?

    A. At 9:40 A.M., John Adams was assaulted on the corner of Frank and Lincoln Avenues by a white male, 5'11", 170 lbs., dressed in gray, suffering a split lip. Mr. Adams lives at 31 20th Street and was transported to St. Mary's Hospital.
    B. At 9:40 A.M., John Adams was assaulted on the corner of Frank and Lincoln Avenues by a white male, 5'11", 170 lbs., dressed in gray, and lives at 31 20th Street. Mr. Adams suffered a split lip and was transported to St. Mary's Hospital.

C. John Adams, who lives at 31 20th Street, was assaulted at 9:40 A.M. on the corner of Frank and Lincoln Avenues by a white male, 5'11", 170 lbs., dressed in gray. Mr. Adams suffered a split lip and was transported to St. Mary's Hospital.

D. Living at 31 20th Street, Mr. Adams suffered a split lip and was transported to St. Mary's Hospital. At 9:40 A.M., Mr. Adams was assaulted by a white male, 5'11", 170 lbs., dressed in gray.

14. The following information was obtained by Police Officer Adams at the scene of an auto accident:

Date of Occurrence:	August 7, 2004
Place of Occurrence:	541 W. Broadway
Time of Occurrence:	12:45 P.M.
Drivers:	Mrs. Liz Smith and Mr. John Sharp
Action Taken:	Summons served to Mrs. Liz Smith

Officer Adams is completing a report on the accident. Which one of the following expresses the above information MOST clearly and accurately?

A. At 541 W. Broadway, Mr. John Sharp and Mrs. Liz Smith had an auto accident at 12:45 P.M. Mrs. Smith received a summons on August 7, 2004.

B. Mrs. Liz Smith received a summons at 12:45 P.M. on August 7, 2004 for an auto accident with Mr. John Sharp at 541 W. Broadway.

C. Mr. John Sharp and Mrs. Liz Smith were in an auto accident. At 541 W. Broadway on August 7, 2004 at 12:45 P.M., Mrs. Smith received a summons.

D. On August 7, 2004 at 12:45 P.M. at 541 W. Broadway, Mrs. Liz Smith and Mr. John Sharp were involved in an auto accident. Mrs. Smith received a summons.

15. Police Officer Gold and his partner were directed by the radio dispatcher to investigate a report of a past burglary. They obtained the following information at the scene:

Date of Occurrence:	April 2, 2004
Time of Occurrence:	Between 7:30 A.M. and 6:15 P.M.
Place of Occurrence:	124 Haring Street, residence of victim
Victim:	Mr. Gerald Palmer
Suspect:	Unknown
Crime:	Burglary
Items Stolen:	Assorted jewelry, $150 cash, TV, VCR

Officer Gold must complete a report on the incident. Which one of the following expresses the above information MOST clearly and accurately?

A. Mr. Gerald Palmer stated that on April 2, 2004, between 7:30 A.M. and 6:15 P.M., while he was at work, someone broke into his house at 124 Haring Street and removed assorted jewelry, a VCR, $150 cash, and a TV.

B. Mr. Gerald Palmer stated while he was at work that somebody broke into his house on April 2, 2004 and between 7:30 A.M. and 6:15 P.M. took his VCR, TV, assorted jewelry, and $150 cash. His address is 124 Haring Street.

C. Between 7:30 A.M. and 6:15 P.M. on April 2, 2004, Mr. Gerald Palmer reported an unknown person at 124 Haring Street took his TV, VCR, $150 cash, and assorted jewelry from his house. Mr. Palmer said he was at work at the time.

D. An unknown person broke into the house at 124 Haring Street and stole a TV, VCR, assorted jewelry, and $150 cash from Mr. Gerald Palmer. The suspect broke in on April 2, 2004 while he was at work, reported Mr. Palmer between 7:30 A.M. and 6:15 P.M.

16. While on patrol, Police Officers Morris and Devine receive a call to respond to a reported burglary. The following information relating to the crime was obtained by the Officers:
    Time of Occurrence: 2:00 A.M.
    Place of Occurrence: 2100 First Avenue
    Witness: David Santiago
    Victim: John Rivera
    Suspect: Joe Ryan
    Crime: Burglary, DVD player stolen
    The Officers are completing a report on the incident.
    Which one of the following expresses the above information MOST clearly and accurately?

    A. David Santiago, the witness reported at 2:00 A.M. he saw Joe Ryan leave 2100 First Avenue, home of John Rivera, with a DVD player.
    B. At 2:00 A.M. David Santiago reported that he had seen Joe Ryan go into 2100 First Avenue and steal a DVD player. John Rivera lives at 2100 First Avenue.
    C. David Santiago stated that Joe Ryan burglarized John Rivera's house at 2100 First Avenue. He saw Joe Ryan leaving his house at 2:00 A.M. with a DVD player.
    D. David Santiago reported that at 2:00 A.M. he saw Joe Ryan leave John Rivera's house, located at 2100 First Avenue, with Mr. Rivera's DVD player.

17. When a police officer responds to an incident involving the victim of an animal bite, the officer should do the following in the order given:
    I. Determine the owner of the animal
    II. Obtain a description of the animal and attempt to locate it for an examination if the owner is unknown
    III. If the animal is located and the owner is unknown, comply with the Care and Disposition of Animal procedure
    IV. Prepare a Department of Health Form 480BAA and deliver it to the Desk Officer with a written report
    V. Notify the Department of Health by telephone if the person has been bitten by an animal other than a dog or cat.

    Police Officer Rosario responds to 1225 South Boulevard where someone has been bitten by a dog. He is met by John Miller who informs Officer Rosario that he was bitten by a large German Shepard. Mr. Miller also states that he believes the dog belongs to someone in the neighborhood but does not know who owns it. Officer Rosario searches the area for the dog but is unable to find it.
    What should Officer Rosario do NEXT?

    A. Locate the owner of the animal.
    B. Notify the Department of Health by telephone.
    C. Prepare a Department of Health Form 480BAA.
    D. Comply with the Care and Disposition of Animal procedure.

18. The following details were obtained by Police Officer Howard at the scene of a hit-and-run accident:

    Place of Occurrence: Intersection of Brown Street and Front Street
    Time of Occurrence: 11:15 A.M.
    Victim: John Lawrence
    Vehicle: Red Chevrolet, license plate 727PQA
    Crime: Leaving the scene of an accident

    Officer Howard is completing a report on the incident. Which one of the following expresses the above information MOST clearly and accurately?

    A. A red Chevrolet, license plate 727PQA, hit John Lawrence. It left the scene of the accident at 11:15 A.M. at the intersection of Brown and Front Streets.
    B. At 11:15 A.M., John Lawrence was walking at the intersection of Brown Street and Front Street when he was struck by a red Chevrolet, license plate 727PQA, which left the scene.
    C. It was reported at 11:15 A.M. that John Lawrence was struck at the intersection of Brown Street and Front Street. The red Chevrolet, license plate 727PQA, left the scene.
    D. At the intersection of Brown Street and Front Street, John Lawrence was the victim of a car at 11:15 A.M. which struck him and left the scene. It was a red Chevrolet, license plate 727PQA.

19. Police Officer Donnelly has transported an elderly male to Mt. Hope Hospital after finding him lying on the street. At the hospital, Nurse Baker provided Officer Donnelly with the following information:

    Name: Robert Jones
    Address: 1485 E. 97th St.
    Date of Birth: May 13, 1935
    Age: 73 years old
    Type of Ailment: Heart condition

    Officer Donnelly is completing an Aided Report.
    Which one of the following expresses the above information MOST clearly and accurately?

    A. Mr. Robert Jones, who is 73 years old, born on May 13, 1935, collapsed on the street. Mr. Jones, who resides at 1485 E. 97th Street, suffers from a heart condition.
    B. Mr. Robert Jones had a heart condition and collapsed today on the street, and resides at 1485 E. 97th Street. He was 73 years old and born on May 13, 1935.
    C. Mr. Robert Jones, who resides at 1485 E. 97th Street, was born on May 13, 1935, and is 73 years old, was found lying on the street from a heart condition.
    D. Mr. Robert Jones, born on May 13, 1935, suffers from a heart condition at age 73 and was found lying on the street residing at 1485 E. 97th Street.

20. Police officers on patrol are often called to a scene where a response from the Fire Department might be necessary.
    In which one of the following situations would a request to the Fire Department to respond be MOST critical?

10 (#2)

    A. A film crew has started a small fire in order to shoot a scene on an October evening.
    B. Two manhole covers blow off on a September afternoon.
    C. Homeless persons are gathered around a trash can fire on a February morning.
    D. A fire hydrant has been opened by people in the neighborhood on a July afternoon.

21. Police Officer Johnson arrives at the National Savings Bank five minutes after it has been robbed at gunpoint.
The following are details provided by eyewitnesses: <u>Suspect</u>
Sex: Male
Ethnicity: White
Height: 5'10" to 6'2"
Weight: 180 lbs. to 190 lbs.
Hair Color: Blonde
Clothing: Black jacket, blue dungarees
Weapon: .45 caliber revolver
Officer Johnson is completing a report on the incident.
Which one of the following expresses the above information MOST clearly and accurately?
A white male

    A. weighing 180-190 lbs. robbed the National Savings Bank. He was white with a black jacket with blonde hair, is 5'10" to 6'2", and blue dungarees. The robber was armed with a .45 caliber revolver.
    B. weighing around 180 or 190 lbs. was wearing a black jacket and blue dungarees. He had blonde hair and had a .45 caliber revolver, and was 5'10" to 6'2". He robbed the National Savings Bank.
    C. who was 5'10" to 6'2" and was weighing 180 to 190 lbs., and has blonde hair and wearing blue dungarees and a black jacket with a revolver, robbed the National Savings Bank.
    D. armed with a .45 caliber revolver robbed the National Savings Bank. The robber was described as being between 180-190 lbs., 5'10" to 6'2", with blonde hair. He was wearing a black jacket and blue dungarees.

22. While on patrol, Police Officer Rogers is approached by Terry Conyers, a young woman whose pocketbook has been stolen. Ms. Conyers tells Officer Rogers that the following items were in her pocketbook at the time it was taken:
    4 Traveler's checks, each valued at $20.00
    3 Traveler's checks, each valued at $25.00
    Cash of $212.00
    1 wedding band valued at $450.00
Officer Rogers is preparing a Complaint Report on the robbery.
Which one of the following is the TOTAL value of the property and cash taken from Ms. Conyers?

    A. $707   B. $807   C. $817   D. $837

23. While on patrol, Police Officer Scott is dispatched to respond to a reported burglary. Two burglars entered the home of Mr. and Mrs. Walker and stole the following items:
    3 watches valued at $65.00 each
    1 amplifier valued at $340.00
    1 television set valued at $420.00
    Officer Scott is preparing a Complaint Report on the burglary.
    Which one of the following is the TOTAL value of the property stolen?

    A. $707 B. $825 C. $920 D. $955

24. While on patrol, Police Officer Smith is dispatched to investigate a grand larceny. Deborah Paisley, a businesswoman, reports that her 2000 Porsche was broken into. The following items were taken:
    1 car stereo system valued at $2,950.00
    1 car phone valued at $1,060.00
    Ms. Paisley's attache case valued at $200.00 was also taken from the car in the incident. The attache case contained two new solid gold pens valued at $970.00 each.
    Officer Smith is completing a Complaint Report.
    Which one of the following is the TOTAL dollar value of the property stolen from Ms. Paisley's car?

    A. $5,180 B. $5,980 C. $6,040 D. $6,150

25. Police Officer Grundig is writing a Complaint Report regarding a burglary and assault case. Officer Grundig has obtained the following facts:
    Place of Occurrence: 2244 Clark Street
    Victim: Mrs. Willis
    Suspect: Mr. Willis, victim's ex-husband
    Complaint: Unlawful entry; head injury inflicted with a bat
    Officer Grundig is completing a report on the incident. Which one of the following expresses the above information MOST clearly and accurately?

    A. He had no permission or authority to do so and it caused her head injuries, when Mr. Willis entered his ex-wife's premises. Mrs. Willis lives at 2244 Clark Street. He hit her with a bat.
    B. Mr. Willis entered 2244 Clark Street, the premises of his ex-wife. He hit her with a bat, without permission and authority to do so. It caused Mrs. Willis to have head injuries.
    C. After Mr. Willis hit his ex-wife, Mrs. Willis, at 2244 Clark Street, the bat caused her to have head injuries. He had no permission nor authority do so so.
    D. Mr. Willis entered his ex-wife's premises at 2244 Clark Street without her permission or authority. He then struck Mrs. Willis with a bat, causing injuries to her head.

KEY (CORRECT ANSWERS)

1.	C	11.	B
2.	A	12.	D
3.	B	13.	C
4.	C	14.	D
5.	A	15.	A
6.	B	16.	D
7.	D	17.	C
8.	A	18.	B
9.	C	19.	A
10.	C	20.	B

21. D
22. C
23. D
24. D
25. D

PREPARING WRITTEN MATERIAL

PARAGRAPH REARRANGEMENT
COMMENTARY

The sentences that follow are in scrambled order. You are to rearrange them in proper order and indicate the letter choice containing the correct answer at the space at the right.

Each group of sentences in this section is actually a paragraph presented in scrambled order. Each sentence in the group has a place in that paragraph; no sentence is to be left out. You are to read each group of sentences and decide upon the best order in which to put the sentences so as to form a well-organized paragraph.

The questions in this section measure the ability to solve a problem when all the facts relevant to its solution are not given.

More specifically, certain positions of responsibility and authority require the employee to discover connection between events sometimes, apparently, unrelated. In order to do this, the employee will find it necessary to correctly infer that unspecified events have probably occurred or are likely to occur. This ability becomes especially important when action must be taken on incomplete information.

Accordingly, these questions require competitors to choose among several suggested alternatives, each of which presents a different sequential arrangement of the events. Competitors must choose the MOST logical of the suggested sequences.

In order to do so, they may be required to draw on general knowledge to infer missing concepts or events that are essential to sequencing the given events. Competitors should be careful to infer only what is essential to the sequence. The plausibility of the wrong alternatives will always require the inclusion of unlikely events or of additional chains of events which are NOT essential to sequencing the given events.

It's very important to remember that you are looking for the best of the four possible choices, and that the best choice of all may not even be one of the answers you're given to choose from.

There is no one right way to solve these problems. Many people have found it helpful to first write out the order of the sentences, as they would have arranged them, on their scrap paper before looking at the possible answers. If their optimum answer is there, this can save them some time. If it isn't, this method can still give insight into solving the problem. Others find it most helpful to just go through each of the possible choices, contrasting each as they go along. You should use whatever method feels comfortable and works for you.

While most of these types of questions are not that difficult, we've added a higher percentage of the difficult type, just to give you more practice. Usually there are only one or two questions on this section that contain such subtle distinctions that you're unable to answer confidently. And you then may find yourself stuck deciding between two possible choices, neither of which you're sure about.

EXAMINATION SECTION
TEST 1

DIRECTIONS: Each question consists of several sentences which can be arranged in a logical sequence. For each question, select the choice which places the numbered sentences in the MOST logical sequence. *PRINT THE LETTER OF THE CORRECT ANSWER IN THE SPACE AT THE RIGHT.*

1.
   I. A body was found in the woods.
   II. A man proclaimed innocence.
   III. The owner of a gun was located.
   IV. A gun was traced.
   V. The owner of a gun was questioned.
   The CORRECT answer is:
   A. IV, III, V, II, I
   B. II, I, IV, III, V
   C. I, IV, III, V, II
   D. I, III, V, II, IV
   E. I, II, IV, III, V

   1.____

2.
   I. A man is in a hunting accident.
   II. A man fell down a flight of steps.
   III. A man lost his vision in one eye.
   IV. A man broke his leg.
   V. A man had to walk with a cane.
   The CORRECT answer is:
   A. II, IV, V, I, III
   B. IV, V, I, III, II
   C. III, I, IV, V, II
   D. I, III, V, II, IV
   E. I, III, II, IV, V

   2.____

3.
   I. A man is offered a new job.
   II. A woman is offered a new job.
   III. A man works as a waiter.
   IV. A woman works as a waitress.
   V. A woman gives notice.
   The CORRECT answer is:
   A. IV, II, V, III, I
   B. IV, II, V, I, III
   C. II, IV, V, III, I
   D. III, I, IV, II, V
   E. IV, III, II, V, I

   3.____

4.
   I. A train let the station late.
   II. A man was late for work.
   III. A man lost his job.
   IV. Many people complained because the train was late.
   V. There was a traffic jam.
   The CORRECT answer is:
   A. V, II, I, IV, III
   B. V, I, IV, II, III
   C. V, I, II, IV, III
   D. I, V, IV, II, III
   E. II, I, IV, V, III

   4.____

5.
I. The burden of proof as to each issue is determined before trial and remains upon the same party throughout the trial.
II. The jury is at liberty to believe one witness' testimony as against a number of contradictory witnesses.
III. In a civil case, the party bearing the burden of proof is required to prove his contention by a fair preponderance of the evidence.
IV. However, it must be noted that a fair preponderance of evidence does not necessarily mean a greater number of witnesses.
V. The burden of proof is the burden which rests upon one of the parties to an action to persuade the trier of the facts, generally the jury, that a proposition he asserts is true.
VI. If the evidence is equally balanced, or if it leaves the jury in such doubt as to be unable to decide the controversy either way, judgment must be given against the party upon whom the burden of proof rests.
The CORRECT answer is:
A. III, II, V, IV, I, VI   B. I, II, VI, V, III, IV   C. III, IV, V, I, II, VI
D. V, I, III, VI, IV, II   E. I, V, III, VI, IV, II

6.
I. If a parent is without assets and is unemployed, he cannot be convicted of the crime of non-support of a child.
II. The term *sufficient ability* has been held to mean sufficient financial ability.
III. It does not matter if his unemployment is by choice or unavoidable circumstances.
IV. If he fails to take any steps at all, he may be liable to prosecution for endangering the welfare of a child.
V. Under the penal law, a parent is responsible for the support of his minor child only if the parent is of *sufficient ability*.
VI. An indigent parent may meet his obligation by borrowing money or by seeking aid under the provisions of the Social Welfare Law.
The CORRECT answer is:
A. VI, I, V, III, II, IV   B. I, III, V, II, IV, VI   C. V, II, I, III, VI, IV
D. I, VI, IV, V, II, III   E. II, V, I, III, VI, IV

7.
I. Consider, for example, the case of a rabble rouser who urges a group of twenty people to go out and break the windows of a nearby factory.
II. Therefore, the law fills the indicated gap with the crime of *inciting to riot*.
III. A person is considered guilty of inciting to riot when he urges ten or more persons to engage in tumultuous and violent conduct of a kind likely to create public alarm.
IV. However, if he has not obtained the cooperation of at least four people, he cannot be charged with unlawful assembly.
V. The charge of inciting to riot was added to the law to cover types of conduct which cannot be classified as either the crime of *riot* or the crime of *unlawful assembly*.
VI. If he acquires the acquiescence of at least four of them, he is guilty of unlawful assembly even if the project does not materialize.
The CORRECT answer is:
A. III, V, I, VI, IV, II   B. V, I, IV, VI, II, III   C. III, IV, I, V, II, VI
D. V, I, IV, VI, III, II   E. V, III, I, VI, IV, II

8. I. If, however, the rebuttal evidence presents an issue of credibility, it is for the jury to determine whether the presumption has, in fact, been destroyed.
    II. Once sufficient evidence to the contrary is introduced, the presumption disappears from the trial.
    III. The effect of a presumption is to place the burden upon the adversary to come forward with evidence to rebut the presumption.
    IV. When a presumption is overcome and ceases to exist in the case, the fact or facts which gave rise to the presumption still remain.
    V. Whether a presumption has been overcome is ordinarily a question for the court.
    VI. Such information may furnish a basis for a logical inference.
    The CORRECT answer is:
    A. IV, VI, II, V, I, III   B. III, II, V, I, IV, VI   C. V, III, VI, IV, II, I
    D. V, IV, I, II, VI, III   E. II, III, V, I, IV, VI

9. I. An executive may answer a letter by writing his reply on the face of the letter itself instead of having a return letter typed.
    II. This procedure is efficient because it saves the executive's time, the typist's time, and saves office file space.
    III. Copying machines are used in small offices as well as large offices to save time and money in making brief replies to business letters.
    IV. A copy is made on a copying machine to go into the company files, while the original is mailed back to the sender.
    The CORRECT answer is:
    A. I, II, IV, III   B. I, IV, II, III   C. III, I, IV, II   D. III, IV, II, I

10. I. Most organizations favor one of the types but always include the others to a lesser degree.
    II. However, we can detect a definite trend toward greater use of symbolic control.
    III. We suggest that our local police agencies are today primarily utilizing material control.
    IV. Control can be classified into three types: physical, material, and symbolic.
    The CORRECT answer is:
    A. IV, II, III, I   B. II, I, IV, III   C. III, IV, II, I   D. IV, I, III, II

11. I. Project residents had first claim to this use, followed by surrounding neighborhood children.
    II. By contrast, recreation space within the project's interior was found to be used more often by both groups.
    III. Studies of the use of project grounds in many cities showed grounds left open for public use were neglected and unused, both by residents and by members of the surrounding community.
    IV. Project residents had clearly laid claim to the play spaces, setting up and enforcing unwritten rules for use.
    V. Each group, by experience, found their activities easily disrupted by other groups, and their claim to the use of space for recreation difficult to enforce.

The CORRECT answer is:
A. IV, V, I, II, III
B. V, II, IV, III, I
C. I, IV, III, II, V
D. III, V, II, IV, I

12. I. They do not consider the problems correctable within the existing subsidy formula and social policy of accepting all eligible applicants regardless of social behavior.
    II. A recent survey, however, indicated that tenants believe these problems correctable by local housing authorities and management within the existing financial formula.
    III. Many of the problems and complaints concerning public housing management and design have created resentment between the tenant and the landlord.
    IV. This same survey indicated that administrators and managers do not agree with the tenants.
    The CORRECT answer is:
    A. II, I, III, IV   B. I, III, IV, II   C. III, II, IV, I   D. IV, II, I, III

12.____

13. I. In single-family residences, there is usually enough distance between tenants to prevent occupants from annoying one another.
    II. For example, a certain small percentage of tenant families has one or more members addicted to alcohol.
    III. While managers believe in the right of individuals to live as they choose, the manager becomes concerned when the pattern of living jeopardizes others' rights.
    IV. Still others turn night into day, staging lusty entertainments which carry on into the hours when most tenants are trying to sleep.
    V. In apartment buildings, however, tenants live so closely together that any misbehavior can result in unpleasant living conditions.
    VI. Other families engage in violent argument.
    The CORRECT answer is:
    A. III, II, V, IV, VI, I
    B. I, V, II, VI, IV, III
    C. II, V, IV, I, III, VI
    D. IV, II, V, VI, III, I

13.____

14. I. Congress made the commitment explicit in the Housing Act of 194, establishing as a national goal the realization of a *decent home and suitable environment for every American family*.
    II. The result has been that the goal of decent home and suitable environment is still as far distant as ever for the disadvantaged urban family.
    III. In spite of this action by Congress, federal housing programs have continued to be fragmented and grossly underfunded.
    IV. The passage of the National Housing Act signaled a few federal commitment to provide housing for the nation's citizens.
    The CORRECT answer is:
    A. I, IV, III, II   B. IV, I, III, II   C. IV, I, II, III   D. II, IV, I, III

14.____

15.
I. The greater expense does not necessarily involve *exploitation*, but it is often perceived as exploitative and unfair by those who are aware of the price differences involved, but unaware of operating costs.
II. Ghetto residents believe they are *exploited* by local merchants, and evidence substantiates some of these beliefs.
III. However, stores in low-income areas were more likely to be small independents, which could not achieve the economies available to supermarket chains and were, therefore, more likely to charge higher prices, and the customers were more likely to buy smaller-sized packages which are more expensive per unit of measure.
IV. A study conducted in one city showed that distinctly higher prices were charged for goods sold in ghetto stores in other areas.

The CORRECT answer is:
A. IV, II, I, III   B. IV, I, III, II   C. II, IV, III, I   D. II, III, IV, I

KEY (CORRECT ANSWERS)

1.	C	6.	C	11.	D
2.	E	7.	A	12.	C
3.	B	8.	B	13.	B
4.	B	9.	C	14.	B
5.	D	10.	D	15.	C

PREPARING WRITTEN MATERIAL PARAGRAPH REARRANGEMENT

EXAMINATION SECTION

TEST 1

DIRECTIONS: The sentences that follow are in scrambled order. You are to rearrange them in proper order and indicate the letter choice containing the CORRECT answer. *PRINT THE LETTER OF THE CORRECT ANSWER IN THE SPACE AT THE RIGHT.*

1. Police Officer Jenner responds to the scene of a burglary at 2106 La Vista Boulevard. He is approached by an elderly man named Richard Jenkins, whose account of the incident includes the following five sentences:
   I. I saw that the lock on my apartment door had been smashed and the door was open.
   II. My apartment was a shambles; my belongings were everywhere and my television set was missing.
   III. As I walked down the hallway toward the bedroom, I heard someone opening a window.
   IV. I left work at 5:30 P.M. and took the bus home.
   V. At that time, I called the police.
   The MOST logical order for the above sentence to appear in the report is
   A. I, V, IV, II, III   B. IV, I, II, III, V   C. I, V, II, III, IV   D. IV, III, II, V, I

   1.____

2. Police Officer LaJolla is writing an Incident Report in which back-up assistance was required. The report will contain the following five sentences:
   I. The radio dispatcher asked what my location was and he then dispatched patrol cars for back-up assistance.
   II. At approximately 9:30 P.M., while I was walking my assigned footpost, a gunman fired three shots at me.
   III. I quickly turned around and saw a white male, approximately 5'10", with black hair, wearing blue jeans, a yellow T-shirt, and white sneaker, running across the avenue carrying a handgun.
   IV. When the back-up officers arrived, we searched the area but could not find the suspect.
   V. I advised the radio dispatcher that a gunman had just fired a gun at me, and then I gave the dispatcher a description of the man
   The MOST logical order for the above sentences to appear in the report is:
   A. III, V, II, IV, I   B. II, III, V, I, IV   C. III, II, IV, I, V   D. II, V, I, III, IV

   2.____

3. Police Officer Durant is completing a report of a robbery and assault. The report will contain the following five sentences:
   I. I went to Mount Snow Hospital to interview a man who was attacked and robbed of his wallet earlier that night.
   II. An ambulance arrived at 82nd Street and 3rd Avenue and took an intoxicated, wounded man to Mount Snow Hospital
   III. Two youths attacked the man and stole his wallet.

   3.____

IV. A well-dressed man left Hanratty's Bar very drunk, with his wallet hanging out of his back pocket.
   V. A passerby dialed 911 and requested police and ambulance assistance.
   The MOST logical order for the above sentences to appear in the report is
   A. I, II, IV, III, V   B. IV, III, V, II, I   C. IV, V, II, III, I   D. V, IV, III, II, I

4. Police Officer Boswell is preparing a report of an armed robbery and assault which will contain the following five sentences:
   I. Both men approached the bartender and one of them drew a gun.
   II. The bartender immediately went to grab the phone at the bar.
   III. One of the men leaped over the counter and smashed a bottle over the bartender's head.
   IV. Two men in a blue Buick drove up to the bar and went inside.
   V. I found the cash register empty and the bartender unconscious on the floor, with the phone still dangling off the hook.
   The MOST logical order for the above sentences to appear in the report is
   A. IV, I, II, III, V   B. V, IV, III, I, II   C. IV, III, II, V, I   D. II, I, III, IV, V

5. Police Officer Mitzler is preparing a report of a bank robbery, which will contain the following five sentences:
   I. The teller complied with the instructions on the note, but also hit the silent alarm.
   II. The perpetrator then fled south on Broadway.
   III. A suspicious male entered the bank at approximately 10:45 A.M.
   IV. At this time, an undetermined amount of money has been taken.
   V. He approached the teller on the far right side and handed her a note.
   The MOST logical order for the above sentences to appear in the report is:
   A. III, V, I, II, IV   B. I, III, V, II, IV   C. III, V, IV, I, II   D. III, V, II, IV, I

6. A Police Officer is preparing an Accident Report for an accident which occurred at the intersection of East 119th Street and Lexington Avenue. The report will include the following five sentences:
   I. On September 18, while driving ten children to school, a school bus driver passed out.
   II. Upon arriving at the scene, I notified the dispatcher to send an ambulance.
   III. I notified the parents of each child once I got to the station house.
   IV. He said the school bus, while traveling west on East 119th Street, struck a parked Ford which was on the southwest corner of East 119th Street.
   V. A witness by the name of John Ramos came up to me to describe what happened.
   The MOST logical order for the above sentences to appear in the Accident Report is:
   A. I, II, V, III, IV   B. I, II, V, IV, III   C. II, V, I, III, IV   D. II, V, I, IV, III

7. A Police Officer is preparing a report concerning a dispute. The report will contain the following five sentences:
   I. The passenger got out of the back of the taxi and leaned through the front window to complain to the driver about the fare.

II. The driver of the taxi caught up with the passenger and knocked him to the ground; the passenger then kicked the driver and a scuffle ensued.
III. The taxi drew up in front of the high-rise building and stopped.
IV. The driver got out of the taxi and followed the passenger into the lobby of the apartment building.
V. The doorman tried but was unable to break up the fight, at which point he called the precinct.

The MOST logical order for the above sentences to appear in the report is
   A. III, I, IV, II, V   B. III, IV, I, II, V   C. III, IV, II, V, I   D. V, I, III, IV, II

8. Police Officer Morrow is writing an Incident Report. The report will include the following four sentences:
I. The man reached into his pocket and pulled out a gun.
II. While on foot patrol, I identified a suspect, who was wanted for six robberies in the area, from a wanted picture I was carrying.
III. I drew my weapon and fired six rounds at the suspect, killing him instantly.
IV. I called for back-up assistance and told the man to put his hands up.

The MOST logical order for the above sentences to appear in the report is
   A. II, III, IV, I   B. IV, I, III, II   C. IV, I, II, III   D. II, IV, I, III

9. Sergeant Allen responds to a call at 16 Grove Street regarding a missing child. At the scene, the Sergeant is met by Police Officer Samuels, who gives a brief account of the incident consisting of the following five sentences:
I. I transmitted the description and waited for you to arrive before I began searching the area.
II. Mrs. Banks, the mother, reports that she last saw her daughter Julie about 7:30 A.M. when she took her to school.
III. About 6 P.M., my partner and I arrived at this location to investigate a report of a missing 8-year-old girl.
IV. When Mrs. Banks left her, Julie was wearing a red and white striped T-shirt, blue jeans, and white sneakers.
V. Mrs. Banks dropped her off in front of the playground of P.S. 11.

The MOST logical order for the above sentences to appear in the report is
   A. III, V, IV, II, I   B. III, II, V, IV, I   C. III, IV, I, II, V   D. III, II, IV, I, V

10. Police Officer Franco is completing a report of an assault. The report will contain the following five sentences:
I. In the park I observed an elderly man lying on the ground, bleeding from a back wound.
II. I applied first aid to control the bleeding and radioed for an ambulance to respond.
III. The elderly man stated that he was sitting on the park bench when he was attacked from behind by two males.
IV. I received a report of a man's screams coming from inside the park, and I went to investigate.
V. The old man could not give a description of his attackers.

The MOST logical order for the above sentences to appear in the report is
   A. IV, I, II, III, V   B. V, II, I, IV, II   C. IV, III, V, II, I   D. II, I, V, IV, III

11. Police Officer Williams is completing a Crime Report. The report contains the following five sentences:
    I. As Police Officer Hanson and I approached the store, we noticed that the front door was broken.
    II. After determining that the burglars had fled, we notified the precinct of the burglary.
    III. I walked through the front door as Police Officer Hanson walked around to the back.
    IV. At approximately midnight, an alarm was heard at the Apex Jewelry Store.
    V. We searched the store and found no one.
    The MOST logical order for the above sentences to appear in the report is
        A. I, IV, II, III, V   B. I, IV, III, V, II   C. IV, I, III, II, V   D. IV, I, III, V, II

12. Police Officer Clay is giving a report to the news media regarding someone who has jumped from the Empire State Building. His report will include the following five sentences:
    I. I responded to the 86th floor, where I found the person at the edge of the roof.
    II. A security guard at the building had reported that a man was on the roof at the 86th floor.
    III. At 5:30 P.M., the person jumped from the building.
    IV. I received a call from the radio dispatcher at 4:50 P.M. to respond to the Empire State Building.
    V. I tried to talk to the person and convince him not to jump.
    The MOST logical order for the above sentences to appear in the report is
        A. I, II, IV, III, V   B. III, IV, I, II, V   C. II, IV, I, III, V   D. IV, II, I, V, III

13. The following five sentences are part of a report of a burglary written by Police Officer Reed:
    I. When I arrived at 2400 1st Avenue, I noticed that the door was slightly open.
    II. I yelled out, *Police, don't move!*
    III. As I entered the apartment, I saw a man with a TV set passing through a window to another man standing on a fire escape.
    IV. While on foot patrol, I was informed by the radio dispatcher that a burglary was in progress at 2400 1st Avenue.
    V. However, the burglars quickly ran down the fire escape.
    The MOST logical order for the above sentences to appear in the report is
        A. I, III, IV, V, II   B. IV, I, III, V, II   C. IV, I, III, II, V   D. I, IV, III, II, V

14. Police Officer Jenkins is preparing a report for Lost or Stolen Property. The report will include the following five sentences:
    I. On the stairs, Mr. Harris slipped on a wet leaf and fell on the landing.
    II. It wasn't until he got to the token booth that Mr. Harris realized his wallet was no longer in his back pants pocket.
    III. A boy wearing a football jersey helped him up and brushed off the back of Mr. Harris' pants.
    IV. Mr. Harris states he was walking up the stairs to the elevated subway at Queensborough Plaza.
    V. Before Mr. Harris could thank him, the boy was running down the stairs to the street.

The MOST logical order for the above sentences to appear in the report is
A. IV, III, V, I, II   B. IV, I, III, V, II   C. I, IV, II, III, V   D. I, II, IV, III, V

15. Police Officer Hubbard is completing a report of a missing person. The report will contain the following five sentences:
    I. I visited the store at 7:55 P.M. and asked the employees if they had seen a girl fitting the description I had been given.
    II. She gave me a description and said she had gone into the local grocery store at about 6:15 P.M.
    III. I asked the woman for a description of her daughter.
    IV. The distraught woman called the precinct to report that her daughter, aged 12, had not returned from an errand.
    V. The storekeeper said a girl matching the description had been in the store earlier, but he could not give an exact time.
    The MOST logical order for the above sentences to appear in the report is
    A. I, III, II, V, IV   B. IV, III, II, I, V   C. V, I, II, III, IV   D. III, I, II, IV, V

16. A police officer is completing an entry in his Daily Activity Log regarding traffic summonses which he issued. The following five sentences will be included in the entry:
    I. I was on routine patrol parked 16 yards west of 170th Street and Clay Avenue.
    II. The summonses were issued for unlicensed operator and disobeying a steady red light.
    III. At 8 A.M. hours, I observed an auto traveling westbound on 170th Street not stop for a steady red light at the intersection of Clay Avenue and 170th Street.
    IV. I stopped the driver of the auto and determined that he did not have a valid driver's license.
    V. After a brief conversation, I informed the motorist that he was receiving two summonses.
    The MOST logical order for the above sentences to appear in the report is
    A. I, III, IV, V, II   B. III, IV, II, V, I   C. V, II, I, III, IV   D. IV, V, II, I, III

17. The following sentences appeared on an Incident Report:
    I. Three teenagers who had been ejected from the theater were yelling at patrons who were now entering.
    II. Police Officer Dixon told the teenagers to leave the area.
    III. The teenager said that they were told by the manager to leave the theater because they were talking during the movie.
    IV. The theater manager called the precinct at 10:20 P.M. to report a disturbance outside the theater.
    V. A patrol car responded to the theater at 10:42 P.M. and two police officers went over to the teenagers.
    The MOST logical order for the above sentences to appear in the Incident Report is
    A. I, V, IV, III, II   B. IV, I, V, III, II   C. IV, I, III, V, II   D. IV, III, I, V, II

18. Activity Log entries are completed by police officers. Police Officer Samuels has written an entry concerning vandalism and part of it contains the following five sentences:
    I. The man, in his early twenties, ran down the block and around the corner.
    II. A man passing the store threw a brick through a window of the store.
    III. I arrived on the scene and began to question the witnesses about the incident.
    IV. Malcolm Holmes, the owner of the Fast Service Shoe Repair Store, was working in the back of the store at approximately 3 P.M.
    V. After the man fled, Mr. Holmes called the police.
    The MOST logical order for the above sentences to appear in the Activity Log is
    A. IV, II, I, V, III B. II, IV, I, III, V C. II, I, IV, III, V D. IV, II, V, III, I

19. Police Officer Buckley is preparing a report concerning a dispute in a restaurant. The report will contain the following five sentences:
    I. The manager, Charles Chin, and a customer, Edward Green, were standing near the register arguing over the bill.
    II. The manager refused to press any charges providing Green pay the check and leave.
    III. While on foot patrol, I was informed by a passerby of a disturbance in the Dragon Flame Restaurant.
    IV. Green paid the $15.00 check and left the restaurant.
    V. According to witnesses, the customer punched the owner in the face when Chin asked him for the amount due.
    The MOST logical order for the above sentences to appear in the report is
    A. III, I, V, II, IV B. I, II, III, IV, V C. V, I, III, II, IV D. III, V, II, IV, I

20. Police Officer Wilkins is preparing a report for leaving the scene of an accident. The report will include the following five sentences:
    I. The Dodge struck the right rear fender of Mrs. Smith's 2010 Ford and continued on its way.
    II. Mrs. Smith stated she was making a left turn from 40th Street onto Third Avenue.
    III. As the car passed, Mrs. Smith noticed the dangling rear license plate #412AEJ.
    IV. Mrs. Smith complained to police of back pains and was removed by ambulance to Bellevue Hospital.
    V. An old green Dodge traveling up Third Avenue went through the red light at 40th Street and Third Avenue.
    The MOST logical order for the above sentences to appear in the report is
    A. V, III, I, II, IV B. I, III, II, V, IV C. IV, V, I, II, III D. II, V, I, III, IV

21. Detective Simon is completing a Crime Report. The report contains the following five sentences:
    I. Police Officer Chin, while on foot patrol, heard the yelling and ran in the direction of the man.
    II. The man, carrying a large hunting knife, left the High Sierra Sporting Goods Store at approximately 10:30 A.M.

III. When the man heard Police Officer Chin, he stopped, dropped the knife, and began to cry.
IV. As Police Officer Chin approached the man, he drew his gun and yelled, *Police, freeze.*
V. After the man left the store, he began yelling, over and over, *I am going to kill myself!*

The MOST logical order for the above sentences to appear in the report is
   A. V, II, I, IV, III   B. II, V, I, IV, III   C. II, V, IV, I, III   D. II, I, V, IV, III

22. Police Officer Miller is preparing a Complaint Report which will include the following five sentences:
    I. From across the lot, he yelled to the boys to get away from his car.
    II. When he came out of the store, he noticed two teenage boys trying to break into his car.
    III. The boys fled as Mr. Johnson ran to his car.
    IV. Mr. Johnson stated that he parked his car in the municipal lot behind Tams Department Store.
    V. Mr. Johnson saw that the door lock had been broken, but nothing was missing from inside the auto.

    The MOST logical order for the above sentences to appear in the report is
       A. IV, I, II, V, III   B. II, III, I, V, IV   C. IV, II, I, III, V   D. I, II, III, V, IV

23. Police Officer O'Hara completes a Universal Summons for a motorist who has just passed a red traffic light. The Universal Summons includes the following five sentences:
    I. As the car passed the light, I followed in the patrol car.
    II. After the driver stopped the car, he stated that the light was yellow, not red.
    III. A blue Cadillac sedan passed the red light on the corner of 79th Street and 3rd Avenue at 11:25 P.M.
    IV. As a result, the driver was informed that he did pass a red light and that his brake lights were not working.
    V. The driver in the Cadillac stopped his car as soon as he saw the patrol car, and I noticed that the brake lights were not working.

    The MOST logical order for the above sentences to appear in the Universal Summons is
       A. I, III, V, II, IV   B. III, I, V, II, IV   C. III, I, V, IV, II   D. I, III, IV, II, V

24. Detective Egan is preparing a follow-up report regarding a homicide on 170th Street and College Avenue. An unknown male was found at the scene. The report will contain the following five sentences:
    I. Police Officer Gregory wrote down the names, addresses, and phone numbers of the witnesses.
    II. A 911 operator received a call of a man shot and dispatched Police Officers Worth and Gregory to the scene.
    III. They discovered an unidentified male dead on the street.
    IV. Police Officer Worth notified the Precinct Detective Unit immediately.
    V. At approximately 9:00 A.M., an unidentified male shot another male in the chest during an argument.

The MOST logical order for the above sentences to appear in the report is
A. V, II, III, IV, I   B. II, III, V, IV, I   C. IV, I, V, II, III   D. V, III, II, IV, I

25. Police Officer Tracey is preparing a Robbery Report which will include the following five sentences:
   I. I ran around the corner and observe a man pointing a gun at a taxidriver.
   II. I informed the man I was a police officer and that he should not move.
   III. I was on the corner of 125th Street and Park Avenue when I heard a scream coming from around the corner.
   IV. The man turned around and fired one shot at me.
   V. I fired once, shooting him in the arm and causing him to fall to the ground.
   The MOST logical order for the above sentences to appear in the report is
   A. I, III, IV, II, V   B. IV, V, II, I, III   C. III, I, II, IV, V   D. III, I, V, II, IV

KEY (CORRECT ANSWERS)

1.	B	11.	D
2.	B	12.	D
3.	B	13.	C
4.	A	14.	B
5.	A	15.	B
6.	B	16.	A
7.	A	17.	B
8.	D	18.	A
9.	B	19.	A
10.	A	20.	D

21.	B
22.	C
23.	B
24.	A
25.	C

TEST 2

DIRECTIONS: The sentences that follow are in scrambled order. You are to rearrange them in proper order and indicate the letter choice containing the CORRECT answer. *PRINT THE LETTER OF THE CORRECT ANSWER IN THE SPACE AT THE RIGHT*

1. Police Officer Weiker is completing a Complaint Report which will contain the following five sentences:
   I. Mr. Texlor was informed that the owner of the van would receive a parking ticket and that the van would be towed away.
   II. The police tow truck arrived approximately one half hour after Mr. Texlor complained.
   III. While on foot patrol on West End Avenue, I saw the owner of Rand's Restaurant arrive to open his business.
   IV. Mr. Texlor, the owner, called to me and complained that he could not receive deliveries because a van was blocking his driveway.
   V. The van's owner later reported to the precinct that his van had been stolen, and he was then informed that it had been towed.
   The MOST logical order for the above sentences to appear in the report is
   A. III, V, I, II, IV   B. III, IV, I, II, V   C. IV, III, I, II, V   D. IV, III, II, I, V

   1.____

2. Police Officer Ames is completing an entry in his Activity Log. The entry contains the following five sentences:
   I. Mr. Sands gave me a complete description of the robber.
   II. Alvin Sands, owner of the Star Delicatessen, called the precinct to report he had just been robbed.
   III. I then notified all police patrol vehicles to look for a white male in his early twenties wearing brown pants and shirt, a black leather jacket, and black and white sneakers.
   IV. I arrived on the scene after being notified by the precinct that a robbery had just occurred at the Star Delicatessen.
   V. Twenty minutes later, a man fitting the description was arrested by a police officer on patrol six blocks from the delicatessen.
   The MOST logical order for the above sentences to appear in the Activity Log is
   A. II, I, IV, III, V   B. II, IV, III, I, V   C. II, IV, I, III, V   D. II, IV, I, V, III

   2.____

3. Police Officer Benson is completing a Complaint Report concerning a stolen taxicab, which will include the following five sentences:
   I. Police Officer Benson noticed that a cab was parked next to a fire hydrant.
   II. Dawson *borrowed* the cab for transportation purposes since he was in a hurry.
   III. Ed Dawson got into his car and tried to start it, but the battery was dead.
   IV. When he reached his destination he parked the cab by a fire hydrant and placed the keys under the seat.
   V. He looked around and saw an empty cab with the engine running.
   The MOST logical order for the above sentences to appear in the report is
   A. I, III, II, IV, V   B. III, I, II, V, IV   C. III, V, II, IV, I   D. V, II, IV, III, I

   3.____

4. Police Officer Hatfield is reviewing his Activity Log entry prior to completing a report. The entry contains the following five sentences:
   I. When I arrived at Zand's Jewelry Store, I noticed that the door was slightly open.
   II. I told the burglar I was a police officer and that he should stand still or he would be shot.
   III. As I entered the store, I saw a man wearing a ski mask attempting to open the safe in the back of the store.
   IV. On December 16, 2020, at 1:38 A.M., I was informed that a burglary was in progress at Zand's Jewelry Store on East 59th Street.
   V. The burglar quickly pulled a knife from his pocket when he saw me.
   The MOST logical order for the above sentences to appear in the report is
   A. IV, I, III, V, II   B. I, IV, III, V, II   C. IV, III, II, V, I   D. I, III, IV, V, II

4._____

5. Police Officer Lorenz is completing a report of a murder. The report will contain the following five statements made by a witness:
   I. I was awakened by the sound of a gunshot coming from the apartment next door and I decided to check.
   II. I entered the apartment and looked into the kitchen and the bathroom.
   III. I found Mr. Hubbard's body slumped in the bathtub.
   IV. The door to the apartment was open, but I didn't see anyone.
   V. He had been shot in the head.
   The MOST logical order for the above sentences to appear in the report is
   A. I, III, II, IV, V   B. I, IV, II, III, V   C. IV, II, I, III, V   D. III, I, II, IV, V

5._____

6. Police Officer Baldwin is preparing an accident report which will include the following five sentences:
   I. The old man lay on the ground for a few minutes, but was not physically hurt.
   II. Charlie Watson, a construction worker, was repairing some brick work at the top of a building at 54th Street and Madison Avenue.
   III. Steven Green, his partner, warned him that this could be dangerous, but Watson ignored him.
   IV. A few minutes later, one of the bricks thrown by Watson smashed to the ground in front of an old man, who fainted out of fright.
   V. Mr. Watson began throwing some of the bricks over the side of the building.
   The MOST logical order for the above sentences to appear in the report is
   A. II, V, III, IV, I   B. I, IV, II, V, III   C. III, II, IV, V, I   D. II, III, I, IV, V

6._____

7. Police Officer Porter is completing an Incident Report concerning her rescue of a woman being held hostage by a former boyfriend. Her report will contain the following five sentences:
   I. I saw a man holding .25 caliber gun to a woman's head, but he did not see me.
   II. I then broke a window and gained access to the house.
   III. As I approached the house on foot, a gunshot rang out and I heard a woman scream.
   IV. A decoy van brought me as close as possible to the house where the woman was being held hostage.

7._____

V. I ordered the man to drop his gun, and he released the woman and was taken into custody.

The MOST logical order for the above sentences to appear in the report is
   A. I, III, II, IV, V   B. IV, III, II, I, V   C. III, II, I, IV, V   D. V, I, II, III, IV

8. Police Officer Byrnes is preparing a crime report concerning a robbery. The report will consist of the following five sentences:
   I. Mr. White, following the man's instructions, opened the car's hood, at which time the man got out of the auto, drew a revolver, and ordered White to give him all the money in his pockets.
   II. Investigation has determined there were no witnesses to this incident.
   III. The man asked White to check the oil and fill the tank.
   IV. Mr. White, a gas attendant, states that he was working alone at the gas station when a black male pulled up to the gas pump in a white Mercury.
   V. White was then bound and gagged by the male and locked in the gas station's rest room.

   The MOST logical order for the above sentences to appear in the report is
      A. IV, I, III, II, V   B. III, I, II, V, IV   C. IV, III, I, V, II   D. I, III, IV, II, V

9. Police Officer Gale is preparing a report of a crime committed against Mr. Weston. The report will consist of the following five sentences:
   I. The man, who had a gun, told Mr. Weston not to scream for help and ordered him back into the apartment.
   II. With Mr. Weston disposed of in this fashion, the man proceeded to ransack the apartment.
   III. Opening the door to see who was there, Mr. Weston was confronted by a tall white male wearing a dark blue jacket and white pants.
   IV. Mr. Weston was at home alone in his living room when the doorbell rang.
   V. Once inside, the man bound and gagged Mr. Weston and locked him in the bathroom.

   The MOST logical order for the above sentences to appear in the report is
      A. III, V, II, I, IV   B. IV, III, I, V, II   C. III, V, IV, II, I   D. IV, III, V, I, II

10. A police officer is completing a report of a robbery, which will contain the following five sentences:
    I. Two police officers were about to enter the Red Rose Coffee Shop on 47th Street and 8th Avenue.
    II. They then noticed a male running up the street carrying a brown paper bag.
    III. They heard a woman standing outside the Broadway Boutique yelling that her store had just been robbed by a young man, and she was pointing up the street.
    IV. They caught up with him and made an arrest.
    V. The police officers pursued the male, who ran past them on 8th Avenue.

    The MOST logical order for the above sentences to appear in the report is
       A. I, III, II, V, IV   B. III, I, II, V, IV   C. IV, V, I, II, III   D. I, V, IV, III, II

11. Police Officer Capalbo is preparing a report of a bank robbery. The report will contain the following five statements made by a witness:
    I. Initialing, all I could see were two men, dressed in maintenance uniforms, sitting in the area reserved for bank officers.
    II. I was passing the bank at 8 P.M. and noticed that all the lights were out, except in the rear section.
    III. Then I noticed two other men in the bank, coming from the direction of the vault, carrying a large metal box.
    IV. At this point, I decided to call the police.
    V. I knocked on the window to get the attention of the men in the maintenance uniforms, and they chased the two men carrying the box down a flight of steps.
    The MOST logical order for the above sentences to appear in the report is
    A. IV, I, II, V, III   B. I, III, II, V, IV   C. II, I, III, V, IV   D. II, III, I, V, IV

12. Police Officer Roberts is preparing a crime report concerning an assault and a stolen car. The report will contain the following five sentences:
    I. Upon leaving the store to return to his car, Winters noticed that a male unknown to him was sitting in his car.
    II. The man then re-entered Winters' car and drove away, fleeing north on 2nd Avenue.
    III. Mr. Winters stated that he parked his car in front of 235 East 25th Street and left the engine running while he went into the butcher shop at that location.
    IV. Mr. Robert Gering, a witness, stated that the male is known in the neighborhood as Bobby Rae and is believed to reside at 323 East 114th Street.
    V. When Winters approached the car and ordered the man to get out, the man got out of the auto and struck Winters with his fists, knocking him to the ground.
    The MOST logical order for the above sentences to appear in the report is
    A. III, II, V, I, IV   B. III, I, V, II, IV   C. I, IV, V, II, III   D. III, II, I, V, IV

13. Police Officer Robinson is preparing a crime report concerning the robbery of Mr. Edwards' store. The report will consist of the following five sentences:
    I. When the last customer left the store, the two men drew revolvers and ordered Mr. Edwards to give them all the money in the cash register.
    II. The men proceeded to the back of the store as if they were going to do some shopping.
    III. Janet Morley, a neighborhood resident, later reported that she saw the men enter a green Ford station wagon and flee northbound on Albany Avenue.
    IV. Edwards complied after which the gunmen ran from the store.
    V. Mr. Edwards states that he was stocking merchandise behind the store counter when two white males entered the store.
    The MOST logical order for the above sentences to appear in the report is
    A. V, II, III, I, IV   B. V, II, I, IV, III   C. II, I, V, IV, III   D. III, V, II, I, IV

14. Police Officer Wendell is preparing an accident report for a 6-car accident that occurred at the intersection of Bath Avenue and Bay Parkway. The report will consist of the following five sentences:
    I. A 2016 Volkswagen Beetle, traveling east on Bath Avenue, swerved to the left to avoid the Impala, and struck a 2014 Ford station wagon which was traveling west on Bath Avenue.
    II. The Seville then mounted the curb on the northeast corner of Bath Avenue and Bay Parkway and struck a light pole.
    III. A 2013 Buick Lesabre, traveling northbound on Bay Parkway directly behind the Impala, struck the Impala, pushing it into the intersection of Bath Avenue and Bay Parkway.
    IV. A 2015 Chevy Impala, traveling northbound on Bay Parkway, had stopped for a red light at Bath Avenue.
    V. A 2017 Toyota, traveling westbound on Bath Avenue, swerved to the right to avoid hitting the Ford station wagon, and struck a 2017 Cadillac Seville double-parked near the corner.
    The MOST logical order for the above sentences to appear in the report is
    A. IV, III, V, II, I   B. III, IV, V, II, I   C. IV, III, I, V, II   D. III, IV, V, I, II

15. The following five sentences are part of an Activity Log entry Police Officer Rogers made regarding an explosion:
    I. I quickly treated the pedestrian for the injury.
    II. The explosion caused a glass window in an office building to shatter.
    III. After the pedestrian was treated, a call was placed to the precinct requesting additional police officers to evacuate the area.
    IV. After all the glass settled to the ground, I saw a pedestrian who was bleeding from the arm.
    V. While on foot patrol near 5th Avenue and 53rd Street, I heard a loud explosion.
    The MOST logical order for the above sentences to appear in the report is
    A. II, V, IV, I, III   B. V, II, IV, III, I   C. V, II, I, IV, III   D. V, II, IV, I, III

16. Police Officer David is completing a report regarding illegal activity near the entrance to Madison Square Garden during a recent rock concert. The report will obtain the following five sentences:
    I. As I came closer to the man, he placed what appeared to be tickets in his pocket and began to walk away.
    II. After the man stopped, I questioned him about *scalping* tickets.
    III. While on assignment near the Madison Square Garden entrance, I observed a man apparently selling tickets.
    IV. I stopped the man by stating that I was a police officer.
    V. The man was then given a summons, and he left the area.
    The MOST logical order for the above sentences to appear in the report is
    A. I, III, IV, II, V   B. III, I, IV, V, II   C. III, IV, I, II, V   D. III, I, IV, II, V

17. Police Officer Sampson is preparing a report containing a dispute in a bar. The report will contain the following five sentences:
    I. John Evans, the bartender, ordered the two men out of the bar.
    II. Two men dressed in dungarees entered the C and D Bar at 5:30 P.M.
    III. The two men refused to leave and began to beat up Evans.
    IV. A customer in the bar saw me on patrol and yelled to me to come separate the three men.
    V. The two men became very drunk and loud within a short time.
    The MOST logical order for the above sentences to appear in the report is
    A. II, I, V, III, IV   B. II, III, IV, V, I   C. III, I, II, V, IV   D. II, V, I, III, IV

18. A police officer is completing a report concerning the response to a crime in progress. The report will include the following five sentences:
    I. The officers saw two armed men run out of the liquor store and into a waiting car.
    II. Police Officers Lunty and Duren received the call and responded to the liquor store.
    III. The robbers gave up without a struggle.
    IV. Lunty and Duren blocked the getaway car with their patrol car.
    V. A call came into the precinct concerning a robbery in progress at Jane's Liquor Store.
    The MOST logical order for the above sentence to appear in the report is
    A. V, II, I, IV, III   B. II, V, I, III, IV   C. V, I, IV, II, III   D. I, V, II, III, IV

19. Police Officers Jenkins is preparing a Crime Report which will consist of the following five sentences:
    I. After making inquirie in the vicinity, Smith found out that his next door neighbor, Viola Jones, had seen two local teenagers, Michael Heinz and Vincent Gaynor, smash his car's windshields with a crowbar.
    II. Jones told Smith that the teenagers live at 8700 19th Avenue.
    III. Mr. Smith heard a loud crash at approximately 11:00 P.M., looked out of his apartment window, and saw two white males running away from his car.
    IV. Smith then reported the incident to the precinct, and Heinz and Gaynor were arrested at the address given.
    V. Leaving his apartment to investigate further, Smith discovered that his car's front and rear windshields had been smashed.
    The MOST logical order for the above sentences to appear in the report is
    A. III, IV, V, I, II   B. III, V, I, II, IV   C. III, I, V, II, IV   D. V, III, I, II, IV

20. Sergeant Nancy Winston is reviewing a Gun Control Report which will contain the following five sentences:
    I. The man fell to the floor when hit in the chest with three bullets from 22 caliber gun.
    II. Merriam's 22 caliber gun was seized, and he was given a summons for not having a pistol permit.
    III. Christopher Merriam, the owner of A-Z Grocery, shot a man who attempted to rob him.
    IV. Police Officer Franks responded and asked Merriam for his pistol permit, which he could not produce.

V. Merriam phoned the police to report he had just shot a man who had attempted to rob him.

The MOST logical order for the above sentences to appear in the report is
A. III, I, V, IV, II   B. I, III, V, IV, II   C. III, I, V, II, IV   D. I, III, II, V, IV

21. Detective John Manville is completing a report for his superior regarding the murder of an unknown male who was shot in Central Park. The report will contain the following five sentences:
    I. Police Officers Langston and Cavers responded to the scene.
    II. I received the assignment to investigate the murder in Central Park from Detective Sergeant Rogers.
    III. Langston notified the Detective Bureau after questioning Jason.
    IV. An unknown male, apparently murdered, was discovered in Central Park by Howard Jason, a park employee, who immediately called the police.
    V. Langston and Cavers questioned Jason.

    The MOST logical order for the above sentences to appear in the report is
    A. I, IV, V, III, II   B. IV, I, V, II, III   C. IV, I, V, III, II   D. IV, V, I, III, II

22. A police officer is completing a report concerning the arrest of a juvenile. The report will contain the following five sentences:
    I. Sanders then telephoned Jay's parents from the precinct to inform them of their son's arrest.
    II. The store owner resisted, and Jay then shot him and ran from the store.
    III. Jay was transported directly to the precinct by Officer Sanders.
    IV. James Jay, a juvenile, walked into a candy store and announced a hold-up.
    V. Police Officer Sanders, while on patrol, arrested Jay a block from the candy store.

    The MOST logical order for the above sentences to appear in the report is
    A. IV, V, II, I, III   B. IV, II, V, III, I   C. II, IV, V, III, I   D. V, IV, II, I, III

23. Police Officer Olsen prepared a crime report for a robbery which contained the following five sentences:
    I. Mr. Gordon was approached by this individual who then produced a gun and demanded the money from the cash register.
    II. The man then fled from the scene on foot, southbound on 5th Avenue.
    III. Mr. Gordon was working at the deli counter when a white male, 5'6", 150-160 lbs., wearing a green jacket and blue pants, entered the store.
    IV. Mr. Gordon complied with the man's demands and handed him the daily receipts.
    V. Further investigation has determined there are no other witnesses to this robbery.

    The MOST logical order for the above sentences to appear in the report is
    A. I, III, IV, V, II   B. I, IV, II, III, V   C. III, IV, I, V, II   D. III, I, IV, II, V

24. Police Officer Bryant responded to 285 E. 31st Street to take a crime report of a burglary of Mr. Bond's home. The report will contain a brief description of the incident, consisting of the following five sentences:
   I. When Mr. Bond attempted to stop the burglar by grabbing him, he was pushed to the floor.
   II. The burglar had apparently gained access to the home by forcing open the 2nd floor bedroom window facing the fire escape.
   III. Mr. Bond sustained a head injury in the scuffle, and the burglar exited the home through the front door.
   IV. Finding nothing in the dresser, the burglar proceeded downstairs to the first floor, where he was confronted by Mr. Bond who was reading in the dining room.
   V. Once inside, he searched the drawers of the bedroom dresser.
   The MOST logical order for the above sentences to appear in the report is
   A. V, IV, I, II, III   B. II, V, IV, I, III   C. II, IV, V, III, I   D. III, II, I, V, IV

25. Police Officer Derringer responded to a call of a rape-homicide case in his patrol area and was ordered to prepare an incident report, which will contain the following five sentences:
   I. He pushed Miss Scott to the ground and forcibly raped her.
   II. Mary Scott was approached from behind by a white male, 5'7", 150-160 lbs. wearing dark pants and a white jacket.
   III. As Robinson approached the male, he ordered him to stop.
   IV. Screaming for help, Miss Scott alerted one John Robinson, a local grocer, who chased her assailant as he fled the scene.
   V. The male turned and fired two shots at Robinson, who fell to the ground mortally wounded.
   The MOST logical order for the above sentences to appear in the report is
   A. IV, III, I, II, V   B. II, IV, III, V, I   C. II, IV, I, V, III   D. II, I, IV, III, V

KEY (CORRECT ANSWERS)

1.	B		11	C
2.	C		12	B
3.	C		13	B
4.	A		14.	C
5.	B		15.	D
6.	A		16.	D
7.	B		17.	D
8.	C		18.	A
9.	B		19.	B
10.	A		20.	A

21. C
22. B
23. D
24. B
25. D

PREPARING WRITTEN MATERIAL
EXAMINATION SECTION
TEST 1

DIRECTIONS: The sentences numbered 1 to 10 deal with some phase of police activity. They may be classified most appropriately under one of the following four categories:
- A. *Faulty* because of incorrect grammar
- B. *Faulty* because of incorrect punctuation
- C. *Faulty* because of incorrect use of a word
- D. *Correct*

Examine each sentence carefully. Then, in the correspondingly numbered space on the right, print the capital letter preceding the option which is the best of the four suggested above.

(All incorrect sentences contain only one type of error. Consider a sentence correct if it contains none of the types of errors mentioned, even though there may be other correct ways of expressing the same thought.)

1. The Department Medal of Honor is awarded to a member of the Police Force who distinguishes himself inconspicuously in the line of police duty by the performance of an act of gallantry. 1.____

2. Members of the Detective Division are charged with: the prevention of crime, the detection and arrest of criminals, and the recovery of lost or stolen property. 2.____

3. Detectives are selected from the uniformed patrol forces after they have indicated by conduct, aptitude, and performance that they are qualified for the more intricate duties of a detective. 3.____

4. The patrolman, pursuing his assailant, exchanged shots with the gunman and immortally wounded him as he fled into a nearby building. 4.____

5. The members of the Traffic Division has to enforce the Vehicle and Traffic Law, the Traffic Regulations, and ordinances relating to vehicular and pedestrian traffic. 5.____

6. After firing a shot at the gunman, the crowd dispersed from the patrolman's line of fire. 6.____

7. The efficiency of the Missing Persons Bureau is maintained with a maximum of public personnel due to the specialized training given to its members. 7.____

8. Records of persons arrested for violations of Vehicle and Traffic Regulations are transmitted upon request to precincts, courts, and other authorized agencies. 8.____

2 (#1)

9. The arresting officer done all he could to subdue the perpetrator without physically injuring him. 9._____

10. The Deputy Commissioner is authorized to exercise all of the powers and duties of the Police Commissioner in the latter's absence. 10._____

KEY (CORRECT ANSWERS)

1. C 6. A
2. B 7. C
3. D 8. D
4. C 9. A
5. A 10. D

TEST 2

DIRECTIONS: Questions 1 through 4 consist of sentences concerning criminal law. Some of the sentences contain errors in English grammar or usage, punctuation, spelling, or capitalization. (A sentence does not contain an error simply because it could be written in a different manner.

Choose answer
A. if the sentence contains an error in English grammar or usage
B. if the sentence contains an error in punctuation
C. if the sentence contains an error in spelling or capitalization
D. if the sentence does not contain any errors

1. The severity of the sentence prescribed by contemporary statutes—including both the former and the revised New York Penal Laws—do not depend on what crime was intended by the offender.

2. It is generally recognized that two defects in the early law of *attempt* played a part in the birth of *burglary*: (1) immunity from prosecution for conduct short of the last act before completion of the crime, and (2) the relatively minor penalty imposed for an attempt (its being a common law misdemeanor) vis-à-a the completed offense.

3. The first sentence of the statute is applicable to employees who enter their place of employment, invited guests, and all other persons who have an express or implied license or privilege to enter the premises.

4. Contemporary criminal codes in the United States generally divide burglary into various degrees, differentiating the categories according to place, time, and other attendent circumstances.

1.____
2.____
3.____
4.____

KEY (CORRECT ANSWERS)

1. A
2. D
3. D
4. C

TEST 3

DIRECTIONS: For each of the sentences numbered 1 through 10, select from the options given below the MOST applicable choice, and print the letter of the correct answer in the space at the right.

    A. The sentence is correct.
    B. The sentence contains a spelling error only
    C. The sentence contains an English grammar error only
    D. The sentence contains *both* a spelling error and an English grammar error

1. Every person in the group is going to do his share. 1.____
2. The man who we selected is new to Duke University. 2.____
3. She is the older of the four secretaries on the two staffs that are to be combined. 3.____
4. The decision has to be made between him and I. 4.____
5. One of the volunteers are too young for this complecated task, don't you think? 5.____
6. I think your idea is splindid and it will improve this report considerably. 6.____
7. Do you think this is an exagerated account of the behavior you and me observed this morning? 7.____
8. Our supervisor has a clear idea of excelence. 8.____
9. How many occurences were verified by the observers? 9.____
10. We must complete the typing of the draft of the questionaire by noon tomorrow. 10.____

KEY (CORRECT ANSWERS)

1.	A		6.	B
2.	C		7.	D
3.	C		8.	B
4.	C		9.	B
5.	D		10.	B

TEST 4

DIRECTIONS: Questions 1 through 3 are based on the following paragraph, which consists of three numbered sentences.

Edit each sentence to insure clarity of meaning and correctness of grammar without substantially changing the meaning of the sentence.

Examine each sentence and then select the option which changes the sentence to express BEST the thought of the sentence.

(1) Unquestionably, a knowledge of business and finance is a good advantage to audit committee members but not essential to all members. (2) Other factors also carry weight; for example, at least one member must have the ability to preside over meetings and to discuss things along constructive lines. (3) In the same way, such factors as the amount of time a member can be able to devote to duties or his rating on the score of motivation, inquisitiveness, persistence, and disposition towards critical analysis are important.

1. In the first sentence, the word
   A. "good" should be changed to "distinct"
   B. "good" should be omitted
   C. "and" should be changed to "or"
   D. "are" should be inserted between the words "but" and 'not'

2. In the second sentence, the
   A. word "factors" should be changed to "things"
   B. words "preside over" should be changed to "lead at"
   C. phrase "discuss things" should be changed to "direct the "discussion"
   D. word "constructive" should be changed to "noteworthy"

3. In the third sentence, the
   A. word "amount" should be changed to "period"
   B. words "amount of" should be changed to "length of"
   C. word "can" should be changed to "will"
   D. word "same" should be changed to "similar

KEY (CORRECT ANSWERS)

1. A
2. C
3. C

TEST 5

DIRECTIONS: Each question or incomplete statement is followed by several suggested answers or completions. Select the one that BEST answers the question or completes the statement. *PRINT THE LETTER OF THE CORRECT ANSWER IN THE SPACE AT THE RIGHT.*

1. Of the following, the MOST acceptable close of a business letter would usually be:
   A. Cordially yours,
   B. Respectfully Yours,
   C. Sincerely Yours,
   D. Yours very truly,

   1._____

2. When writing official correspondence to members of the armed forces, their titles should be used
   A. both on the envelope and in the inside address
   B. in the inside address, but not on the envelope
   C. neither on the envelope nor in the inside address
   D. on the envelope but not in the inside address

   2._____

3. Which one of the following is the LEAST important advantage of putting the subject of a letter in the heading to the right of the address? It
   A. makes filing of the copy easier
   B. makes more space available in the body of the letter
   C. simplifies distribution of letters
   D. simplifies determination of the subject of the letter

   3._____

4. Generally, when writing a letter, the use of precise words and concise sentences is
   A. *good*, because less time will be required to write the letter
   B. *bad*, because it is most likely that the reader will think the letter is unimportant and will not respond favorably
   C. *good*, because it is likely that your desired meaning will be conveyed to the reader
   D. *bad*, because your letter will be too brief to provide adequate information

   4._____

5. Of the following, it is MOST appropriate to use a form letter when it is necessary to answer many
   A. requests or inquiries from a single individual
   B. follow-up letters from individuals requesting additional information
   C. requests or inquiries about a single subject
   D. complaints from individuals that they have been unable to obtain various types of information

   5._____

KEY (CORRECT ANSWERS)

1. D
2. A
3. B
4. C
5. C

TEST 6

DIRECTIONS: Each question or incomplete statement is followed by several suggested answers or completions. Select the one that BEST answers the question or completes the statement. *PRINT THE LETTER OF THE CORRECT ANSWER IN THE SPACE AT THE RIGHT.*

1. The one of the following sentences which is LEAST acceptable from the viewpoint of correct usage is:
   A. The police thought the fugitive to be him.
   B. The criminals set a trap for whoever would fall into it.
   C. It is ten years ago since the fugitive fled from the city.
   D. The lecturer argued that criminals are usually cowards.
   E. The police removed four bucketfuls of earth from the scene of the crime.

   1._____

2. The one of the following sentences which is LEAST acceptable from the viewpoint of correct usage is:
   A. The patrolman scrutinized the report with great care.
   B. Approaching the victim of the assault, two bruises were noticed by the patrolman.
   C. As soon as I had broken down the door, I stepped into the room.
   D. I observed the accused loitering near the building, which was closed at the time.
   E. The storekeeper complained that his neighbor was guilty of violating a local ordinance.

   2._____

3. The one of the following sentences which is LEAST acceptable from the viewpoint of correct usage is:
   A. I realized immediately that he intended to assault the woman, so I disarmed him.
   B. It was apparent that Mr. Smith's explanation contained many inconsistencies.
   C. Despite the slippery condition of the street, he managed to stop the vehicle before injuring the child.
   D. Not a single one of them wish, despite the damage to property, to make a formal complaint.
   E. The body was found lying on the floor.

   3._____

KEY (CORRECT ANSWERS)

1. C
2. B
3. D

PREPARING WRITTEN MATERIAL
EXAMINATION SECTION
TEST 1

Questions 1-15.

DIRECTIONS: For each of Questions 1 through 15, select from the options given below the MOST applicable choice, and mark your answer accordingly.
    A. The sentence is correct.
    B. The sentence contains a spelling error only.
    C. The sentence contains an English grammar error only.
    D. The sentence contains both a spelling error and an English grammar error.

1. He is a very dependible person whom we expect will be an asset to this division.
2. An investigator often finds it necessary to be very diplomatic when conducting an interview.
3. Accurate detail is especially important if court action results from an investigation.
4. The report was signed by him and I since we conducted the investigation jointly.
5. Upon receipt of the complaint, an inquiry was begun.
6. An employee has to organize his time so that he can handle his workload efficiantly.
7. It was not apparent that anyone was iving at the address given by the client.
8. According to regulations, there is to be at least three attempts made to locate the client.
9. Neither the inmate nor the correction officer was willing to sign a formal statement.
10. It is our opinion that one of the persons interviewed were lying.
11. We interviewed both clients and departmental personel in the course of this investigation.
12. It is concievable that further research might produce additional evidence.
13. There are too many occurences of this nature to ignore.

14. We cannot accede to the candidate's request. 14._____

15. The submission of overdue reports is the reason that there was a delay in completion of this investigation. 15._____

Questions 16-25.

DIRECTIONS: Each of Questions 16 through 25 may be classified under one of the following four categories:
    A. Faulty because of incorrect grammar or sentence structure.
    B. Faulty because of incorrect punctuation.
    C. Faulty because of incorrect spelling.
    D. Correct

Examine each sentence carefully to determine under which of the above four options it is best classified. Then, in the space at the right, write the letter preceding the option which is the BEST of the four suggested above. Each incorrect sentence contains but one type of error. Consider a sentence to be correct if it contains none of the types of errors mentioned, even though there may be other correct ways of expressing the same thought.

16. Although the department's supply of scratch pads and stationary have diminished considerably, the allotment for our division has not been reduced. 16._____

17. You have not told us whom you wish to designate as your secretary. 17._____

18. Upon reading the minutes of the last meeting, the new proposal was taken up for consideration. 18._____

19. Before beginning the discussion, we locked the door as a precautionery measure. 19._____

20. The supervisor remarked, "Only those clerks, who perform routine work, are permitted to take a rest period." 20._____

21. Not only will this duplicating machine make accurate copies, but it will also produce a quantity of work equal to fifteen transcribing typists. 21._____

22. "Mr. Jones," said the supervisor, "we regret our inability to grant you an extention of your leave of absence. 22._____

23. Although the employees find the work monotonous and fatigueing, they rarely complain. 23._____

24. We completed the tabulation of the receipts on time despite the fact that Miss Smith our fastest operator was absent for over a week. 24._____

25. The reaction of the employees who attended the meeting, as well as the reaction of those who did not attend, indicates clearly that the schedule is satisfactory to everyone concerned.

25.____

KEY (CORRECT ANSWERS)

1.	D	11.	B
2.	A	12.	B
3.	A	13.	B
4.	C	14.	A
5.	A	15.	C
6.	B	16.	A
7.	B	17.	D
8.	C	18.	A
9.	A	19.	C
10.	C	20.	B

21.	A
22.	C
23.	C
24.	B
25.	D

TEST 2

Questions 1-15.

DIRECTIONS: Questions 1 through 15 consist of two sentences. Some are correct according to ordinary formal English usage. Others are incorrect because they contain errors in English usage, spelling, or punctuation. Consider a sentence correct if it contains no errors in English usage, spelling, or punctuation, even if there may be other ways of writing the sentence correctly. Mark your answer:
- A. If only sentence I is correct.
- B. If only sentence II is correct.
- C. If sentences 1 and II are correct.
- D. If neither sentence I nor II is correct.

1.
   I. The influence of recruitment efficiency upon administrative standards is readily apparant.
   II. Rapid and accurate thinking are an essential quality of the police officer.

2.
   I. The administrator of a police department is constantly confronted by the demands of subordinates for increased personnel in their respective units.
   II. Since a chief executive must work within well-defined fiscal limits, he must weigh the relative importance of various requests.

3.
   I. The two men whom the police arrested for a parking violation were wanted for robbery in three states.
   II. Strong executive control from the top to the bottom of the enterprise is one of the basic principals of police administration.

4.
   I. When he gave testimony unfavorable to the defendant loyalty seemed to mean very little.
   II. Having run off the road while passing a car, the patrolman gave the driver a traffic ticket.

5.
   I. The judge ruled that the defendant's conversation with his doctor was a privileged communication.
   II. The importance of our training program is widely recognized; however, fiscal difficulties limit the program's effectiveness.

6.
   I. Despite an increase in patrol coverage, there were less arrests for crimes against property this year.
   II. The investigators could hardly have expected greater cooperation from the public.

7.
   I. Neither the patrolman nor the witness could identify the defendant as the driver of the car.
   II. Each of the officers in the class received their certificates at the completion of the course.

8. I. The new commander made it clear that those kind of procedures would no longer be permitted.
   II. Giving some weight to performance records is more advisable than making promotions solely on the basis of test scores.

8._____

9. I. A deputy sheriff must ascertain whether the debtor, has any property.
   II. A good deputy sheriff does not cause histerical excitement when he executes a process.

9._____

10. I. Having learned that he has been assigned a judgment debtor, the deputy sheriff should call upon him.
    II. The deputy sheriff may seize and remove property without requiring a bond.

10._____

11. I. If legal procedures are not observed, the resulting contract is not enforseable.
    II. If the directions from the creditor's attorney are not in writing, the deputy sheriff should request a letter of instructions from the attorney.

11._____

12. I. The deputy sheriff may confer with the defendant and enter this defendants' place of business.
    II. A deputy sheriff must ascertain from the creditor's attorney whether the debtor has any property against which he may proceede.

12._____

13. I. The sheriff has a right to do whatever is necessary for the purpose of executing the order of the court.
    II. The written order of the court gives the sheriff general authority and he is governed in his acts by a very simple principal.

13._____

14. I. Either the patrolman or his sergeant are always ready to help the public.
    II. The sergeant asked the patrolman when he would finish the report.

14._____

15. I. The injured man could not hardly talk.
    II. Every officer had ought to had in their reports on time.

15._____

Questions 16-26.

DIRECTIONS: For each of the sentences given below, numbered 16 through 25, select from the following choices the MOST correct choice and print your choice in the space at the right. Select as your answer:
    A. If the statement contains an unnecessary word or expression
    B. If the statement contains a slang term or expression ordinarily not acceptable in government report writing.
    C. If the statement contains an old-fashioned word or expression, where a concrete, plain term would be more useful.
    D. If the statement contains no major faults.

16. Every one of us should try harder.

16._____

17. Yours of the first instant has been received.

17._____

18. We will have to do a real snow job on him. 18.____
19. I shall contact him next Thursday. 19.____
20. None of us were invited to the meeting with the community. 20.____
21. We got this here job to do. 21.____
22. She could not help but see the mistake in the checkbook. 22.____
23. Don't bug the Director about the report. 23.____
24. I beg to inform you that your letter has been received. 24.____
25. This project is all screwed up. 25.____

KEY (CORRECT ANSWERS)

1.	D		11.	B
2.	C		12.	D
3.	A		13.	A
4.	D		14.	D
5.	B		15.	D
6.	B		16.	D
7.	A		17.	C
8.	D		18.	B
9.	D		19.	D
10.	C		20.	D

21.	B
22.	D
23.	B
24.	C
25.	B

TEST 3

DIRECTIONS: Questions 1 through 25 are sentences taken from reports. Some are correct according to ordinary English usage. Others are incorrect because they contain errors in English usage, spelling, or punctuation. Consider a sentence correct if it contains no errors in English usage, spelling, or punctuation, even if there may be other ways of writing the sentence correctly. Mark your answer:
- A. If only sentence I is correct
- B. If only sentence II is correct
- C. If sentences I and II are correct
- D. If neither sentence I nor II is correct

1. I. The Neighborhood Police Team Commander and Team Patrolmen are encouraged to give to the public the widest possible verbal and written disemination of information regarding the existence and purposes of the program.
    II. The police must be vitally interelated with every segment of the public they serve.

2. I. If social gambling, prostitution, and other vices are to be prohibited, the law makers should provide the manpower and method for enforcement.
    II. In addition to checking on possible crime locations such as hallways, roofs yards and other similar locations, Team Patrolmen are encouraged to make known their presence to members of the community.

3. I. The Neighborhood Police Team Commander is authorized to secure, the cooperation of local publications, as well as public and private agencies, to further the goals of the program.
    II. Recruitment from social minorities is essential to effective police work among minorities and meaningful relations with them.

4. I. The Neighborhood Police Team Commander and his men have the responsibility for providing patrol service within the sector territory on a twenty-four hour basis.
    II. While the patrolman was walking his beat at midnight he noticed that the clothing stores' door was partly open.

5. I. Authority is granted to the Neighborhood Police Team to device tactics for coping with the crime in the sector.
    II. Before leaving the scene of the accident, the patrolman drew a map showing the positions of the automobiles and indicated the time of the accident as 10 M. in the morning.

6. I. The Neighborhood Police Team Commander and his men must be kept apprised of conditions effecting their sector.
    II. Clear, continuous communication with every segment of the public served based on the realization of mutual need and founded on trust and confidence is the basis for effective law enforcement.

7. I. The irony is that the police are blamed for the laws they enforce when they are doing their duty.
    II. The Neighborhood Police Team Commander is authorized to prepare and distribute literature with pertinent information telling the public whom to contact for assistance.

    7._____

8. I. The day is not far distant when major parts of the entire police compliment will need extensive college training or degrees.
    II. Although driving under the influence of alcohol is a specific charge in making arrests, drunkenness is basically a health and social problem.

    8._____

9. I. If a deputy sheriff finds that property he has to attach is located on a ship, he should notify his supervisor.
    II. Any contract that tends to interfere with the administration of justice is illegal.

    9._____

10. I. A mandate or official order of the court to the sheriff or other officer directs it to take into possession property of the judgment debtor.
    II. Tenancies from month-to-month, week-to-week, and sometimes year-to-year are termenable.

    10._____

11. I. A civil arrest is an arrest pursuant to an order issued by a court in civil litigation.
    II. In a criminal arrest, a defendant is arrested for a crime he is alleged to have committed.

    11._____

12. I. Having taken a defendant into custody, there is a complete restraint of personal liberty.
    II. Actual force is unnecessary when a deputy sheriff makes an arrest.

    12._____

13. I. When a husband breaches a separation agreement by failing to supply to the wife the amount of money to be paid to her periodically under the agreement, the same legal steps may be taken to enforce his compliance as in any other breach of contract.
    II. Having obtained the writ of attachment, the plaintiff is then in the advantageous position of selling the very property that has been held for him by the sheriff while he was obtaining a judgment.

    13._____

14. I. Being locked in his desk, the investigator felt sure that the records would be safe.
    II. The reason why the witness changed his statement was because he had been threatened.

    14._____

15. I. The investigation had just began then an important witness disappeared.
    II. The check that had been missing was located and returned to its owner, Harry Morgan, a resident of Suffolk County, New York.

    15._____

16. I. A supervisor will find that the establishment of standard procedures enables his staff to work more efficiently.
    II. An investigator hadn't ought to give any recommendations in his report if he is in doubt.

17. I. Neither the investigator nor his supervisor is ready to interview the witness.
    II. Interviewing has been and always will be an important asset in investigation.

18. I. One of the investigator's reports has been forwarded to the wrong person.
    II. The investigator stated that he was not familiar with those kind of cases.

19. I. Approaching the victim of the assault, two large bruises were noticed by me.
    II. The prisoner was arrested for assault, resisting arrest, and use of a deadly weapon.

20. I. A copy of the orders, which had been prepared by the captain, was given to each patrolman.
    II. It's always necessary to inform an arrested person of his constitutional rights before asking him any questions.

21. I. To prevent further bleeding, I applied a tourniquet to the wound.
    II. John Rano a senior officer was on duty at the time of the accident.

22. I. Limiting the term "property" to tangible property, in the criminal mischief setting, accords with prior case law holding that only tangible property came within the purview of the offense of malicious mischief.
    II. Thus, a person who intentionally destroys the property of another, but under an honest belief that he has title to such property, cannot be convicted of criminal mischief under the Revised Penal Law.

23. I. Very early in it's history, New York enacted statutes from time to time punishing, either as a felony or as a misdemeanor, malicious injuries to various kinds of property: piers, boos, dams, bridges, etc.
    II. The application of the statute is necessarily restricted to trespassory takings with larcenous intent: namely with intent permanently or virtually permanently to "appropriate" property or "deprive" the owner of its use.

24. I. Since the former Penal Law did not define the instruments of forgery in a general fashion, its crime of forgery was held to be narrower than the common law offense in this respect and to embrace only those instruments explicitly specified in the substantive provisions.
    II. After entering the barn through an open door for the purpose of stealing, it was closed by the defendants.

25. I. The use of fire or explosives to destroy tangible property is proscribed by the criminal mischief provisions of the Revised Penal Law.
    II. The defendant's taking of a taxicab for the immediate purpose of affecting his escape did not constitute grand larceny.

25._____

KEY (CORRECT ANSWERS)

1.	D	11.	C
2.	D	12.	B
3.	B	13.	C
4.	A	14.	D
5.	D	15.	B
6.	D	16.	A
7.	C	17.	C
8.	D	18.	A
9.	C	19.	B
10.	D	20.	C

21.	A
22.	C
23.	B
24.	A
25.	A

TEST 4

Questions 1-4.

DIRECTIONS: Each of the two sentences in Questions 1 through 4 may be correct or may contain errors in punctuation, capitalization, or grammar. Mark your answer:
- A. If there is an error only in sentence I
- B. If there is an error only in sentence II
- C. If there is an error in both sentences I and II
- D. If both sentences are correct.

1. I. It is very annoying to have a pencil sharpener, which is not in working order.
   II. Patrolman Blake checked the door of Joe's Restaurant and found that the lock has been jammed.

2. I. When you are studying a good textbook is important.
   II. He said he would divide the money equally between you and me.

3. I. Since he went on the city counci a year ago, one of his primary concerns has been safety in the streets.
   II. After waiting in the doorway for about 15 minutes, a black sedan appeared.

Questions 4-8.

DIRECTIONS: Each of the sentences in Questions 4 through 8 may be classified under one of the following four categories:
- A. Faulty because of incorrect grammar
- B. Faulty because of incorrect punctuation
- C. Faulty because of incorrect capitalization or incorrect spelling
- D. Correct

Examine each sentence carefully to determine under which of the above four options it is BEST classified. Then, in the space at the right, print the capitalized letter preceding the option which is the BEST of the four suggested above. Each faulty sentence contains but one type of error. Consider a sentence to be correct if it contains none of the types of errors mentioned, even though there may be other correct ways of expressing the same thought.

4. They told both he and I that the prisoner had escaped.

5. Any superior officer, who, disregards the just complaints of his subordinates, is remiss in the performance of his duty.

6. Only those members of the national organization who resided in the Middle west attended the conference in Chicago.

7. We told him to give the investigation assignment to whoever was available.

8. Please do not disappoint and embarass us by not appearing in court.

Questions 9-13

DIRECTIONS: Each of Questions 9 through 13 consists of three sentences lettered A, B, and C. In each of these questions, one of the sentences may contain an error in grammar, sentence structure, or punctuation, or all three sentences may be correct. If one of the sentence in a question contains an error in grammar, sentence structure, or punctuation, print in the space at the right the capital letter preceding the sentence which contains the error. If all three sentences are correct, print the letter D.

9. A. Mr. Smith appears to be less competent than I in performing these duties. 9.____
    B. The supervisor spoke to the employee, who had made the error, but did not reprimand him.
    C. When he found the book lying on the table, he immediately notified the owner.

10. A. Being locked in the desk, we were certain that the papers would not be taken. 10.____
    B. It wasn't I who dictated the telegram; I believe it was Eleanor.
    C. You should interview whoever comes to the office today.

11. A. The clerk was instructed to set the machine on the table before summoning the manager. 11.____
    B. He said that he was not familiar with those kind of activities.
    C. A box of pencils, in addition to erasers and blotters, was included in the shipment of supplies.

12. A. The supervisor remarked, "Assigning an employee to the proper type of work is not always easy." 12.____
    B. The employer found that each of the applicants were qualified to perform the duties of the position.
    C. Any competent student is permitted to take this course if he obtains the consent of the instructor.

13. A. The prize was awarded to the employee whom the judges believed to be most deserving. 13.____
    B. Since the instructor believes his book is the better of the two, he is recommending it for use in the school.
    C. It was obvious to the employees that the completion of the task by the scheduled date would require their working overtime.

Questions 14-20.

DIRECTIONS: In answering Questions 14 through 20, choose the sentence which is BEST from the point of view of English usage suitable for a business report.

14. A. The client's receiving of public assistance checks at two different addresses were disclosed by the investigation.
    B. The investigation disclosed that the client was receiving public assistance checks at two different addresses.
    C. The client was found out by the investigation to be receiving public assistance checks at two different addresses.
    D. The client has been receiving public assistance checks at two different addresses, disclosed the investigation.

14.____

15. A. The investigation of complaints are usually handled by this unit, which deals with internal security problems in the department.
    B. This unit deals with internal security problems in the department usually investigating complaints.
    C. Investigating complaints is this unit's job, being that it handles internal security problems in the department.
    D. This unit deals with internal security problems in the department and usually investigates complaints.

15.____

16. A. The delay in completing this investigation was caused by difficulty in obtaining the required documents from the candidate.
    B. Because of difficulty in obtaining the required documents from the candidate is the reason that there was a delay in completing this investigation.
    C. Having had difficulty in obtaining the required documents from the candidate, there was a delay in completing this investigation.
    D. Difficulty in obtaining the required documents from the candidate had the affect of delaying the completion of this investigation.

16.____

17. A. This report, together with documents supporting our recommendation, are being submitted for your approval.
    B. Documents supporting our recommendation is being submitted with the report for your approval.
    C. This report, together with documents supporting our recommendation, is being submitted for your approval.
    D. The report and documents supporting our recommendation is being submitted for your approval.

17.____

18. A. The chairman himself, rather than his aides, has reviewed the report.
    B. The chairman himself, rather than his aides, have reviewed the report.
    C. The chairmen, not the aide, has reviewed the report.
    D. The aide, not the chairmen, have reviewed the report.

18.____

19. A. Various proposals were submitted but the decision is not been made.
    B. Various proposals has been submitted but the decision has not been made.
    C. Various proposals were submitted but the decision is not been made.
    D. Various proposals have been submitted but the decision has not been made.

20. A. Everyone were rewarded for his successful attempt.
    B. They were successful in their attempts and each of them was rewarded.
    C. Each of them are rewarded for their successful attempts.
    D. The reward for their successful attempts were made to each of them.

21. The following is a paragraph from a request for departmental recognition consisting of five numbered sentences submitted to a Captain for review. These sentences may or may not have errors in spelling, grammar, and punctuation:
    (1) The officers observed the subject Mills surreptitiously remove a wallet from the woman's handbag and entered his automobile. (2) As they approached Mills, he looked in their direction and drove away. (3) The officers pursued in their car. (4) Mills executed a series of complicated manuvers to evade the pursuing officers. (5) At the corner of Broome and Elizabeth Streets, Mills stopped the car, got out, raised his hands and surrendered to the officers.
    Which one of the following BEST classifies the above with regard to spelling, grammar, and punctuation?
    A. 1, 2, and 3 are correct, but 4 and 5 have errors.
    B. 2, 3, and 5 are correct, but 1 and 4 have errors.
    C. 3, 4, and 5 are correct, but 1 and 2 have errors.
    D. 1, 2, 3, and 5 are correct, but 4 has errors.

22. The one of the following sentences which is grammatically PREFERABLE to the others is:
    A. Our engineers will go over your blueprints so that you may have no problems in construction.
    B. For a long time he had been arguing that we, not he, are to blame for the confusion.
    C. I worked on his automobile for two hours and still cannot find out what is wrong with it.
    D. Accustomed to all kinds of hardships, fatigue seldom bothers veteran policemen.

23. The MOST accurate of the following sentences is:
    A. The commissioner, as well as his deputy and various bureau heads, were present.
    B. A new organization of employers and employees have been formed.
    C. One or the other of these men have been selected.
    D. The number of pages in the book is enough to discourage a reader.

24. The MOST accurate of the following sentences is:
    A. Between you and me, I think he is the better man.
    B. He was believed to be me.
    C. Is it us that you wish to see?
    D. The winners are him and her.

KEY (CORRECT ANSWERS)

1.	C	11.	B
2.	A	12.	B
3.	C	13.	D
4.	A	14.	B
5.	B	15.	D
6.	C	16.	A
7.	D	17.	C
8.	C	18.	A
9.	B	19.	D
10.	A	20.	B

21. B
22. A
23. D
24. A

PREPARING WRITTEN MATERIAL

EXAMINATION SECTION

TEST 1

DIRECTIONS: Each question or incomplete statement is followed by several suggested answers or completions. Select the one that BEST answers the question or completes the statement. *PRINT THE LETTER OF THE CORRECT ANSWER IN THE SPACE AT THE RIGHT.*

1. The one of the following sentences which is LEAST acceptable from the viewpoint of correct usage is:
   A. The police thought the fugitive to be him.
   B. The criminals set a trap for whoever would fall into it.
   C. It is ten years ago since the fugitive fled from the city.
   D. The lecturer argued that criminals are usually cowards.
   E. The police removed four bucketfuls of earth from the scene of the crime.

1.____

2. The one of the following sentences which is LEAST acceptable from the viewpoint of correct usage is:
   A. The patrolman scrutinized the report with great care.
   B. Approaching the victim of the assault, two bruises were noticed by the patrolman.
   C. As soon as I had broker down the door, I stepped into the room.
   D. I observed the accused loitering near the building, which was closed at the time.
   E. The storekeeper complained that his neighbor was guilty of violating a local ordinance.

2.____

3. The one of the following sentences which is LEAST acceptable from the viewpoint of correct usage is:
   A. I realized immediately that he intended to assault the woman, so I disarmed him.
   B. It was apparent that Mr. Smith's explanation contained many inconsistencies.
   C. Despite the slippery condition of the street, he managed to stop the vehicle before injuring the child.
   D. Not a single one of them wish, despite the damage to property, to make a formal complaint.
   E. The body was found lying on the floor.

3.____

4. The one of the following sentences which contains NO error in usage is:
   A. After the robbers left, the proprietor stood tied in his chair for about two hours before help arrived.
   B. In the cellar I found the watchman's hat and coat.
   C. The persons living in adjacent apartments stated that they had heard no unusual noises.

4.____

D. Neither a knife or any firearms were found in the room.
E. Walking down the street, the shouting of the crowd indicated that something was wrong.

5. The one of the following sentences which contains NO error in usage is:
   A. The policeman lay a firm hand on the suspect's shoulder.
   B. It is true that neither strength nor agility are the most important requirement for a good patrolman.
   C. Good citizens constantly strive to do more than merely comply the restraints imposed by society.
   D. No decision was made as to whom the prize should be awarded.
   E. Twenty years is considered a severe sentence for a felony.

6. Which of the following sentences is NOT expressed in standard English usage?
   A. The victim reached a pay-phone booth and manages to call police headquarters.
   B. By the time the call was received, the assailant had left the scene.
   C. The victim has been a respected member of the community for the past eleven years.
   D. Although the lighting was bad and the shadows were deep, the storekeeper caught sight of the attacker.
   E. Additional street lights have since been installed, and the patrols have been strengthened.

7. Which of the following sentences is NOT expressed in standard English usage?
   A. The judge upheld the attorney's right to question the witness about the missing glove.
   B. To be absolutely fair to all parties is the jury's chief responsibility.
   C. Having finished the report, a loud noise in the next room startled the sergeant.
   D. The witness obviously enjoyed having played a part in the proceedings.
   E. The sergeant planned to assign the case to whoever arrived first.

8. In which of the following sentences is a word misused?
   A. As a matter of principle, the captain insisted that the suspect's partner be brought for questioning.
   B. The principle suspect had been detained at the station house for most of the day.
   C. The principal in the crime had no previous criminal record, but his closest associate had been convicted of felonies on two occasions.
   D. The interest payments had been made promptly, but the firm had been drawing upon the principal for these payments.
   E. The accused insisted that his high school principal would furnish him a character reference.

9. Which of the following statements is ambiguous?
   A. Mr. Sullivan explained why Mr. Johnson had been dismissed from his job.
   B. The storekeeper told the patrolman he had made a mistake.
   C. After waiting three hours, the patients in the doctor's office were sent home.
   D. The janitor's duties were to maintain the building in good shape and to answer tenants' complaints.
   E. The speed limit should, in my opinion, be raised to sixty miles an hour on that stretch of road.

9._____

10. In which of the following is the punctuation or capitalization faulty?
   A. The accident occurred at an intersection in the Kew Gardens section of Queens, near the bus stop.
   B. The sedan, not the convertible, was struck in the side.
   C. Before any of the patrolmen had left the police car received an important message from headquarters.
   D. The dog that had been stolen was returned to his master, John Dempsey, who lived in East Village.
   E. The letter had been sent to 12 Hillside Terrace, Rutland, Vermont 05702.

10._____

Questions 11-25.

DIRECTIONS: Questions 11 through 25 are to be answered in accordance with correct English usage; that is, standard English rather than nonstandard or substandard. Nonstandard and substandard English includes words or expressions usually classified as slang, dialect, Illiterate, etc., which are not generally accepted as correct in current written communication. Standard English also requires clarity, proper punctuation and capitalization and appropriate use of words. Write the letter of the sentence NOT expressed in standard English usage in the space at the right

11. A. There were three witnesses to the accident.
    B. At least three witnesses were found to testify for the plaintiff.
    C. Three of the witnesses who took the stand was uncertain about the defendant's competence to drive.
    D. Only three witnesses came forward to testify for the plaintiff.
    E. The three witnesses to the accident were pedestrians.

11._____

12. A. The driver had obviously drunk too many martinis before leaving for home.
    B. The boy who drowned had swum in these same waters many times before.
    C. The petty thief had stolen a bicycle from a private driveway before he was apprehended.
    D. The detectives had brung in the heroin shipment they intercepted.
    E. The passengers had never ridden in a converted bus before.

12._____

13. A. Between you and me, the new platoon plan sounds like a good idea.
     B. Money from an aunt's estate was left to his wife and he.
     C. He and I were assigned to the same patrol for the first time in two months.
     D. Either you or he should check the front door of that store.
     E. The captain himself was not sure of the witness's reliability.

14. A. The alarm had scarcely begun to ring when the explosion occurred.
     B. Before the firemen arrived at the scene, the second story had been destroyed.
     C. Because of the dense smoke and heat, the firemen could hardly approach the now-blazing structure.
     D. According to the patrolman's report, there wasn't nobody in the store when the explosion occurred.
     E. The sergeant's suggestion was not at all unsound, but no one agreed with him.

15. A. The driver and the passenger they were both found to be intoxicated.
     B. The driver and the passenger talked slowly and not too clearly.
     C. Neither the driver nor his passengers were able to give a coherent account of the accident.
     D. In a corner of the room sat the passenger, quietly dozing.
     E. the driver finally told a strange and unbelievable story, which the passenger contradicted.

16. A. Under the circumstances I decided not to continue my examination of the premises.
     B. There are many difficulties now not comparable with those existing in 1960.
     C. Friends of the accused were heard to announce that the witness had better been away on the day of the trial.
     D. The two criminals escaped in the confusion that followed the explosion.
     E. The aged man was struck by the considerateness of the patrolman's offer.

17. A. An assemblage of miscellaneous weapons lay on the table.
     B. Ample opportunities were given to the defendant to obtain counsel.
     C. The speaker often alluded to his past experience with youthful offenders in the armed forces.
     D. The sudden appearance of the truck aroused my suspicions.
     E. Her studying had a good affect on her grades in high school.

18. A. He sat down in the theater and began to watch the movie.
     B. The girl had ridden horses since she was four years old.
     C. Application was made on behalf of the prosecutor to cite the witness for contempt.
     D. The bank robber, with his two accomplices, were caught in the act.
     E. His story is simply not credible.

19. A. The angry boy said that he did not like those kind of friends.
     B. The merchant's financial condition was so precarious that he felt he must avail himself of any offer of assistance.
     C. He is apt to promise more than he can perform.
     D. Looking at the messy kitchen, the housewife felt like crying.
     E. A clerk was left in charge of the stolen property.

20. A. His wounds were aggravated by prolonged exposure to sub-freezing temperatures.
     B. The prosecutor remarked that the witness was not averse to changing his story each time he was interviewed.
     C. The crime pattern indicated that the burglars were adapt in the handling of explosives.
     D. His rigid adherence to a fixed plan brought him into renewed conflict with his subordinates.
     E. He had anticipated that the sentence would be delivered by noon.

21. A. The whole arraignment procedure is badly in need of revision.
     B. After his glasses were broken in the fight, he would of gone to the optometrist if he could.
     C. Neither Tom nor Jack brought his lunch to work.
     D. He stood aside until the quarrel was over.
     E. A statement in the psychiatrist's report disclosed that the probationer vowed to have his revenge.

22. A. His fiery and intemperate speech to the striking employees fatally affected any chance of a future reconciliation.
     B. The wording of the statute has been variously construed.
     C. The defendant's attorney, speaking in the courtroom, called the official a demagogue who contempuously disregarded the judge's orders.
     D. The baseball game is likely to be the most exciting one this year.
     E. The mother divided the cookies among her two children.

23. A. There was only a bed and a dresser in the dingy room.
     B. John was one of the few students that have protested the new rule.
     C. It cannot be argued that the child's testimony is negligible; it is, on the contrary, of the greatest importance.
     D. The basic criterion for clearance was so general that officials resolved any doubts in favor of dismissal.
     E. Having just returned from a long vacation, the officer found the city unbearably hot.

24. A. The librarian ought to give more help to small children.
     B. The small boy was criticized by the teacher because he often wrote careless.
     C. It was generally doubted whether the women would permit the use of her apartment for intelligence operations.
     D. The probationer acts differently every time the officer visits him.
     E. Each of the newly appointed officers has 12 years of service.

25. A. The North is the most industrialized region in the country.
     B. L. Patrick Gray 3d, the bureau's acting director, stated that, while "rehabilitation is fine" for some convicted criminals, "it is a useless gesture for those who resist every such effort."
     C. Careless driving, faulty mechanism, narrow or badly kept roads all play their part in causing accidents.
     D. The childrens' books were left in the bus.
     E. It was a matter of internal security; consequently, he felt no inclination to rescind his previous order.

KEY (CORRECT ANSWERS)

1.	C	11.	C
2.	B	12.	D
3.	D	13.	B
4.	C	14.	D
5.	E	15.	A
6.	A	16.	C
7.	C	17.	E
8.	B	18.	D
9.	B	19.	A
10.	C	20.	C

21.	B
22.	E
23.	B
24.	B
25.	D

TEST 2

DIRECTIONS: Each question or incomplete statement is followed by several suggested answers or completions. Select the one that BEST answers the question or completes the statement. *PRINT THE LETTER OF THE CORRECT ANSWER IN THE SPACE AT THE RIGHT.*

Questions 1-6.

DIRECTIONS: Each of Questions 1 through 6 consists of a statement which contains a word (one of those underlined) that is either incorrectly used because it is not in keeping with the meaning the quotation is evidently intended to convey, or is misspelled. There is only one INCORRECT word in each quotation. Of the four underlined words, determine if the first one should be replaced by the word lettered A, the second replaced by the word lettered B, the third replaced by the word lettered C, or the fourth replaced by the word lettered D.

1. Whether one depends on fluorescent or artificial light or both, adequate standards should be maintained by means of systematic tests.   1.____
   A. natural   B. safeguards   C. established   D. routine

2. A police officer has to be prepared to assume his knowledge as a social scientist in the community.   2.____
   A. forced   B. role   C. philosopher   D. street

3. It is practically impossible to indicate whether a sentence is too long simply by measuring its length.   3.____
   A. almost   B. tell   C. very   D. guessing

4. Strong leaders are required to organize a community for delinquency prevention and for dissemination of organized crime and drug addiction.   4.____
   A. tactics   B. important   C. control   D. meetings

5. The demonstrators who were taken to the Criminal Courts building in Manhattan (because it was large enough to accommodate them), contended that the arrests were unwarranted.   5.____
   A. demonstraters   B. Manhatten
   C. accomodate   D. unwarranted

6. They were guaranteed a calm atmosphere, free from harassment, which would be conducive to quiet consideration of the indictments.   6.____
   A. guarenteed   B. atmspher
   C. harassment   D. inditements

263

Questions 7-11.

DIRECTIONS: Each of Questions 7 through 11 consists of a statement containing four words in capital letters. One of these words in capital letters is not in keeping with the meaning which the statement is evidently intended to carry. The four words in capital letters in each statement are reprinted after the statement. Print the capital letter preceding the one of the four words which does MOST to spoil the true meaning of the statement in the space at the right.

7. Retirement and pension systems are essential not only to provide employees with with a means of support in the future, but also to prevent longevity and CHARITABLE considerations from UPSETTING the PROMOTIONAL opportunities RETIRED members of the career service. 7.____
   A. charitable   B. upsetting   C. promotional   D. retired

8. Within each major DIVISION in a properly set up public or private organization, provision is made so that each NECESSARY activity is CARED for and lines of authority and responsibility are clear-cut and INFINITE. 8.____
   A. division   B. necessary   C. cared   D. infinite

9. In public service, the scale of salaries paid must be INCIDENTAL to the services rendered, with due CONSIDERATION for the attraction of the desired MANPOWER and for the maintenance of a standard of living COMMENSURATE with the work to be performed. 9.____
   A. incidental   B. consideration
   C. manpower   D. commensurate

10. An understanding of the AIMS of an organization by the staff will AID greatly in increasing the DEMAND of the correspondence work of the office, and will to a large extent DETERMINE the nature of the correspondence. 10.____
    A. aims   B. aid   C. demand   D. determine

11. BECAUSE the Civil Service Commission strongly feels that the MERIT system is a key factor in the MAINTENANCE of democratic government, it has adopted as one of its major DEFENSES the progressive democratization of its own procedures in dealing with candidates for positions in the public service. 11.____
    A. Because   B. merit   C. maintenance   D. defenses

Questions 12-14.

DIRECTIONS: Questions 12 through 14 consist of one sentence each. Each sentence contains an incorrectly used word. First, decide which is the incorrectly used word. Then, from among the options given, decide which word, when substituted for the incorrectly used word, makes the meaning of the sentence clear.
EXAMPLE:
The U.S. national income exhibits a pattern of long term deflection.
   A. reflection   B. subjection   C. rejoicing   D. growth

The word *deflection* in the sentence does not convey the meaning the sentence evidently intended to convey. The word *growth* (Answer D), when substituted for the word *deflection*, makes the meaning of the sentence clear. Accordingly, the answer to the question is D.

12. The study commissioned by the joint committee fell compassionately short of the mark and would have to be redone.
    A. successfully B. insignificantly
    C. experimentally D. woefully

13. He will not idly exploit any violation of the provisions of the order.
    A. tolerate B. refuse C. construe D. guard

14. The defendant refused to be virile and bitterly protested service.
    A. irked B. feasible C. docile D. credible

Questions 15-25.

DIRECTIONS: Questions 15 through 25 consist of short paragraphs. Each paragraph contains one word which is INCORRECTLY used because it is NOT in keeping with the meaning of the paragraph. Find the word in each paragraph which is INCORRECTLY used and then select as the answer the suggested word which should be substituted for the incorrectly used word.

SAMPLE QUESTION:
In determining who is to do the work in your unit, you will have to decide just who does what from day to day. One of your lowest responsibilities is to assign work so that everybody gets a fair share and that everyone can do his part well.
    A. new B. old C. important D. performance

EXPLANATION:
The word which is NOT in keeping with the meaning of the paragraph is *lowest*. This is the INCORRECTLY used word. The suggested word *important* would be in keeping with the meaning of the paragraph and should be substituted for *lowest*. Therefore, the CORRECT answer is choice C.

15. If really good practice in the elimination of preventable injuries is to be achieved and held in any establishment, top management must refuse full and definite responsibility and must apply a good share of its attention to the task.
    A. accept B. avoidable C. duties D. problem

16. Recording the human face for identification is by no means the only service performed by the camera in the field of investigation. When the trial of any issue takes place, a word picture is sought to be distorted to the court of incidents, occurrences, or events which are in dispute.
    A. appeals B. description C. portrayed D. deranged

17. In the collection of physical evidence, it cannot be emphasized too strongly that a haphazard systematic search at the scene of the crime is vital. Nothing must be overlooked. Often the only leads in a case will come from the results of this search.
    A. important   B. investigation
    C. proof   D. thorough

17._____

18. If an investigator has reason to suspect that the witness is mentally stable, or a habitual drunkard, he should leave no stone unturned in his investigation to determine if the witness was under the influence of liquor or drugs, or was mentally unbalanced either at the time of the occurrence to which he testified or at the time of the trial.
    A. accused   B. clue   C. deranged   D. question

18._____

19. The use of records is a valuable step in crime investigation and is the main reason every department should maintain accurate reports. Crimes are not committed through the use of departmental records alone but from the use of all records, of almost every type, wherever they may be found and whenever they give any incidental information regarding the criminal.
    A. accidental   B. necessary   C. reported   D. solved

19._____

20. In the years since passage of the Harrison Narcotic Act of 1914, making the possession of opium amphetamines illegal in most circumstances, drug use has become a subject of considerable scientific interest and investigation. There is at present a voluminous literature on drug use of various kinds.
    A. ingestion   B. derivatives   C. addiction   D. opiates

20._____

21. Of course, the fact that criminal laws are extremely patterned in definition does not mean that the majority of persons who violate them are dealt with as criminals. Quite the contrary, for a great many forbidden acts are voluntarily engaged in within situations of privacy and go unobserved and unreported.
    A. symbolic   B. casual   C. scientific   D. broad-gauged

21._____

22. The most punitive way to study punishment is to focus attention on the pattern of punitive action: to study how a penalty is applied, too study what is done to or taken from an offender.
    A. characteristic   B. degrading   C. objective   D. distinguished

22._____

23. The most common forms of punishment in times past have been death, physical torture, mutilation, branding, public humiliation, fines, forfeits of property, banishment, transportation, and imprisonment. Although this list is by no means differentiated, practically every form of punishment has had several variations and applications.
    A. specific   B. simple   C. exhaustive   D. characteristic

23._____

24. There is another important line of inference between ordinary and professional criminals, and that is the source from which they are recruited. The professional criminal seems to be drawn from legitimate employment and, in many instances, from parallel vocations or pursuits.
    A. demarcation   B. justification   C. superiority   D. reference

24._____

25. He took the position that the success of the program was insidious on getting additional revenue.
    A. reputed   B. contingent   C. failure   D. indeterminate

25._____

KEY (CORRECT ANSWERS)

1.	A	11.	D
2.	B	12.	D
3.	B	13.	A
4.	C	14.	C
5.	D	15.	A
6.	C	16.	C
7.	D	17.	D
8.	D	18.	C
9.	A	19.	D
10.	C	20.	B

21.	D
22.	C
23.	C
24.	A
25.	B

TEST 3

DIRECTIONS: Each question or incomplete statement is followed by several suggested answers or completions. Select the one that BEST answers the question or completes the statement. *PRINT THE LETTER OF THE CORRECT ANSWER IN THE SPACE AT THE RIGHT.*

Questions 1-5.

DIRECTIONS: Questions 1 through 5 are to be answered on the basis of the following.

You are a supervising officer in an investigative unit. Earlier in the day, you directed Detectives Tom Dixon and Sal Mayo to investigate a reported assault and robbery in a liquor store within your area of jurisdiction.

Detective Dixon has submitted to you a preliminary investigative report containing the following information:

- At 1630 hours on 2/20, arrived at Joe's Liquor Store at 350 SW Avenue with Detective Mayo to investigate A & R.
- At store interviewed Rob Ladd, store manager, who stated that he and Joe Brown (store owner) had been stuck up about ten minutes prior to our arrival.
- Ladd described the robbers as male whites in their late teens or early twenties. Further stated that one of the robbers displayed what appeared to be an automatic pistol as he entered the store, and said, *Give us the money or we'll kill you.* Ladd stated that Brown then reached under the counter where he kept a loaded .38 caliber pistol. Several shots followed, and Ladd threw himself to the floor.
- The robbers fled, and Ladd didn't know if any money had been taken.
- At this point, Ladd realized that Brown was unconscious on the floor and bleeding from a head wound.
- Ambulance called by Ladd, and Brown was removed by same to General Hospital.
- Personally interviewed John White, 382 Dartmouth Place, who stated he was inside store at the time of occurrence. White states that he hid behind a wine display upon hearing someone say, *Give us the money.* He then heard shots and saw two young men run from the store to a yellow car parked at the curb. White was unable to further describe auto. States the taller of the two men drove the car away while the other sat on passenger side in front.
- Recovered three spent .38 caliber bullets from premises and delivered them to Crime Lab.
- To General Hospital at 1800 hours but unable to interview Brown, who was under sedation and suffering from shock and a laceration of the head.
- Alarm #12487 transmitted for car and occupants.
- Case Active.

Based solely on the contents of the preliminary investigation submitted by Detective Dixon, select one sentence from the following groups of sentences which is MOST accurate and is grammatically correct.

1. A. Both robbers were armed.
    B. Each of the robbers were described as a male white.
    C. Neither robber was armed.
    D. Mr. Ladd stated that one of the robbers was armed.

2. A. Mr. Brown fired three shots from his revolver.
    B. Mr. Brown was shot in the head by one of the robbers.
    C. Mr. Brown suffered a gunshot wound of the head during the course of the robbery.
    D. Mr. Brown was taken to General Hospital by ambulance.

3. A. Shots were fired after one of the robbers said, *Give us the money or we'll kill you.*
    B. After one of the robbers demanded the money from Mr. Brown, he fired a shot.
    C. The preliminary investigation indicated that although Mr. Brown did not have a license for the gun, he was justified in using deadly physical force.
    D. Mr. Brown was interviewed at General Hospital.

4. A. Each of the witnesses were customers in the store at the time of occurrence.
    B. Neither of the witnesses interviewed was the owner of the liquor store.
    C. Neither of the witnesses interviewed were the owner of the store.
    D. Neither of the witnesses was employed by Mr. Brown.

5. A. Mr. Brown arrived at General Hospital at about 5:00 P.M.
    B. Neither of the robbers was injured during the robbery.
    C. The robbery occurred at 3:30 P.M on February 10.
    D. One of the witnesses called the ambulance.

Questions 6-10.

DIRECTIONS: Each of Questions 6 through 10 consists of information given in outline form and four sentences labeled A, B, C, and D. For each question, choose the one sentence which CORRECTLY expresses the information given in outline form and which also displays PROPER English usage.

6. Client's Name: Joanna Jones
    Number of Children: 3
    Client's Income: None
    Client's Marital Status: Single

    A. Joanna Jones is an unmarried client with three children who have no income.
    B. Joanna Jones, who is single and has no income, a client she has three children.
    C. Joanna Jones, whose three children are clients, is single and has no income.
    D. Joanna Jones, who has three children, is an unmarried client with no income.

7. Client's Name: Bertha Smith
   Number of Children: 2
   Client's Rent: $1050 per month
   Number of Rooms: 4

   A. Bertha Smith, a client, pays $1050 per month for her four rooms with two children.
   B. Client Bertha Smith has two children and pays $1050 per month for four rooms.
   C. Client Bertha Smith is paying $1050 per month for two children with four rooms.
   D. For four rooms and two children client Bertha Smith pays $1050 per month.

7.____

8. Name of Employee: Cynthia Dawes
   Number of Cases Assigned: 9
   Date Cases were Assigned: 12/16
   Number of Assigned Cases Completed: 8

   A. On December 16, employee Cynthia Dawes was assigned nine cases; she has completed eight of these cases.
   B. Cynthia Dawes, employee on December 16, assigned nine cases, completed eight.
   C. Being employed on December 16, Cynthia Dawes completed eight of nine assigned cases.
   D. Employee Cynthia Dawes, she was assigned nine cases and completed eight, on December 16.

8.____

9. Place of Audit: Broadway Center
   Names of Auditors: Paul Cahn, Raymond Perez
   Date of Audit: 11/20
   Number of Cases Audited: 41

   A. On November 20, at the Broadway Center 41 cases was audited by auditors Paul Cahn and Raymond Perez.
   B. Auditors Raymond Perez and Paul Cahn has audited 41 cases at the Broadway Center on November 20.
   C. At the Broadway Center, on November 20, auditors Paul Cahn and Raymond Perez audited 41 cases.
   D. Auditors Paul Cahn and Raymond Perez at the Broadway Center, on November 20, is auditing 41 cases.

9.____

10. Name of Client: Barbra Levine
    Client's Monthly Income: $2100
    Client's Monthly Expenses: $4520

    A. Barbra Levine is a client, her monthly income is $2100 and her monthly expenses is $4520.
    B. Barbra Levine's monthly income is $2100 and she is a client, with whose monthly expenses are $4520.

10.____

C. Barbra Levine is a client whose monthly income is $2100 and whose monthly expenses are $4520.
D. Barbra Levine, a client, is with a monthly income which is $2100 and monthly expenses which are $4520.

Questions 11-13.

DIRECTIONS: Questions 11 through 13 involve several statements of fact presented in a very simple way. These statements of fact are followed by 4 choices which attempt to incorporate all of the facts into one logical statement which is properly constructed and grammatically correct.

11. I. Mr. Brown was sweeping the sidewalk in front of his house.
    II. He was sweeping it because it was dirty.
    III. He swept the refuse into the street.
    IV. Police Officer gave him a ticket.

    Which one of the following BEST presents the information given above?
    A. Because his sidewalk was dirty, Mr. Brown received a ticket from Officer Green when he swept the refuse into the street.
    B. Police Officer Green gave Mr. Brown a ticket because his sidewalk was dirty and he swept the refuse into the street.
    C. Police Officer Green gave Mr. Brown a ticket for sweeping refuse into the street because his sidewalk was dirty.
    D. Mr. Brown, who was sweeping refuse from his dirty sidewalk into the street, was given a ticket by Police Officer Green.

12. I. Sergeant Smith radioed for help.
    II. The sergeant did so because the crowd was getting larger.
    III. It was 10:00 A.M. when he made his call.
    IV. Sergeant Smith was not in uniform at the time of occurrence.

    Which one of the following BEST presents the information given above?
    A. Sergeant Smith, although not on duty at the time, radioed for help at 10 o'clock because the crowd was getting uglier.
    B. Although not in uniform, Sergeant Smith called for help at 10:00 A.M. because the crowd was getting uglier.
    C. Sergeant Smith radioed for help at 10:00 A.M. because the crowd was getting larger.
    D. Although he was not in uniform Sergeant Smith radioed for help at 10:00 A.M. because the crowd was getting larger.

13. I. The payroll office is open on Fridays.
    II. Paychecks are distributed from 9:00 A.M. to 12 Noon.
    III. The office is open on Fridays because that's the only day the payroll staff is available.
    IV. It is open for the specified hours in order to permit employees to cash checks at the bank during lunch hour.

The choice below which MOST clearly and accurately presents the above idea is:
   A. Because the payroll office is open on Fridays from 9:00 A.M. to 12 Noon, employees can cash their checks when the payroll staff is available.
   B. Because the payroll staff is only available on Fridays until noon, employees can cash their checks during their lunch hour.
   C. Because the payroll staff is available only on Fridays, the office is open from 9:00 A.M. to 12 Noon to allow employees to cash their checks.
   D. Because of payroll staff availability, the payroll office is open on Fridays. It is open from 9:00 A.M. to 12 Noon so that distributed paychecks can be cashed at the bank while employees are on their lunch hour.

Questions 14-16.

DIRECTIONS: In each of Questions 14 through 6, the four sentences are from a paragraph in a report. They are not in the right order. Which of the following arrangements is the BEST one?

14. I. An executive may answer a letter by writing his reply on the face of the letter itself instead of having a return letter typed.
   II. This procedure is efficient because it saves the executive's time, the typist's time, and saves office file space.
   III. Copying machines are used in small offices as well as large offices to save time and money in making brief replies to business letters.
   IV. A copy is made on a copy machine to go into the company files, while the original is mailed back to the sender.

The CORRECT answer is:
A. I, II, IV, III   B. I, IV, II, III   C. III, I, IV, II   D. III, IV, II, I

15. I. Most organizations favor one of the types but always include the others to a lesser degree.
   II. However, we can detect a definite trend toward greater use of symbolic control.
   III. We suggest that our local police agencies are today primarily utilizing material control.
   IV. Control can be classified into three types: physical, material, and symbolic.

The CORRECT answer is:
A. IV, II, III, I   B. II, I, IV, III   C. III, IV, II, I   D. IV, I, III, II

16. I. They can and do take advantage of ancient political and geographical boundaries, which often give them sanctuary from effective policy activity.
   II. This country is essentially a country of small police forces, each operating independently within the limits of its jurisdiction.
   III. The boundaries that define and limit police operations do not hinder the movement of criminals, of course.
   IV. The machinery of law enforcement in America is fragmented, complicated, and frequently overlapping.

The CORRECT answer is:
A. III, I, IV   B. II, IV, I, III   C. IV, II, III, I   D. IV, III, II, I

17. Examine the following sentence, and then choose from below the words which should be inserted in the blank spaces to produce the best sentence.
    The unit has exceeded _____ goals and the employees are satisfied with _____ accomplishments.
    A. their, it's   B. it's; it's   C. its, there   D. its, their

18. Examine the following sentence, and then choose from below the words which should be inserted in the blank spaces to produce the best sentence.
    Research indicates that employees who _____ no opportunity for close social relationships often find their work unsatisfying, and this _____ of satisfaction often reflects itself in low production.
    A. have; lack   B. have; excess   C. has; lack   D. has; excess

19. Words in a sentence must be arranged properly to make sure that the intended meaning of the sentence is clear.
    The sentence below that does NOT make sense because a clause has been separated from the word on which its meaning depends is:
    A. To be a good writer, clarity is necessary.
    B. To be a good writer, you must write clearly.
    C. You must write clearly to be a good writer.
    D. Clarity is necessary to good writing.

Questions 20-21.

DIRECTIONS: Each of Questions 20 and 21 consists of a statement which contains a word (one of those underlined) that is either incorrectly used because it is not in keeping with the meaning the quotation is evidently intended to convey, or is misspelled. There is only one INCORRECT word in each quotation. Of the four underlined words, determine if the first one should be replaced by the word lettered A, the second one replaced by the word lettered B, the third one replaced by the word lettered C, or the fourth one replaced by the word lettered D.

20. The alleged killer was occasionally permitted to excercise in the corridor.
    A. alledged   B. ocasionally   C. permited   D. exercise

21. Defense counsel stated, in affect, that their conduct was permissible under the First Amendment.
    A. council   B. effect   C. there   D. permissable

Question 22.

DIRECTIONS: Question 22 consists of one sentence. This sentence contains an incorrectly used word. First, decide which is the incorrectly used word. Then, from among the options given, decide which word, when substituted for the incorrectly used word, makes the meaning of the sentence clear.

22. As today's violence has no single cause, so its causes have no single scheme. 22.____
    A. deference   B. cure   C. flaw   D. relevance

23. In the sentence, *A man in a light-grey suit waited thirty-five minutes in the ante-room for the all-important document*, the word IMPROPERLY hyphenated is 23.____
    A. light-grey   B. thirty-five
    C. ante-room   D. all-important

24. In the sentence, *The candidate wants to file his application for preference before it is too late*, the word *before* is used as a(n) 24.____
    A. preposition   B. subordinating conjunction
    C. pronoun   D. adverb

25. In the sentence, *The perpetrators ran from the scene*, the word *from* is a 25.____
    A. preposition   B. pronoun   C. verb   D. conjunction

KEY (CORRECT ANSWERS)

1. D
2. D
3. A
4. B
5. D

6. D
7. B
8. A
9. C
10. C

11. D
12. D
13. D
14. C
15. D

16. C
17. D
18. A
19. A
20. D

21. B
22. B
23. C
24. B
25. A

www.ingramcontent.com/pod-product-compliance
Lightning Source LLC
Chambersburg PA
CBHW081759300426
44116CB00014B/2171